ANDRÉ MALRAUX

André Malraux

ANDRÉ
MALRAUX

DENIS BOAK

SENIOR LECTURER IN
MODERN FRENCH LITERATURE
UNIVERSITY OF HULL

OXFORD
AT THE CLARENDON PRESS
1968

Oxford University Press, Ely House, London W. 1

GLASGOW NEW YORK TORONTO MELBOURNE WELLINGTON
CAPE TOWN SALISBURY IBADAN NAIROBI LUSAKA ADDIS ABABA
BOMBAY CALCUTTA MADRAS KARACHI LAHORE DACCA
KUALA LUMPUR HONG KONG TOKYO

Ce

PRINTED IN GREAT BRITAIN
AT THE UNIVERSITY PRESS, OXFORD
BY VIVIAN RIDLER
PRINTER TO THE UNIVERSITY

FOR

ESTELLE

PREFACE

THIS book owes its origin to a remark by Roger Martin du Gard in 1955. At the time, as a raw research student, I had recently begun a study of his works; and, through a chance meeting with a lady who knew the Martin du Gard family, I was fortunate enough to be invited along to have a chat with him at his *pied-à-terre* in the rue du Dragon one summer morning. Knowing his reluctance to be interviewed, I was already somewhat intimidated when I rang the bell at the appointed time. I was still more apprehensive when, no doubt knowing the Sorbonne rule that living authors could not be subjects of theses, he promptly accused me of anticipating his death within the next year or two. However, I managed to convince him that, since the thesis I proposed was for Cambridge, not the Sorbonne, I had no such hopes; and I think that he was probably, in a period of general neglect of his work, somewhat gratified at my interest. This did not prevent him from growling good-naturedly, before we started to talk about his own works, that the novelist I should be working on was not himself but André Malraux. Since completing my study of Martin du Gard I have followed his suggestion.

I mention Martin du Gard for another reason. Greatly impressed by *Jean Barois*, I had been slightly disappointed at my first contact with *Les Thibault*, which seemed, then, slow-moving and lacking in action. The contrast with *La Condition humaine*, which I had read with much enthusiasm about the same time, no doubt strengthened this feeling. But as I reread Martin du Gard (all his works three times, and some four or five), my opinion rose steadily: at every reading I found new things to admire, and I became more and more impressed by the quality of his writing. With Malraux, however, this has not been so. Except for *La Condition humaine* and *L'Espoir*, rereading has, unfortunately, tended to lower my opinion—at times sharply—as a certain thinness of texture, mixed with what I can only call pretentiousness, has intruded on appreciation. This is not to say that my attitude is now hostile; indeed, there is little point in destructive criticism. Nevertheless, the present study is intended as critical in the fullest sense; I have attempted to see Malraux's work in as wide a perspective as I can, and I have not hesitated to make value judgements of various kinds. Made from a relativist standpoint, they implicate only myself, and are persuasive, not conclusive. Malraux seems, indeed, an exemplary case with which to face those critics, perhaps still the majority, who believe in absolute standards, or who may never have considered the epistemological status of the value judgement: among the very critics whose admiration for Malraux is strongest, there is little agreement about the relative standing of his works. For some, *La Condition humaine* is his masterpiece; for others, *L'Espoir*; some prefer *Les Noyers de l'Altenburg*; while still others regard *Les Voix du silence* as one of the most important books of the century. With this last group I find myself in more radical disagreement, since this opinion seems to be less an aesthetic than an intellectual judgement, and one perhaps based on an inadequate knowledge of the context and antecedents of Malraux's art philosophy.

This is a further reason why I believe a detached study of Malraux is valuable at the present time. Quite a number of books on Malraux, and still more articles, have appeared in the last few years; many of them contain excellent and thorough-going analyses of his works and the ideas he has used in them. But the critical sense has perhaps sometimes been deficient: if long on *explication*, many of these writers seem to me to have been short on *jugement* and evaluation, and sometimes also they have tended to ignore, in either the English or the French sense, the full literary and intellectual background of Malraux's work. But surely literature is only artificially a discipline of its own (and much more so French Literature, English Literature, or German Literature, as separate disciplines); to *le musée imaginaire* we must now add *la bibliothèque imaginaire*, since the creative writer—or critic—of today has at his disposal the entire range, not merely of the world's literature, but of all its books of all kinds.[1] Literature is but a part,

---

[1] Since writing this sentence, I find that I have been anticipated in this image by Professor Harry Levin (*Contexts of Criticism*, p. 255).

if the most significant one, of the totality of culture and intellectual activity, and as a consequence the study of literature is an
integral part of cultural and intellectual history. By viewing it this
way we can bring it together with the other humanities and social
sciences. And it is from this viewpoint that, in my opinion,
Malraux can most profitably be treated. Although, as a writer, he
is in many ways atypical and non-representative, as a twentieth-
century figure he can only be properly evaluated in the context of
the principal currents of modern thought, from psychology to art
history. Not that I think that he is himself primarily a psychologist
or art historian; I hope in fact to show that he is not. But an appreciation of his work involves contact with many fields outside the
purely literary one, since Malraux has used ideas in his works as
extensively as any writer of the century, and, if few of them were
actually generated by him, all bear the distinctive stamp of his
style.

The method I have used is chronological; with the apparent
exception of *La Voie royale*, which I treat first among Malraux's
novels since there can be little doubt that it was first in conception.
The chronological method is, of course, merely one among many
ways of treating a writer; but in a general study it seems to me to
be the most useful as well as the most straightforward. In Malraux's particular case there has been in the past some tendency to
throw all his novels together, and to extract a general 'philosophy'
or 'meaning' from them. Obviously the works have much in
common, above all their peculiarly 'heroic' accent, but there is also
a fairly clear development from the Surrealist-type prose poems
of the early 1920s, through the broad Nietzschean ideas of the two
essays, the application of these ideas to the novel in *La Voie royale*,
the involvement in politics, growing gradually greater until
L'Espoir becomes a *roman engagé* designed for immediate political
effect, then the sharp break away from politics and heroism in *Les
Noyers de l'Altenburg*. Finally, in the post-war period, Malraux
abandons the novel and turns back to Nietzschean concepts in developing his philosophy of art, returning at the same time from
the more normal humanism of *Les Noyers* towards an earlier, more
heroic, vision. To ignore this movement, caused by an interplay of

his own intellectual development and of outside events, is, I would suggest, to reduce sharply the potentialities of appreciation of Malraux's work.

For convenience, quotations and titles in German have been given in English, except for standard terms such as *Weltanschauung*. I should like to thank Professors John Cruickshank, I. D. McFarlane, and Garnet Rees for their kindness in reading the first draft, and for the many helpful suggestions they have made; and Professors W. M. Frohock and D. J. Enright for assistance on points of detail. I should also like to thank the University of Hong Kong and the staff of its Library for generous financial aid and practical help in obtaining research materials; and my wife for preparing the index. An earlier version of Chapter 2 appeared in *French Studies*, and of parts of Chapters 1 and 9 in the *Modern Language Review*; I should like to thank the Editors of these journals for permission to use this material. Thanks are also due to Messrs. Bernard Grasset and Gallimard for permission to quote from Malraux's works.

The first volume of Malraux's *Antimémoires* came out only after the present book had gone to press. However, this fascinating volume, consisting more of reflections on experience than of traditional autobiography—somewhat on the lines of Claude Lévi-Strauss's *Tristes Tropiques*—, contains relatively little material bearing on its author as artist, and nothing which seems to invalidate any of my main arguments and conclusions.

D. B.

CONTENTS

BIOGRAPHICAL SUMMARY

(This summary is limited to biographical facts which appear to be beyond dispute. Malraux's works are given in the year of publication, not of composition.)

1901   Born in Paris.
       Secondary education; leaves school without the *baccalauréat*.

1919-22 Works as *chineur* for a Paris bookseller; moves on to publishing work for Kra; first articles and stories published in minor *avant-garde* reviews.

1920   First marriage, to Clara Goldschmidt.

1923-4 Trip to Cambodia in search of ruined Khmer statues; Malraux arrested and convicted for looting a historical monument, later released (on a technicality).

1925-6 Second visit to Indo-China; political activity in Saigon.

1926   *La Tentation de l'Occident.*

1927-58 Publishing work with the house of Gallimard; with many intervals.

1927   *D'une jeunesse européenne.*

1928   *Les Conquérants.*

1930   *La Voie royale.*

1933   *La Condition humaine.*

1934   Flies over the Arabian desert with Corniglion-Molinier; claims to have discovered the legendary city of the Queen of Sheba.
       Goes to Berlin with Gide to assist defendants in the Reichstag Fire trial.

1935   *Le Temps du mépris.*

1936   Visit to Moscow.

1936-7 Serves actively in the Spanish Civil War.

1937-9 Propaganda and fund-raising activities for the Spanish Republican Government in Europe and the U.S.A.

1937   *L'Espoir*, made into a film by Malraux himself in 1938-9.

1939-40 Serves in a tank unit in the French army.

1940   Captured by Germans; escapes.

1941-4 Resistance activity; becomes a Maquis leader.

1943   *Les Noyers de l'Altenburg.*

1944-5 Colonel in reconstituted French army; commands a brigade.

1945–6   Minister of Information under General de Gaulle.

1946–58 In 1946 resigns with de Gaulle, whom he constantly supports; returns to power with him in 1958.

1947–9   *La Psychologie de l'Art.*

1951   *Les Voix du silence.*

1957   *La Métamorphose des dieux.*

1958   Minister Delegate, later Minister of State for Cultural Affairs.

I

INTRODUCTION

AT first sight it seems almost incredible that any man living, whose life and background are reasonably accessible to biographers, should nevertheless be enveloped in legend and mystery. Yet not many hard facts are known about much of Malraux's career; and the legend, where it has been investigated in detail, has often proved to correspond only very vaguely to the reality. There is no full biography available, although much light on the early years has now been cast by three recent books.[1]

It is not the intention of the present work to attempt a biography, although a full and detailed account would obviously be fascinating. And who would not wish for an autobiography, especially after the signal success achieved by Simone de Beauvoir, Sartre, and also Malraux's own first wife Clara, in this field? At the same time, one can scarcely ignore Malraux's life completely, on the ground that his works stand by themselves and are unaffected in value by his biography. From one point of view this is obviously true; yet, from another, Malraux has deliberately attempted to create his own life as an artistic entity in its own right; in his article on T. E. Lawrence he states this unequivocally:

[1] A. Vandegans, *La Jeunesse littéraire d'André Malraux*; W. G. Langlois, *André Malraux: The Indo-China Adventure*; and above all Clara Malraux's second volume of autobiography, *Nos vingt ans*. The account which, according to Malraux himself, was the best (up to 1963: cf. J. Hoffmann, *L'Humanisme de Malraux*, p. 391) is Janet Flanner's *New Yorker* profile, reprinted in her *Men and Monuments*. She succeeds in getting the best of both worlds by retailing many of the wildest elements of the legend, such as Malraux's ability to speak fifteen languages, lightly deprecating such exaggerations, while accepting other features, like his photographic memory, which—one reads—enables him to emerge from an art gallery and list large numbers of paintings in order of hanging. But it is doubtful whether we really approach an understanding of either the man or the writer more closely by this type of rather slick writing, by such descriptive traits as 'the cold, impassioned face of a Renaissance *condottiere*', or by being told of Malraux's inability to remember how old he is except once a year, on his birthday.

'La grande personnalité telle que la rêvait confusément Lawrence
—telle que la conçoivent beaucoup d'entre nous—c'était une
vérité incarnée, devenue vivante: Nietzsche devenu Zarathustra.'[1]
An obvious parallel is with Byron. Byron's reputation in the world
has always depended much more on his legend than on his actual
works, which many of those who are prepared to use his name
have never properly read—to the point where many a student, first
settling down to study Byron, is amazed or disappointed to discover that in many ways he is hardly a typical Romantic at all.
Byron, in fact, made his life itself into a work of art; and no doubt
this is one reason why his reputation has consistently been higher
in the rest of Europe than in Britain: a mixture of legend and
translation meant that the Byron judged abroad was not the same
man as the one read in the original. This naturally implied a good
deal of conscious intention, and even deliberate pose: Childe
Harold, who began as a projection of Byron's own desires, ended
up by becoming the reality of the legend: Byron transformed into
Childe Harold, like Nietzsche into Zarathustra—or Malraux into
Garine or Vincent Berger.

This conscious shaping of his life, to impress others, seems the
key to much of the Malraux legend. Life becomes an embodiment
of will, and Malraux resembles the King of the Sedangs of whom
Perken speaks in *La Voie royale*: 'un homme avide de jouer sa
biographie, comme un acteur joue un rôle.'[2] This attitude towards his life no doubt only crystallized into a deliberate creation
of legend late in the 1920s, by which time Malraux, through his
publishing work, must have become familiar with modern

---

[1] 'N'était-ce donc que cela?', *Saisons*, no. 3, Winter 1946–7, pp. 22–3. Cf. also
the study of Laclos (in *Tableau de la littérature française*, vol. 2, Paris, 1939)—
probably Malraux's most perceptive piece of literary criticism. Here he interprets
Valmont and Mme de Merteuil in a similar way: both act according to a 'mythical' view of themselves—'c'est l'image mythique qui informe l'image vivante;
celle-ci devenant son modèle en action, confronté à la vie, incarné' (p. 382). The
means of transferring the 'mythical' image to actual behaviour is the exercise of
will. Cf. also Clappique, perhaps the most striking personality in all Malraux's
novels, precisely because of his mythomania, which Malraux analyses in some detail. Clappique, by lying, 'entrait dans un monde où la vérité n'existait plus. Ce
n'était ni vrai, ni faux, mais vécu' (*La Condition humaine*, Livre de Poche edn.,
p. 209).   [2] *La Voie royale*, Livre de Poche edn., p. 12.

publicity methods and the techniques now generally known as
'image-formation'. But even before this there is an unmistakable
element of intentional pose in many of Malraux's activities: even
the photographs taken of him as a young man show that he was
very alive to appearances—with his eyes deliberately searching
penetratingly into the camera. (Malraux must be one of the most
photographed writers of the century.) And Clara Malraux relates
a curious incident when Malraux, shortly after meeting her in
1920, took her to a *bal-musette* in a rather sordid quarter of Paris;
on leaving, Malraux was shot at by an unrecognized assailant, and
immediately drew a revolver from his own pocket and fired back.[1]
Not the least curious feature of this anecdote is that the nineteen-
year-old Malraux should, in peace-time Paris, have been armed;
and the adoption of a role is clear.

Malraux's attitude to his life—this creation of the legend—may
perhaps be characterized as 'rationalized mythomania'; and it is
largely responsible for the inadequacy of the biographical material.
I have suggested elsewhere that T. E. Lawrence was probably
Malraux's model in the early 1920s, shortly after Lowell Thomas's
popular lectures had begun to make the Englishman internationally
famous.[2] Lawrence, whose legend was at that time accepted as
established fact, seems to have become something of an exemplary
figure for the young Malraux, and desire to emulate Lawrence,
who was after all only thirteen years older than himself, may
partly have motivated his sudden decision in 1923 to abandon
literary activities in Paris and seek adventure in the Far East.[3] The
parallel goes deeper: Malraux has always admitted being fascinated
by Lawrence, and even claimed to have written a book on him, of
which one apparent chapter was published as an article in 1946.[4]

[1] C. Malraux, *Apprendre à vivre*, p. 280.
[2] 'Malraux and T. E. Lawrence', *Modern Language Review*, Apr. 1966, pp.
218–24.
[3] Clara Malraux, in her fascinating account, has added a more pressing reason
for the young couple's departure for the East: they had lost all their—or rather her
—money in unfortunate speculations on the Bourse, and set off, just like Claude
Vannec, to recoup their fortunes by obtaining and selling Khmer statuary (*Nos
vingt ans*, pp. 109–12).
[4] *Saisons*, no. 3, Winter 1946–7, pp. 9–24. Since Malraux has never been slow to
publish, it is doubtful whether he in fact ever wrote more than this section.

In both men we find a keen intellectual pride, coupled with a certain contempt for formal academic values, seen as pedantry. Both went to found their careers on archaeological expeditions in the East; partly, perhaps, because the Near East had, as it were, been pre-empted by Lawrence, Malraux chose the Far East. He was not a trained archaeologist, despite the legend,[1] and like Lawrence took a decidedly cavalier attitude both to professional methods and to normal conceptions of ownership of finds.

It is in terms of the creation of legend that the parallel is most revealing. It is now clear that Lawrence was mainly responsible for his own legend, even during the Arabian campaign itself, when he posed to the visiting Thomas, then a war correspondent, as a 'Prince of Arabia'.[2] Lawrence, in short, seems a clear case of mythomania. Many of his wilder claims, from adolescence onwards, are only explicable on this assumption; and to say this is not to deny his achievements, which were very real. But there is a gap between the facts and the legend, a compulsion to embroider on reality, even though this compulsion may itself have been the dynamic which produced the reality. As the ship's captain puts it in *La Voie royale*, 'Tout aventurier est né d'un mythomane',[3] and Malraux's psychological insight here is convincing. Lawrence seems to have realized very rapidly that actions alone are not enough to create a lasting reputation, and was a precursor of the modern technique of 'projecting the image'. As Aldington has pointed out, the various anecdotes which composed the Lawrence legend, and which always redounded to his own credit, could in the main have had no other source than himself, however much he

---

[1] A. Vandegans, in 'Malraux a-t-il fréquenté les grandes écoles', *Revue des langues vivantes*, xxvi, pp. 336–40, shows fairly conclusively that any study Malraux put in at the Sorbonne, École du Louvre, or École Nationale des Langues Orientales Vivantes, entirely escaped the notice of the authorities. He may have attended occasional lectures, but nothing more. Despite this, Malraux's entry in *Who's Who in France*, 1963–4, includes the mention: 'Diplômé de l'École Nationale des Langues Orientales Vivantes'.

[2] Cf. Richard Aldington's debunking biography, *Lawrence of Arabia*. Whatever Aldington's excesses—and his book is vitiated by an unusually violent personal hostility to his subject—he has established enough facts to prove his case in general terms.

[3] *La Voie royale*, p. 16.

might later deny them, or however contradictory they might be, since he had been the sole person present, or the only one who knew his identity.

The Malraux legend is clearly similar. He has rarely gone to the extent of denying anything about his life; indeed, his flat refusal even to answer questions about his private life is well known. The result is that various contradictory accounts are in circulation; but, as with Lawrence, the original source for many of these can only have been Malraux himself. Above all, respectable works of reference differ on simple questions of fact, such as the year of his birth; yet they usually rely on the subject himself for factual information. It is hard to understand how Malraux's year of birth can be recorded as 1895, instead of 1901, with the obvious difficulties such a date raises—such as First World War service—unless it had been supplied by Malraux himself. This particular instance is no longer in doubt; but similar basic points of uncertainty still exist. Was Malraux's father's name Fernand, or Georges, or Fernand-Georges? Was he a banker? Or a businessman? Or an official in Indo-China? Did he commit suicide? Did Malraux himself marry Josette Clotis, who was killed in a railway accident in 1944? And what are we to make of his statement to Edmund Wilson that his interest in Goya dates from his capture (by whom?) in the Spanish Civil War, and imprisonment in Madrid, in Goya's 'House of the Deaf Man'?[1] Questions like these could be settled by Malraux in five minutes, and one is forced to conclude that he prefers an aura of uncertainty about his life. He must be regarded as at least negatively responsible for his legend.

The accusation of mythomania is certainly one which Malraux's critics have not hesitated to use against him;[2] and it also receives some confirmation from his first wife Clara.[3] And one of her novels, *Par de plus longs chemins*,[4] is simply the story that a woman tells of her liaison with a young archaeologist named Bernard,

[1] E. Wilson, *The Bit between my Teeth*, p. 143.
[2] e.g. C. Roy, *Descriptions critiques*, vol. 1, p. 225; or even F. Mauriac, *Journal*, vol. 2, p. 221: 'Quoi qu'il ait raconté de lui, nous ne l'avons jamais cru à fait . . . il faut qu'il nous trompe: son démon l'exige.'
[3] e.g. *Apprendre à vivre*, p. 270; *Nos vingt ans*, pp. 41-2, 84, 189.
[4] Paris, 1953.

whom she accompanies on an expedition to Persia. Bernard, depicted as much more the adventurer than the careful scientist,
becomes bored with progress in Persia, and sets off with his mistress and a young Persian Jew to search for the ruins of Alexandria
of the Caucasus, in Afghanistan. Only after the other two have
gleaned the necessary information is Bernard able to discover
sensational Graeco-Buddhist sculptures dating from the early
Christian era. At this point he falls seriously ill; a revolt by the
Moslem labourers, intent on destroying these heathen idols, is
averted by the efforts of the narrator; and, with the help of the
Persian, the two reach India with the sculptures. The rest of the
story is taken up with the narrator's gradual disillusionment with
Bernard, who, in describing his exploits in Afghanistan, gives himself all the credit, and makes no mention of the Persian, and later
even of the narrator herself. The resemblance to Malraux is undeniable; and it seems that he himself made an expedition to
Afghanistan between 1928 and 1932 (although this whole episode
is clouded in typical mystery), where he obtained some of the
'Gandharan' Graeco-Buddhist sculptures discussed and illustrated
in *Les Voix du silence*. Bernard has courage, imagination, and
initiative; and the narrator wonders why he needs to tell tales that
the listeners often know to be untrue, as when he claims to have
directed Hittite excavations in Turkey, or stories about a shaman
(a subject recurring in *Les Noyers de l'Altenburg*). He is obviously
building a fictional world around his own fantasies, from which
she is excluded: 'Tu ne pénétreras pas jusqu'à moi, me dit chaque
mot qui ne correspondant pas à la réalité, crée un univers dont je
suis exclue. . . .'[1] This world of fantasy is partly a compensation for
something lacking in his real life, and partly a spur to his ambitions,
which drive him on to compete with his own exaggerations
and lies. The narrator investigates his background, and concludes
that his childhood had been made miserable by the separation of
his parents; he had therefore banished the unpleasant reality and
replaced it by a background, or rather various backgrounds, of his
own imagining. Bernard's enormous ambition is summed up in
terms of monumental egoism and emotional aridity: 'il était plus

[1] *Par de plus longs chemins*, p. 56.

important de survivre cinq cents ou mille ans dans la mémoire humaine que quelques jours dans le cœur des voisins.'[1]

This story can clearly not be accepted as absolute fact; the portrait of Bernard is so hostile that one wonders how the narrator, herself shown, incidentally, as almost without faults, could have tolerated him so long. Nevertheless, there is obviously something in it; and the explanation of Bernard's behaviour through humiliation suffered in childhood brings us back again to Lawrence. It is now well known that Lawrence was illegitimate, the son of an Irish baronet; and it is widely accepted that his whole personality was deeply affected by the sense of humiliation and the ambivalent feelings towards his parents which knowledge of this produced in him. Now in Malraux also there are signs of some emotional crisis in late adolescence, in which difficulties with his parents played a major part. Why else should he be apparently earning part of his own living, buying rare books on the *quais*, and reselling them to a dealer, instead of following the normal pattern and registering at the Sorbonne?[2] Presumably because there had been some kind of a break. At all events, Malraux shares Lawrence's reticence about his family background; and his life shows a consistent effort to break away from this environment, from his unusually early marriage—at 19—onwards.[3]

There is of course nothing unusual in all this; for the young would-be artist or writer difficulties with parents have been almost mandatory from the Romantic epoch onwards. Malraux's initial career in no way deviates from the normal development. Like Barbusse, Romains, Duhamel, or Mauriac, he made his début by writing poetry (there is really no other way of characterizing his early work—or for that matter that of any writers of the Dadaist/Surrealist type). The situation was no doubt

[1] Ibid., p. 14.
[2] According to M. Vandegans (*La Jeunesse littéraire d'André Malraux*, pp. 18–19), after his parents had separated, Malraux lived first with his mother, then one of his grandmothers, receiving a certain amount of financial aid from both his father and his maternal grandmother.
[3] Lawrence took the name of Shaw, apparently out of admiration for Bernard Shaw; Malraux, taking the name of one of his own heroes, later became Colonel Berger.

8 INTRODUCTION

somewhat exacerbated by Malraux's age: as Professor Frohock stresses, he just missed the First World War.[1] His attitude to violence is very different from that of his immediate elders; indeed, one may say that much of the frivolity and nihilism of Dadaism and Surrealism was a reaction against the war by young men who did not take active part in it.

It seems certain, though, that Malraux's early literary attempts did not bring him the hoped-for success; although he managed to bring out a few works here and there in little magazines, others either were never published at all, or (like *Royaume farfelu*) had to wait until he had an established reputation in the late 1920s. Most of his initial publications are reviews, not creative works, and there is an air of dilettantism about much of this early literary activity.[2] It is this situation of unfulfilled ambition which preceded, and no doubt was partly a cause of, his first expedition to the East in 1923. This view of Malraux's youthful career indicates, I think, his need to find something with which to identify himself. Indeed, the most fruitful interpretation of these early years seems to be through the suggestion that Malraux's problems—and all witnesses seem agreed that he was nervous to the point of near-neurosis—were largely a question of ego-identity. As Erik Erikson, the chief proponent of this neo-Freudian school of 'ego-psychology', puts it, an identity crisis takes place in 'that period of the life cycle when each youth must forge for himself some central perspective and direction, some working unity, out of the effective remnants of his childhood and the hopes of his anticipated adulthood'.[3] Although aspects of the theory seem doubtful—and

[1] W. M. Frohock, *André Malraux and the Tragic Imagination*, p. 10.

[2] Vandegans (op. cit., p. 50) talks of 'une crise de dandysme' in 1920, while Clara Malraux also mentions her former husband's love of 'luxe' and 'parures' (*Apprendre à vivre*, p. 280). Vandegans (pp. 22–9) also describes some of Malraux's early publishing activities: among others, volumes of erotica, and 'inédits' of Laforgue, the latter savagely attacked by G. Jean-Aubry, both for the numerous errors and for the fact that the so-called 'inédits' were merely lifted from ephemeral reviews of the past. Malraux responded equally warmly, though he had no real defence; we may suspect that his hostile attitude to formal scholarship was sharpened by this episode.

[3] E. Erikson, *Young Man Luther*, p. 12. Cf. also Erikson's other books: *Childhood and Society* (1950), and *Identity and the Life Cycle* (1959). Malraux has in fact been all of the following at one time or another: book dealer, editor, poet, publisher,

this interpretation of Malraux can be no more than a hypothesis—much of his life can be viewed as an attempt to give himself satisfactory identity, even, perhaps, in the earlier novels, by identifying himself with his own heroes. 'Role-diffusion' is the technical term which covers such efforts to establish oneself in widely differing fields; and it is of course a cliché to call Malraux an adventurer. But, outside the deliberate creation of legend, precisely such activity is the hallmark of his entire career: what can only be called large-scale opportunism, the assumption of a number of widely varied, grandiose roles.

Here I wish to take up the question of Malraux's Communism. Although it seems fairly certain that he was never a party member (if he had been, surely someone would have used this fact against him during his later career?), it seems impossible to deny that he worked for the Communist cause as actively, and with as good effect, as if he had been, for the better part of twenty years.[1] And by now he has worked well over twenty years against it. In view of this it seems pointless to claim—as have Communists and anti-Communists alike—that his political attitude has never basically changed.[2] It is arguable, certainly, that Malraux's psychological attitude has not changed, based throughout as it is on a powerful belief in will and individualism; but this is not to say that his political statements and actions have always been consistent. Communism and Gaullism have little in common except their authoritarian approach. The contradiction between Malraux's view in 1934 that the future of culture lies in the hands of the explorer, archaeologist, detainee, novelist, reviewer, aviator, revolutionary, politician, orator, soldier, guerilla leader, minister, philosopher—and he has adopted other roles besides, such as that of military historian and strategist. Cf. his preface to General P. E. Jacquot, *Essai de stratégie occidentale.* (There may be another touch of Lawrence in this last role.) Naturally his status in many of these roles has never gone beyond the amateur.

[1] On the other hand, both he and his wife became members of the Cholon (Saigon) branch of the Kuomintang (C. Malraux, *Nos vingt ans,* p. 180).

[2] It appears to be a variation of the general dialectical attitude to contradictions, 'resolving' them with terms such as 'subjectively wrong but objectively right', to view Malraux's political attitudes in the 1930s and 1950s as consistent. To the non-dialectical observer such an analysis seems, like Sartre's statement after the Hungarian revolution of 1956, 'I was wrong but I was right to be wrong', merely a monumental example of *mauvaise foi.*

U.S.S.R., the only Socialist State, and his claim in 1949 that only
an anti-Communist Europe can preserve the intellectual and cultural values of the world, is formal, and cannot be resolved by any
dialectical sleight-of-hand. Equally, Malraux's support of Vietnamese nationalism in the 1920s contrasts bluntly with his careful
avoidance of the Vietnam issue in 1946.

Malraux's Communist sympathies appear, indeed, to have been
the direct result of his expedition to Cambodia to acquire Khmer
sculptures, and the humiliation he suffered in the arrest and trial
following this not entirely creditable episode. Before leaving for
the East Malraux had shown little sign of left-wing sympathies;
his interests were mostly artistic and literary, and his tastes much
the same as those of any other young man from the same environment and milieu:[1] apart from the Surrealists, France, Barrès, Gide,
Claudel, Suarès, Maurras, Valéry, and Gobineau, and, among older
writers, Hugo, Michelet, Stendhal, Dostoevsky, and above all
Nietzsche.[2] There is a distinct tinge of the political Right in these,
confirmed by Malraux's 1923 preface to Maurras's *Mademoiselle
Monk*, eulogistic in tone, which ends with the uncompromising
declaration: 'Charles Maurras est une des plus grandes forces in-
tellectuelles d'aujourd'hui.'[3] The most likely hypothesis for
Malraux's sudden plunge into revolutionary activities about 1924
is his imprisonment and the resentment it caused in him, turning
him violently against the French colonial régime in Indo-China
and bringing him together with other elements equally opposed:
Vietnamese nationalists, many of whom were already Marxist
sympathizers.[4] In the ideology of Marxism, Malraux was presumably able to find an emotional satisfaction which lasted him for
fifteen years, despite the difficulties of reconciling it with a
Nietzschean belief in will and individualism. Certainly, on any
view, this Cambodian episode is the origin of the obsession with
humiliation, often noted by critics, which marks most of his

[1] Among the Surrealists proper, of course, artistic revolt frequently took on
Communist overtones—without necessarily implying any genuine understanding
of Marxism.   [2] Vandegans, op. cit., p. 58.
[3] Preface to C. Maurras, *Mademoiselle Monk*, p. 9.
[4] Since the above was originally written, Clara Malraux has confirmed this
hypothesis (*Nos vingt ans*, pp. 179–80).

novels; and one might even surmise that much of *La Voie royale* is
a more successful re-enactment of the events leading to his arrest in
Pnom-Penh in 1923, an attempt to conjure the reality by making
Claude Vannec's efforts meet with greater success.[1]

Malraux's two expeditions to the East were fundamental in developing the novelist he afterwards became. Both were, from the
point of view of accomplishing his immediate purposes, miserable
failures. The first brought him no valuable Khmer statues, but a
mortifying trial from which he was lucky to escape with a suspended gaol sentence; the rather unscrupulous political journalism
in which he indulged in Saigon during his second trip seems not
only to have had its ludicrous aspect—Malraux challenging an adversary to a duel with swords—but also to have achieved little
immediate political result. M. Vandegans is surely right when he
speaks here of a 'traumatisme' of failure reflected in the novels.[2]
From the purely personal point of view Malraux, once back in
France, had every reason to gild the image a little, to take full advantage of the publicity which his expeditions had afforded him,
and, later, to allow it to be believed that his China novels were
eye-witness accounts of real events in which he himself had taken
a leading role. But in the East he at least gained a setting: and the
application of naturalism to the exotic produced an effect of seedy
authenticity, in powerful contrast to the artificial and deliberately
romantic exoticism of earlier writers like Loti or Victor Segalen.
To this descriptive technique, now familiar in novelists such as
Graham Greene—to say nothing of producers of thrillers—but
nevertheless much more original in the 1920s, we must add
staccato dialogue, elliptical sentences, and an apparent disregard
of traditional novel form, all of which bear little or no relation to
Malraux's Surrealist prose poems. Most important of all, however,
was probably the very tension set up in Malraux's own personality
between his newly-developed Communist sympathies and his
established belief in will, and his obsession with death and failure.[3]

[1] One need hardly add that conjectures of this kind about the origin of a novel
have no bearing on any value-judgement which might be made about it.
[2] Op. cit., pp. 246, 254.
[3] Peter Quennell's theory, in *The Sign of the Fish*, pp. 15–26, that emotional conflict is the dynamic behind artistic creation, is no doubt too sweeping if applied to

Without his journeys to the East and his Marxist sympathies he would have had neither theme nor setting for *Les Conquérants* and *La Condition humaine* (whatever their exact autobiographical contents as they stand); yet, if he had become a fully fledged Communist without any individualistic leanings, they could scarcely have risen above the level of propaganda. And without contact with nationalists and revolutionaries, and personal experience of subversive political activity, he would hardly have had any characters to portray. Although creative imagination, not personal experience, is what makes a writer, the imagination needs some sort of experience to feed on, and the circumstances of Malraux's life and sympathies were able to provide this; his rejection of the novel form since 1945 may also be linked with a paucity of suitable experiential material.[1]

Back in France after his Far-Eastern exploits, Malraux's career as a writer went much more smoothly. He had the entry to the *N.R.F.*, and soon began to work for Gallimard as a publisher as well as a reviewer, although, probably because of pre-existing contracts with Grasset, *La Condition humaine* in 1933 was the first of his own novels to appear with the Gallimard imprint.[2] Yet there are still many mysterious episodes in his life in the years until 1935. There is the expedition to Afghanistan, mentioned above, and a possible visit to Shanghai; indeed, according to M. Hoffmann, he visited the whole world except for South America and Oceania, although no details are given.[3] From 1936 his movements are fairly clearly documented: a trip to Moscow, to further a

all artistic creation (and evidently derives from the Romantic theory that all art is expression). Nevertheless in many cases it is enlightening: above all in Flaubert, torn between Romantic nostalgia and the 'reality principle'.

    [1] A comparison with Hemingway may be made here. The last twenty years of Hemingway's life are marked by a search for new experience to write about, with a varying degree of success. (The same problem no doubt faces all writers to a greater or lesser extent; but the novelist who has taken vigorous action as his main theme is confronted with it more directly.)

    [2] At least sixteen book reviews signed by Malraux were published in the *N.R.F.* between 1927 and 1932; after then he was evidently able to dispense with routine reviewing. With a few exceptions, they cannot be said to stand out from other reviews in the same volumes.

    [3] J. Hoffmann, *L'Humanisme de Malraux*, p. 2.

typically grandiose design: a new—Marxist—*Encyclopédie*, the supreme intellectual achievement of the century, with world-wide contributors, to be published in four languages—Russian, English, French, and Spanish. (In the end, nothing came of it.)[1] In the same year the Spanish Civil War broke out and he promptly began work for the Republican air force; his work both as organizer and as a crew member is well known. The Nazi–Soviet Pact of 1939, or possibly even Spanish experiences earlier, finally disillusioned him with the Communist party, and there is no sign of any political views whatever in *Les Noyers de l'Altenburg*, written in 1941. In that year he began to resist actively, and by 1944 had become a Maquis colonel, keeping his rank when the French army was reorganized after the Liberation, and commanding a French unit in the Vosges. (In 1939–40 he had served in the tanks as a simple ranker, before escaping after the defeat.) In 1944 Malraux first met General de Gaulle, to whom he has shown complete and irreproachable loyalty ever since, both in power and out of it.

Malraux's political career since 1945, and especially since 1958, when he has been continuously in office, is not really germane to a literary study, and need not detain us long. No politician, of whatever party, can expect to escape criticism; and in addition there has been a tendency, as so often in France, for political bias to colour literary judgements on Malraux's work. To the extreme Left, Malraux is a renegade and turncoat, as might be supposed; this puts him in such distinguished company as Gide, Arthur Koestler, and a host of others. Liberal opinion has been dismayed and disappointed by Malraux's continued presence in a government which has introduced censorship in literature, and which seems to it little interested in the ordinary liberal conception of democracy. A common view has been that Malraux's support of President de Gaulle, and his rumoured position as the latter's closest adviser, are more a feather in the President's cap than his own.[2] But all this is perhaps a naïve attitude, depending on the

---

[1] Cf. E. Sinkó, *Roman eines Romans*, p. 333.

[2] De Gaulle's alleged comment on first meeting Malraux in 1944, 'Enfin, voilà un homme!', seems perhaps a little too reminiscent of Napoleon's (reputed) words on meeting Goethe, 'Voilà un homme!', to be fully credible. At any rate, it is difficult to imagine de Gaulle himself relating this anecdote.

assumption that all left-wing and liberal attitudes are identical. All the evidence from Malraux's actions and writings is that he has never had much time for liberal democracy; in the 1920s he was fascinated by violence, while *Les Conquérants* and *L'Espoir* in particular show a keen interest, almost to the point of obsession, in intrigue, power techniques, and the manipulation, forcible if necessary, of social groups and public opinion: in a word, in the belief that the end justifies the means. Psychologically, his position has been authoritarian throughout. Certainly Malraux has moved sharply from Left to Right in politics; but this has been, especially in France, so common a development among writers as to be almost typical. Indeed, it is the move in the opposite direction, from Right to Left, in such writers as Hugo, Anatole France, and Gide that would seem to require more explanation. Similarly, the transition from the erotic theorist of the earlier years—witness not only his own novels, but also the preface to *L'Amant de Lady Chatterley*—to the apparent supporter of literary censorship is not too difficult to understand on psychological grounds, despite the surface inconsistency.

Positive cultural achievements in Malraux's political career have been the establishment of the Maisons de Culture and the revitalization of the Comédie Française; and no doubt cultural considerations have been taken more seriously in the Fifth Republic than in its predecessor. This is all to the good, though there is an accompanying danger: state encouragement in the arts, theoretically admirable, may have less desirable results if private support should therefore peter out and official encouragement become insistent and selective. Without needing to cite contemporary totalitarian examples, one need only go back a century in France itself and consider Berlioz's lifelong struggle to gain acceptance. There is, as yet, no guarantee that the standard values of 'modern' art accepted by Malraux will survive any more than the standard values of the art of the Second Empire have done; and there has been perhaps a disquieting resemblance between the pomp of Louis-Napoléon and such ceremonies as Malraux's 'act of solemn national homage' at his funeral oration for Braque, delivered in the Louvre courtyard with full military honours. Others of

Malraux's colourful gestures have verged on the comic. The idea of having the Opéra ceiling repainted by Marc Chagall—in imitation of Lenin, incidentally, who had likewise commissioned Chagall to paint frescoes in the Jewish Theatre in Moscow[1]—led to the somewhat ludicrous result that the ceiling would be painted by a 'ghost' artist, while the 77-year-old Chagall, unwilling to spend many of his last days lying on his back painting a ceiling *à la* Michaelangelo, merely sketched the design and signed the finished work. There has, in fact, been a fairly constant stream of comic anecdotes about Malraux—doubtless often apocryphal; and since 1958 his legend has had to contend with a debunking 'anti-legend' in such journals as *Le Canard Enchaîné*.

All in all, it is possible to doubt whether Malraux's political career will aid his artistic posterity. On the whole, artists have not played an impressive role when they have achieved political power, despite the courage they may have shown. This is especially true of French writers—for example Chateaubriand or Lamartine —and their political attitudes have often seemed more admirable in opposition: Hugo hurling imprecations at Louis-Napoléon from his exile is a more impressive figure than Hugo the life-senator of the Third Republic. Sartre has claimed that no writer should be a 'technicien' of the government: 'son rôle ne se confond pas avec celui des dirigeants.'[2] This remark would sound better if there were no savour of sour grapes about it: Sartre did his best to become a political figure in 1949 when he helped to found the R.D.R., and to what end if he did not hope, however vainly as it turned out, for political power? One might in fact argue against Sartre himself that the writer, as writer, has no business being a 'technicien' of the opposition either. *Engagement*, in reality, is present in all artists, more or less,[3] and its explicit

---

[1] Cf. L. Guissard, *Écrits en notre temps*, p. 245.

[2] S. de Beauvoir, *La Force des choses*, p. 427.

[3] As Roger Martin du Gard put it, 'Toute littérature qui vaut quelque chose, dont l'auteur a une personnalité, est *engagée*, même les *Fables* de La Fontaine . . .' (letter to J.-J. Thierry, quoted in *N.N.R.F.*, December 1958, p. 1015). Cf. also Sainte-Beuve's profound judgement, that men of letters should avoid politics, since otherwise they tend to strike attitudes and derive from practical affairs the emotions of fancy; in a word they dramatize their situations and adopt roles not strictly their own.

affirmation by Sartre seems to have sapped his creative energies without any positive political results as compensation. In Malraux's case, many admirers of his novels have felt a distinct regret, even irritation, that he has abandoned imaginative literature to such an extent since the war. Despite a certain impatience with execution in *Les Noyers de l'Altenburg*, it seems unlikely that he simply felt that he had written himself out. And his whole pre-occupation with legend may ultimately prove to do him a dis-service, despite its power, especially in his earlier career, as a dynamic. Malraux may have wished to become the Byron of the twentieth century, but legends are dangerous attributes and may recoil on their possessors: the fate of d'Annunzio, who since his death has undergone metamorphosis from the 'hero of Fiume'—itself an issue utterly forgotten—to a kind of comic Casanova, whose works, whatever their value, are never even read. In the end Malraux's artistic reputation will have to depend on his works, rather than on the legend; and the former, unlike the latter, are open to detailed analysis and appreciation.

One feature of Malraux's political career is, however, highly important in understanding his thought. This is that the conception of art as the ultimate *anti-destin* is not, as many critics have assumed, Malraux's last word. We so far wait in vain for the second volume of *La Métamorphose des dieux*. Given the chance of exchanging contemplation of art for political action in 1958, he did not hesitate. He evidently takes his position and responsibilities as Minister very seriously, and his career since the downfall of the Fourth Republic makes it clear that action is more important to him than art—given the choice. Indeed, one might even go further and glance back at 1945, with Malraux just appointed Minister under de Gaulle for the first time. At that point he could scarcely have anticipated the General's resignation so soon afterwards, and must have looked forward to some considerable period of political office; and it might be argued that the development of earlier ideas into a dramatic philosophy of art is at least partly due to a period of forced inaction and disappointment, in which contemplation of art was particularly attractive to him.

Taken all in all, Malraux presents a compelling rather than an

appealing personality. No doubt this is as he would wish it, preferring public respect and admiration to sympathy and affection.
Numerous writers have borne witness to his scintillating conversation: to take only one example, Stephen Spender, who met
Malraux at the Madrid Writers' Congress in 1937, thought him
the outstanding figure there, and 'the most brilliant and dynamic
conversationalist I had met'.[1] Others, while paying their due to the
hypnotic quality of Malraux's talk (monologue rather than conversation), have found it unsettling as well as overpowering.[2]
Malraux seems, indeed, to have spent much of his life keyed up to
a state of nervous tension far more intense than the average man
could tolerate, and, as a personality, he both fascinates and
dominates.

One of the elements of the Malraux legend which is still most
widely current is the vision of 'Malraux le témoin', or the belief
that his novels are largely autobiographical, fairly straightforward
transcriptions of personal experience into the novel form. Yet this
is in fact not so. There is a good deal of autobiographical material
in *La Voie royale*, but the climax of the novel has no equivalent in
Malraux's own experiences in Cambodia. In *Les Conquérants* there
is a background of settings—Singapore, Saigon, Hong Kong, and
Canton itself—which are evidently genuine; though it seems certain that Malraux was not in Canton at the time of the events
described there.[3] The first edition of *La Condition humaine* contained various signs that its author was unfamiliar with Shanghai,

[1] S. Spender, *World within World*, pp. 239–40. It is only fair to add that
Spender also thought the whole Madrid Congress—to a great extent Malraux's
own propaganda achievement—somewhat grotesque and irrelevant to the Civil
War then in progress. Malraux has rarely been able to refuse a grandiose gesture,
though this may very well have been a strength as well as a weakness.

[2] A friend of mine, who had the good fortune to attend Malraux's press con-
ference during his visit to Peking in 1965, described Malraux's manner as 'dream-
ing out loud'. My friend added that he thought the Chinese officials present could
rarely have been so bewildered.

[3] Cf. Frohock, op. cit., p. 16. My own investigations on the spot in Hong Kong
have been entirely negative: no one I met had any knowledge of Malraux as either
Kuomintang or Communist agent. This does not prove very much, except
possibly that his role—if he had one at all—must have been very minor. It is in any
case difficult to believe that either the Nationalists, with their distrust of all
foreigners, or the Communists, with their strict discipline, would have entrusted

and it seems that he never visited it until 1931.[1] Models for certain of the characters in this novel have, it is true, been found, yet mostly they are people Malraux had known in Europe, not in Asia at all. *Le Temps du mépris* has quite openly nothing to do with Malraux's personal experience; on the other hand, the aviation episodes in *L'Espoir* may well have been based on personal experience—but these form only a fraction of the total novel.[2] In *Les Noyers de l'Altenburg* only the experiences of the narrator in the opening and closing sections can be directly based on Malraux's own lived experience;[3] they certainly have the ring of truth, but the centre of gravity of the novel, as it stands, is in the central sections dealing with Vincent Berger. On the whole, then, Malraux has written his novels using the same creative processes as any other novelist: the characters, events, and settings he presents have their origin in a complex mixture of first-hand and vicarious experience, bolstered by pure imagination, and transformed into an autonomous existence in the act of composition. There is nothing strange about this; and indeed, even if Malraux's novels were directly autobiographical, the fact of their being so might well be to their disadvantage, since their creative content would be correspondingly reduced. However, the point should perhaps be stressed, since certain critics have attempted to maintain that the authenticity which they claim to have perceived in the novels gives them a uniquely representative value.[4] This claim cannot resist analysis:

important work to a relative newcomer and non-party-member.

[1] e.g. Malraux originally put the city on the Yangtse River, whereas anyone at all familiar with Shanghai must have known that the river there is the Whangpoo. Sinkó (op. cit., p. 189) describes meeting in Moscow a Mr. Tru, the Chinese translator of *La Condition humaine*, who complained that the book was full of topographical blunders. Malraux had given him *carte blanche* to correct them, but there were so many that it was impossible. Cf. also C. Malraux, *Nos vingt ans*, p. 129.

[2] Certain episodes at least (such as the 'descent from the mountain') were described as fact by Malraux before the publication of the novel. Cf. Sinkó, op. cit., p. 438; and F. Mauriac, *Journal*, vol. 2, p. 222.

[3] Clara Malraux tells us that many of the details of Dietrich Berger's life were taken from Malraux's own grandfather (*Nos vingt ans*, pp. 93–4).

[4] e.g. H. M. Chevalier, in his introduction to the American edition of *La Condition humaine*, New York, 1934, where he states that Malraux had lived through and participated in the events depicted in the novel, and speaks of 'heroes who have a complete validity for our time'.

although Malraux's experiences undoubtedly shaped his work, as we have seen, by giving him both his settings and some of his themes, and although a knowledge of Malraux's biography may well help appreciation of the novels, the fact remains that 'authenticity' in the strict autobiographical sense is a criterion which cannot be applied to any work of fiction without an immediate and inescapable contradiction. As novels, Malraux's books can be judged in no other way than any other novel.

Malraux's 'Surrealist' writings have generally been dismissed as little more than juvenilia. Recently André Vandegans has made a valiant attempt to 'rehabilitate' these works: 'Leur étude est une introduction indispensable à la connaissance historique et esthétique de l'œuvre malrucienne.'[1] Indeed, M. Vandegans would go further and conclude, from his analysis of the three 'Surrealist' works, that Malraux's work forms a unity: 'il n'y a qu'un seul Malraux.'[2] Not the least merit of M. Vandegans's book is that it makes available to the general reader long extracts and summaries of works difficult to obtain, and his careful and patient study both of the early writings and of Malraux's own life during the years before 1928 is a model of literary scholarship. Yet I cannot feel that he has proved his case. From the beginning the odds are against him: Malraux himself obviously has no wish to include these writings in the accepted corpus of his work. The first, *Lunes en papier*, was published in a small edition in 1921, illustrated with engravings by Fernand Léger which would have a fair claim to be no less valuable than Malraux's text. The book has not, so far, been reprinted. The succeeding work, *Écrit pour une idole à trompe*, was only partially published—and, indeed, never finished. The critics who have studied the completed fragments have been able to do so only through Malraux's generosity in lending them a typescript. The final work, *Royaume farfelu*, of which the first draft dated back to 1920, came out under the Gallimard imprint in 1928, the same year that the same house serialized *Les Conquérants* in the *N.R.F.*, before the novel was published by Grasset in book form. Its comparative lack of success (Bernard Groethuysen, reviewing the

[1] Vandegans, op. cit., p. 11.   [2] Ibid., p. 12.

two books in the *N.R.F.* of April 1929, simply refused to give it serious attention, devoting practically all his space to *Les Conquérants*) possibly had something to do with Malraux's complete abandonment of 'Surrealist' works—and of attempts to publish other *œuvres de tiroir* written in the early 1920s. It is clear that at any time in the last twenty years Malraux's reputation, let alone his connexions with Gallimard, would have made republication perfectly straightforward—if he had wished it. The inference must be that he did not.

I have used the word 'Surrealist' to describe this early phase of Malraux's work, but in inverted commas, since he appears to have moved only on the fringes of the Surrealist movement proper, and in any case to have been influenced before its beginning at the end of 1921 by Dadaism, and, as Vandegans has pointed out, even by German Expressionism.[1] Nevertheless for practical purposes these early writings of Malraux can legitimately be called Surrealistic, since they share the principal characteristics of other works produced by writers in the movement. *Lunes en papier*, to take the best example, is a complicated fantasy with grotesque imagery (although in a prefatory note Malraux warns us that 'il n'y a aucun symbole dans ce livre'), relying chiefly for its aesthetic impact on effects of shock and unexpected juxtaposition of language and events. Perhaps nearly all Surrealist writings could be defined as *écrits gratuits*: certainly this is the most striking feature of *Lunes*, of which the plot, if such it can be called, is an attack on Death by a company of balloons, who mysteriously turn into fruits, then imaginary beings.[2] Among the images encountered are noses transformed into billiard cues, the genius of a lake, which is a living pin-cushion in the shape of a cat, stuffed alligators flying about, and phosphorescent mushrooms, while Death is personified in a dinner jacket. The gratuitousness of the whole work is almost absolute, and the reader is placed in a position familiar to anybody who has been faced with any Surrealist art: if gratuitousness is accepted as an artistic premiss, then few if any standards of judge-

[1] Vandegans, op. cit., pp. 157–9.
[2] For a full and sympathetic analysis, see ibid., especially pp. 95–140. Cf. also Frohock, op. cit., pp. 21–4.

ment remain possible. Originality of image seems swiftly to descend into a wild search for gimmicks, while criteria of crafts-manship can be little in evidence. Pure gratuitousness, indeed, as an aesthetic ideal, must be a dead end. There is, moreover, a certain conventionality about many Surrealistic works, including those of Malraux, a certain sameness; one might go so far as to say that a theory of art putting the highest premium on unrestrained indi-viduality ends by depriving works of precisely what individuality they might otherwise have possessed. Certainly it is very difficult to identify Surrealistic works unless the name of the writer is already known.

We may, I think, add to this a consideration affecting Malraux perhaps more than others. One of the main principles of the Surrealist aesthetic was that both the rational and the conscious should be scrupulously avoided. Malraux, as is not surprising given the deep Nietzschean influence he was already feeling, his belief in will as the chief dynamic of personality, is clearly torn between the ideal of unrestrained subconscious fantasy, and the desire to con-trol his writings to the utmost. Professor Frohock has commented that Malraux was writing before 'the great Surrealist year of 1924' and that 'doubtless his manner seemed fresher then than it does now'.[1] This is probably true; but also one of the features that strike the present-day reader is a rather self-conscious artificiality in *Lunes*. There are, it is true, evident obsessions, above all with violence, torture, and massacres,[2] but on the whole the spon-taneous outpouring of the subconscious is notably lacking.[3] And, as with any highly self-conscious writing, there is a strong tendency

[1] Ibid., p. 24.

[2] Cf. C. Roy, op. cit., p. 226: 'Le fait premier de Malraux, c'est la fascination de la guerre, du sang, des supplices et de la mort, de préférence dans un décor éclatant et bizarre, *lointain*.'

[3] It is, of course, arguable that few of the Surrealists had any deep comprehension of the (Freudian) concept of the subconscious, or of the unconscious, and that they merely used the words, particularly the former, as blanket terms to cover all fan-tasies, whether unconscious or not. Again, the unconscious seems a most dubious foundation for any aesthetic, since the contribution—and consequently the value —of the artist is reduced to a minimum. The same applies to the Romantic faith in pure inspiration—in which this particular Surrealist tenet seems to have origi-nated: as an aesthetic principle it suffers from the same defect.

towards preciosity (despite appearances, Surrealism probably owes more to Symbolism than is sometimes recognized).
These strictures are generally true of all Malraux's early work,
though less so in the case of *Royaume farfelu*, in which fantasy is
more restrained, as there is a reasonably clear line of plot and the
characters are at least human.

For Malraux's early work really to sustain Vandegans's claim,
it would have to contain the essence of his later novels, or at least
be shown as absolutely essential to his further development as a
writer. But this is not so. Neither the political preoccupations nor
the metaphysical anxieties which provide practically all Malraux's
later themes are to be discerned in the early fantasies. All we
are left with is fascination with violence and death (the exotic is
not a point in common, since in the fantasies it is entirely imaginary, while in the novels the appearance of objective description
is the aim). Nor can there be said to be the unity of Malraux's work
which Vandegans also distinguishes: after *Royaume farfelu*
Surrealism is repudiated just as utterly as his apparently right-
wing sympathies on his first visit to Indo-China. If these early
works had been written by any writer except Malraux they would
probably have been long since forgotten. As it is, they betray an
immaturity just as striking as the wide powers of expression and
confident touch of the later Malraux. Far from casting valuable
light on the mature novels, the early fantasies seem more likely
to make one marvel that the same man could have produced
both. Clearly, in these early stages Malraux had literary ambitions
which were not matched by any sense of self-criticism; he really
had little to write about, and was content to imitate the contemporary idiom.[1]

The second stage of Malraux's work is more interesting. This is
represented by the two works, *La Tentation de l'Occident* and
D'une jeunesse européenne. The first, appearing as a separate book

---

[1] It is interesting that when, about 1922 or 1923, Malraux first came into contact with the *N.R.F.*, Jacques Rivière refused some of his work, 'prétextant qu'un
jour, quand leur auteur aurait à son actif des œuvres de poids, il regretterait d'avoir
livré au public ce qui n'était que fantaisie, sans conséquence' (*Nos vingt ans*, p. 57).

in 1926 under the Grasset imprint, consists of a series of letters between a young Chinese, Ling, visiting Europe, and a young Frenchman, A. D., touring China and the East. This form is, of course, merely a device to add interest to a number of general ideas which are Malraux's real preoccupation: at the end, the work bears the dates 1921–5, and thus would seem to embody the fruits of its author's meditations during that period. The book might be compared to (and be partly derived from) Montesquieu's *Lettres persanes*, although it lacks the latter's wit and satire, and limits itself almost entirely to the two correspondents. Seriousness is, indeed, the main feature of the work, which resolves itself very largely into an application of certain Nietzschean ideas to the traditional antithesis between Europe and the Orient. It is thus less original than might at first appear.

Malraux's principal concern is not so much his analysis of the East, which is mainly conventional and therefore less interesting, as his attempt at dissection of the Western mentality. The Orient, as A. D. sees it and as it emerges from Ling's reflections on Europe, is very much the same as that of earlier Western commentators, such as Count Keyserling. Meditation is contrasted with the Western thirst for action, lack of self-consciousness with Occidental moral doubt and sense of sin. A Nietzschean belief in will dominates the European: the Chinese feels himself merged into the world, the European distinct from it. The former's ideal is *sagesse*, the latter's is *gloire*: calm contrasted with movement, and above all with intensity. This vision of the East is a long way away from Malraux's political activity in Indo-China, and we may suppose that this part of the book antedates this plunge into action, a whole-hearted attempt to transform the East according to Western ideas.[1] Towards the end of the book there are, indeed, some considerations on the contemporary political situation in China, when A. D. meets one Wang-Loh: Wang-Loh's reflections are fairly close to the tone of *Les Conquérants*, but seem something of an afterthought to the main ideas discussed in *La Tentation*, and

[1] It is sometimes forgotten that Marxism in China is merely one of many European intellectual exports: vastly more successful in diffusion, certainly, but none the less European.

may well be posterior to the bulk of the book. Wang-Loh sees
Chinese thinkers as both seduced and repelled by Western ideas.
Their country is in moral ruins because of the decay of Confu-
cianism, and its former cultural traditions are dying away. Almost
in contradiction to views expressed earlier in the book, he com-
plains that no one understands any more 'la parfaite assimilation
du monde par l'homme' (p. 174)—the same merging with the
world already mentioned. The younger generations are, above all,
inspired by a thirst for destruction. Ling, in his answer, agrees:
'C'est de l'injustice que nos millions de malheureux ont conscience, et non de la justice; de la souffrance, et non du bonheur'
(p. 191); and he also talks of the Canton revolutionary government, which is challenging Britain and adopting Western technology.

The main part of the book, however, is written in much more
general terms: although Ling visits Rome and Athens as well as
France, his reflections contain almost no topical references. He
begins by rejecting material civilization, unlike the Canton
nationalists, in favour of spiritual values: 'Je vois dans l'Europe une
barbarie attentivement ordonnée, où l'idée de la civilisation et
celle de l'ordre sont chaque jour confondues' (p. 29). (This idea can
be found in both Spengler and Keyserling, among many others;
no doubt it came to them through Nietzsche, but it is also a
typically Romantic attitude.) Western man, believing that to be
means to act, is consumed with passion and suffering: in Spenglerian terms, he is primarily Faustian.[1] But Ling's meditations
largely spring from the two fields of art and sexuality, and, indeed,
it is the latter which leads him to the often-quoted formulation of
the absurd: 'au centre de l'homme européen, dominant les grands
mouvements de sa vie, est une absurdité essentielle' (p. 72). The
context of the formulation is important: against the simple
Oriental view of sexuality as physical pleasure, unsullied by any
purely mental idea of love, the European subordinates his sexual

---

[1] Although *The Decline of the West* was only fully translated into French in
1931–3, Malraux must certainly have been familiar with Spengler's basic concepts,
which had been very much in the air since the end of the First World War; and
there is, perhaps, a Spenglerian echo in his very title here.

life to his imagination and thereby to his will. This is, of course, very close to the conception of the erotic in *La Voie royale*, or in Ferral in *La Condition humaine*; but it is both curious and noteworthy that Malraux at this time seems a good deal more critical of this erotic ideal than in the later works. The same is true of the reflections on art, which point forward to the post-war art philosophy, but which often seem to reject it in advance. Thus Ling, after spending an afternoon in the Louvre, feels profoundly depressed: 'A leur maladroite réunion, que je préfère ce que montrent les fenêtres! . . . Vos musées n'apportent point de plaisir. . . . Le musée enseigne, hélas! ce qu'attendent de la beauté des "étrangers". Il incite à comparer, et amène à sentir surtout, dans une œuvre nouvelle, la différence qu'elle apporte' (pp. 114–15). This is precisely the objection raised by the severest critics of *Les Voix du silence*. Ling is even more devastating when he considers the whole Western obsession with its past: 'Parmi les gestes les plus tragiques et les plus vains des hommes, aucun, jamais, ne m'a paru plus tragique et plus vain que celui par lequel vous interrogez toutes vos ombres illustres, race vouée à la puissance, race désespérée . . .' (p. 106). Thus, although Malraux is using Nietzsche's conception of art as metaphysical solace, and of history as dynamic myth, he seems extremely doubtful about their ultimate validity. (It is, of course, arguable that Ling and A. D. do not necessarily represent Malraux's own beliefs; but since the two are in agreement in their diagnosis of the Occident, this argument loses a good deal of its force. There is no genuine confrontation of opposing views as in the novels, especially *Les Noyers de l'Altenburg*.)

The Nietzschean idea that underlies the whole work is that God is dead. Malraux, indeed, develops this further. Western man is governed by his mental life: 'L'intensité que les idées créent en vous me semble . . . expliquer votre vie mieux qu'elles-mêmes. La réalité absolue a été pour vous Dieu, puis l'homme; mais *l'homme est mort*, après Dieu, et vous cherchez avec angoisse celui à qui vous pourriez confier son étrange héritage' (p. 166). Here we have not only the germ of the *anti-destin*—dismissed, incidentally, by Ling without much more ado—but also the rejection of humanism together with that of Christianity. Ling has no more confidence than Nietzsche in rational philosophies, despite their popularity: 'Vos petits essais de structure pour des nihilismes modérés ne me semblent plus destinés à une longue existence. . . . La vision de tous ces hommes appliqués à maintenir l'Homme qui leur permet de surmonter la pensée et de vivre, tandis que le monde sur lequel il règne leur devient, de jour en jour, étranger, est sans doute la dernière vision que j'emporterai de l'Occident' (pp. 166-7).

La Tentation de l'Occident leaves the reader with a curiously negative impression. Malraux accepts Nietzsche's destructive analysis of modern European society, and, indeed, refines on it, but is much more reluctant to substitute for it, at this stage, an ethic of heroism. The same negative attitude emerges from D'une jeunesse européenne, a fairly short essay of less than 4,000 words, published in the Cahiers verts in 1927. Here Malraux is considerably more direct, since there is no question of any fictional form; although some of the same lyricism, and indulgence in generalizations and abstract ideas, tend slightly to confuse his line of argument. European man is seen as searching to rid himself of his existing civilization, including the Christian tradition, and wishing to create his own values, even his own reality, instead: 'Il semble donc que le principal effort du monde moderne doive tendre à la création de sa réalité' (p. 139). Thus an absolute individualism has to replace the empty humanism which has itself replaced religious belief; and Nietzsche is representative of modern man in this: 'Si Nietzsche trouve tant d'échos dans les cœurs désespérés, c'est qu'il n'est lui-même que l'expression de leur désespoir et de leur violence' (p. 139). This individualism will be based on will and action—already Malraux has no time for the unconscious or subconscious—but can only lead to a perception of the absurd through the absolute contingency of the individual personality: 'Pousser à l'extrême la recherche de soi-même, en acceptant son propre monde, c'est tendre à l'absurde' (p. 144). No ultimate meaning in life can be discovered by this means:

. . . nous voici au point où l'individualisme triomphant veut prendre de lui-même une conscience plus nette. Chargé des passions successives

des hommes, il a tout anéanti, sauf lui-même; élevé par les plus hauts
esprits de notre époque, précédé par la folie de Nietzsche et paré de la
dépouille des dieux, le voici devant nous, et nous ne voyons en lui qu'un
triomphateur aveugle. (pp. 145–6)

Malraux's reflections are clearly metaphysical here, not political.
He goes on to emphasize the barrenness of the contemporary
situation: 'Notre époque, où rôdent encore tant d'échos, ne veut
pas avouer sa pensée nihiliste, destructrice, foncièrement négative'
(p. 148). The only possible escape from destiny, that is, from time,
might be through a private world of art, and Malraux comments
that a good deal of European art, such as the plastic art of Eastern
Europe and poetry everywhere, depends on the use of the fantastic (he is taking Surrealism as the prevailing movement in
poetry). But this does not alter the main conclusion, which is in
fact a question mark, refusing all positive solutions, yet having
nothing to put in their place: 'A quel destin est donc vouée cette
jeunesse violente, merveilleusement armée contre elle-même, et
délivrée de la basse vanité de nommer grandeur le dédain d'une
vie à laquelle elle ne sait pas se lier?' (p. 153). Malraux has not yet
tried to work out a Marxist *Weltanschauung*: *La Tentation* is essentially a transitional work. Beginning with a prologue, which is
still very much in the earlier 'Surrealist' style, Malraux then turns
his back on his previous work completely, devoting himself to an
elaboration of general ideas. The section introducing Wang-Loh
seems to have been appended as an afterthought, as we have seen,
while the whole book ends on a deliberately lyrical note which
again is not much in keeping with the analytical mood of most of
the letters, though occasionally both correspondents launch into
similar purple passages. It appears that Malraux was still feeling his
way. Surrealism had proved a false start,[1] and his imaginative

[1] It remains, of course, to explain why Malraux continued working at *Royaume
farfelu* even after his second visit to the East, in 1925–6, and after the publication of
La Tentation de l'Occident. There is, however, no insuperable difficulty here.
Royaume farfelu was in the main an old text which Malraux was revising specifically
for publication. Above all, Malraux has never shown signs of reluctance to launch
into print, as the number and variety of his minor publications illustrate (cf. the
excellent bibliography in Hoffmann, op. cit.), and it is understandable that he was
unwilling to waste usable manuscripts, even if his primary interests had changed.
There is no evidence that he began new 'Surrealist' works after 1925.

powers and feeling for poetic prose found much better scope in contexts where fantasy was closely limited. The final passage of *La Tentation* has often been quoted: 'Lucidité avide, je brûle encore devant toi, flamme solitaire et droite, dans cette lourde nuit ou [*sic*] le vent jaune crie comme dans toutes ces nuits étrangères où le vent du large répétait autour de moi l'orgueilleuse clameur de la mer stérile . . .' (p. 205). Clearly we have here the germ of the poetic imagery—sound and silence, light and darkness—of the novels. On the other hand, the passage bears no relevance to the ideas in the book—any more than does the prologue. Other passages approach very closely the style and tone of *Les Voix du silence*, and show clearly how Malraux's attitude to art and history at this time was already one of lyrical emotion, rather than cold rational appraisal:

Le temps à ces pierres attaché se divertit à ramener leur fruste gloire aux limites du pittoresque méditerranéen. Et, parfois, devant ce jeu trop lucide d'un temps occidental et facétieux, je voyais se mêler le souvenir de Rome à celui d'Alexandrie, luxe et vulgarité, idoles dans le soleil du matin et violentes foules blanches sur de vastes places. (p. 52)

Malraux's powers of expression have greatly developed in this second stage, and he also has more to say and greater confidence in his material. Yet general ideas alone do not make literature (and Malraux's ideas here were doubtless much more derivative than he thought). To some extent the exchange of letters provides a more satisfactory literary vehicle than a straightforward essay; but any dramatic effects are prevented by the lack of any clash between the two correspondents, who are both patently Malraux himself. And the ideas are too general, therefore too abstract, to communicate most effectively. The success of *La Tentation* and *D'une jeunesse* was only moderate, as one might expect. Though the former, particularly, contains—unlike the 'Surrealist' fantasies—the germ of much of Malraux's later work, it is only when he found a precise concrete situation, and developed a number of reasonably well-differentiated characters, that he really came into his own.

2

LA VOIE ROYALE

LA VOIE ROYALE, although appearing only in 1930 and thus the
second in order of Malraux's major novels, bears all the
signs of having been conceived, and perhaps largely written,
before *Les Conquérants* (1928). The duality of theme, the keen tension between the political and the metaphysical, that characterizes
Les Conquérants and *La Condition humaine* (1933) is not present;
whereas a certain clumsiness of narrative technique, and naivety in
psychological analysis, amounting at times almost to a parody of
Malraux's later idiom—'Claude avait été séduit d'abord par le ton
de sa voix (c'était la seule personne du bateau qui prononçât le
mot: énergie, avec simplicité)' (p. 11)[1]—and the fact that Malraux
himself excluded the novel from the *Pléiade* edition of his novels in
1947, are evidence for this view.[2] We may, indeed, surmise that
Malraux initially found difficulty in completing his novel and put
it aside until later. A note at the end of the original edition of the
novel runs: '*La Voie royale* constitue le Tome premier des *Puissances
du Désert*, dont cette initiation tragique n'est que le prologue.'
Nothing has come to light of the other novels included in this
rather ambitious plan (unless the unidentified narrator of *Les*

[1] Quotations are taken from the *Livre de Poche* edition.
[2] In fact, Malraux seems to have both confirmed and denied this chronology.
In 1961, in a letter to M. Hoffmann, he stated very firmly, '*La Voie royale* a été
écrite après les *Conquérants*' (quoted in Hoffmann, op. cit., p. 134). Earlier Claude
Mauriac, presumably acting on first-hand information, states that '*La Voie royale*
fut le premier roman conçu et même ébauché par notre auteur' (*Malraux ou le mal
du héros*, p. 36). Evidently Malraux had begun his novel, but had lost interest in it
temporarily. Another minor bibliographical problem is why Malraux, already a
member of Gallimard's staff, should nevertheless have published *La Voie royale*
with Grasset: we now know that as early as 1925 he had signed a contract with
Grasset for three books (C. Malraux, *Nos vingt ans*, p. 278). This being so, he may
well have taken up again an abandoned book to execute this option obligation.

Conquérants is in fact supposed to be Claude Vannec), and we must conclude that conception was not followed by execution. Certainly, it is easy to see why he did not pursue the series further, since his interests had moved sharply over towards revolutionary politics (of which there is no sign in *La Voie royale*). Again, it is difficult to understand why Malraux should choose an almost identical opening for both *La Voie royale* and *Les Conquérants*, with tension gradually mounting during a long sea journey out to the East, unless he thought that this was one of the better features of the uncompleted *Voie*, worth preserving in his next attempt. We may conclude that Malraux's literary career in the 1920s was largely concerned with the search for an adequate vehicle for the themes that gradually came to obsess him; he had to publish—like any young writer—where and how he could, and the evident order of his development—Surrealist, then metaphysical, then politico-metaphysical—is not necessarily reflected in the order of publication of his works.

The general title, *Les Puissances du Désert*, not particularly apt for Cambodia alone, and probably inspired by Malraux's admiration for Lawrence, seems to indicate that his major theme was to be the adventurer struggling with his destiny in the shape of a hostile Nature—*le désert*. Later, this hostile Nature disappears from Malraux's work: the encounter with destiny remains, but the circumstances will change to the field of revolution. The struggle with destiny—'le combat décisif avec l'ange', as Malraux himself called it in his article on Lawrence[1]—forms the essence of *La Voie royale*. By a *dédoublement* somewhat similar to the relationship between Garine and the narrator of *Les Conquérants*, there are two protagonists: Perken, a Danish adventurer who governs an almost independent *domaine* in up-country Thailand, and Claude Vannec, officially a trained archaeologist, *chargé de mission*, yet whose ideas of archaeological investigation seem to go little further than the desire to plunder any finds for his own financial profit. In his attitude there is scarcely any notion of systematic excavation to increase knowledge of the Khmer civilization, merely a crude thirst for treasure-hunting; and it is possible to sympathize with the

---

[1] 'N'était-ce donc que cela?', *Saisons*, no. 3, p. 12.

Director of the French Institute in Saigon, despite Malraux's obvious attempt to satirize him as unimaginative and deliberately obstructive, when he refuses Claude more than token assistance.

The plot of the novel appears, at first sight, to be Claude's search for ruined Khmer temples along the former Royal Road—which gives the novel its title—in Cambodia, in order to remove and to sell any remaining sculptures to dealers in Europe. Yet this is no more than an introduction to, even a pretext for the main theme: Perken's pushing of the struggle against destiny to its absolute limits and the apparent victory of his will over the 'other', only to find that at the very moment of success the absurd reasserts itself and slowly kills him, the novel ending with his death. The novel is formally divided into four main parts, while each part is again subdivided into sections of roughly conventional chapter length (and occasionally dramatic episodes are rather arbitrarily split to produce these sections). The first part of the novel covers the sea journey from Djibouti, during which Claude makes Perken's acquaintance, and enlists him to join in the expedition in Cambodia in exchange for half the profits. The numerous conversations between the two men, as their sense of comradeship grows, permit Malraux to treat various themes: the erotic, the absurd, the destructive effects of time, the relationship between the *moi* and *autrui*.

In the second part of the book, which is considerably shorter, the two men are able, after an initial failure, to discover and to detach from the gigantic stone blocks of a half-buried ruin the sculptures they covet; this marks their material success, which is immediately followed by a further obstacle, when they are promptly deserted by the Cambodian peasants whom Claude has hitherto been able to requisition. They are now far in the jungle, and, since any removal of the sculptures has been expressly forbidden by the French authorities, they decide to push further forward through unpacified areas to Siam, from where they will be able to ship the carvings back to Europe. At the same time Perken wishes to search for Grabot, another adventurer of his own kind, who is rumoured to dominate certain tribes in this area, but from whom no news has come for some time. This move forms the third and crucial part of the novel, with the focus of interest switched sharply away from the archaeological to the metaphysical. On arrival in the village of Moï warriors, Grabot is discovered, not as a chief, but as a blinded slave set to a treadmill. As the tribesmen prepare to attack, Perken, at the point of highest tension in the book, walks almost unarmed to their ranks and succeeds in bargaining for their free passage and Grabot's subsequent release. This triumph of will marks his apparent victory over destiny—but, by a deliberate irony, at the very moment when he walks across to the natives, he stumbles on a war-dart embedded in the ground. The resulting wound in his knee becomes fatally infected, and by the time the two men and their Cambodian servant reach Thailand, Perken is doomed. There is no escape, even temporary, from his consciousness of death: the section ends with Perken procuring a woman for a last erotic experience, only to find that she too remains irrevocably 'other' and unreachable. In the final section, again shorter, Perken decides to move north to his own territory, but on the way is given unmistakable signs of his fallen prestige, and finally dies, watched by Claude. Death has now ceased to be an abstract concept, and has become instead the ultimate personal experience, as Perken's last words show:

'Il n'y a pas . . . de mort. . . . Il y a seulement . . . *moi*. . . .' Un doigt se crispa sur la cuisse.
'. . . *moi* . . . *qui vais mourir*. . . .' (p. 182)

La Voie royale is essentially conceived in terms of will: the Nietzschean affiliation is evident. Both Perken and Claude are embodiments of will, with very few qualities, either physical or psychological, that are unrelated; while Grabot too, as described to Claude by Perken, has conceived his life in the same terms. Professor Frohock has pointed out the confusion in narrative viewpoint in the novel:[1] we see the action through Claude's eyes until the discovery of the sculptures, at which point Malraux requires introspection by Perken, and from then on the viewpoint alternates between the two. Frequently it becomes difficult to de-

---

[1] *André Malraux and the Tragic Imagination*, p. 50.

tect at first reading which of the two is analysing his thoughts at any given moment, both are so alike in their 'lucidity' (and, perhaps, insufficiently differentiated from Malraux himself). This difficulty is only increased by the fact that the psychological analysis is carried out almost entirely in terms of will seeking to impose itself on everything else, even the physical body of the protagonist. Dissociation of the self from everything—the plant, insect, and animal worlds, from other men, from its own physical envelope—leads to a kind of Cartesian split; and identification of the self with will is deliberate: 'Une fois de plus il se trouve planté dans le sol, vaincu par la chair, par les viscères, par tout ce qui peut se révolter contre l'homme' (p. 132). The immediate consequence is a world composed of obstacles, to be overcome by the use of will; and therefore a world of constant struggle and violence, seen as heroism. The novel, indeed, seems to be constructed round certain key scenes, all of them acts of will: Claude's effort while clambering along the temple façade, the discovery and removal of the carvings, the finding of Grabot and Perken's domination of the Moïs, and finally Perken's exercise of will *in extremis*, until conquered by death—this last providing Malraux's initial formulation of the tragic. This world of obstacles is exemplified in countless images, as when Claude looks at the block of stone from which he wishes to hack off the carvings: 'Cette pierre était là, opiniâtre, être vivant, passif et capable de refus' (p. 80). At times, even, emphasis on volition is pushed beyond the limits of plausibility, or exaggerated to the point of parody, as when Perken feels almost glad as he considers his wound: '[il] était saturé d'impatience, mais sans angoisse: de nouveau en face d'un adversaire, cet adversaire fût-il son propre sang' (p. 153). Again, it may turn into a kind of masochism, as the individual is driven to ever more difficult physical feats in order to prove his will-power to himself. Grabot has blinded himself deliberately in one eye in order to revenge himself on a medical officer, and again has had himself stung by a scorpion in order to overcome his fear of these creatures:

Pour avoir éprouvé une violente répulsion nerveuse en en voyant un, il est allé se faire piquer exprès. Se refuser au monde, c'est toujours se faire souffrir terriblement pour se prouver sa force. Il y a dans tout cela un immense orgueil primitif, mais à quoi la vie et pas mal de souffrance ont fini par donner une forme. . . . (pp. 97–98)

(This particular incident may well have been inspired by Lawrence deliberately driving himself to the limits of physical endurance.) The purely physical aspect of courage is more dominant here than in the later novels, where it takes on a more intellectual shape, if for no other reason than because of the nature of the obstacles which the individual has to overcome. Here the main antagonist is Nature, and the tribesmen form part of Nature, or the jungle, more or less in the same way that insects or animals do ; later the antagonists are other men, set as firmly in the background of society as Malraux's heroes themselves.

Introduction of the term 'orgueil' is significant: pride is inextricably mixed with will, and the result is a ferocious egoism. The only escape from this egoism occurs when the individual can respect his equal in will and courage, in what one might call a kind of mutual admiration. This is no less at the root of Perken's feelings for Grabot than of Claude's relationship with the Dane. After Perken has been told by the doctors that he has no hope of recovery, Claude catches his glance: 'Il y avait en ce regard une complicité intense où se heurtait la poignante fraternité du courage et la compassion, l'union animale des êtres devant la chair condamnée' (pp. 153–4). Here we have in embryo the *fraternité virile* which will become a key concept in the political novels, but as yet with no component of revolutionary comradeship. It is, nevertheless, noteworthy that this conception of fraternity should be closely linked to the idea of death: for Malraux, obsession with mortality is a crucial element in man's sense of his destiny— another term pervading his later work, though rarely defined with any precision—while dignity in the face of death becomes his vision of tragedy. This dignity, however, is an active, not a passive, conception: man must struggle and exert his will right up to the moment of expiry, and Perken, doomed, remembers one of his ancestors who had achieved an exemplary death:

Il se souvint de l'un de ses oncles, hobereau danois qui après mille folies s'était fait ensevelir sur son cheval mort soutenu par des pieux, en

roi hun, attentif durant son agonie à chasser par la volonté de ne pas
crier une seule fois, malgré l'appel de tous ses nerfs, l'effroyable
épouvante qui secouait ses épaules comme une danse de Saint-Guy. . . .
(p. 174)

Death can thus be given a positive value: as Perken has already reflected, 'Il se peut que faire sa mort me semble beaucoup plus important que faire sa vie...' (p. 164); although he has already, early
in the novel, dismissed suicide in a typically pithy formula: 'Celui
qui se tue court après une image qu'il s'est formée de lui-même:
on ne se tue jamais que pour *exister*' (p. 13).

The encounter with death is also the source of the absurd: the
disproportion between man's concerns and struggles, and the
pointlessness of his ultimate extinction, since no transcendental
religious belief can preserve him from this defeat. Ultimately all is
vain in the face of death: not only the whole of Perken's previous
life and actions, but also Claude's sentiment of fraternity—
Perken, in his last moments, looks at him as if he were 'étranger
comme un être d'un autre monde' (p. 182, with what are in fact
the last words of the novel)—and the whole of human thought are
utterly powerless against the brute existential fact of personal
death; and the consummation of the novel can be found in
Claude's perception of this, as he sits with Perken, 'face à face avec
la vanité d'être homme, malade de silence et de l'irréductible
accusation du monde qu'est un mourant qu'on aime' (p. 182). This
idea is developed in the following lyrical passage—perhaps also
confused, since it is not clear whether these are Perken's thoughts
in his delirium, or Claude's as he watches:

Presque tous ces corps, perdus dans la nuit d'Europe ou le jour d'Asie,
écrasés eux aussi par la vanité de leur vie, pleins de haine pour ceux qui
au matin se réveilleraient, se consolaient avec des dieux. Ah! qu'il en
existât, pour pouvoir, au prix des peines éternelles, hurler, comme ces
chiens, qu'aucune pensée divine, qu'aucune récompense future, que rien
ne pouvait justifier la fin d'une existence humaine, pour échapper à la
vanité de le hurler au calme absolu du jour, à ces yeux fermés, à ces dents
ensanglantées qui continuaient à déchiqueter la peau! ... Échapper à
cette tête ravagée, à cette défaite monstrueuse! (p. 182)

But the hope of conquering death is in vain: there can be no

escape from the ultimate meaninglessness of life. It might be asked
at this point why, since the absurdity of life is a basic *donnée* of
Malraux's *Weltanschauung*, any attempt at all should be made to
fight against it. Indeed, Perken provokes destiny and brings on his
death before his normal span. The answer is clearly that the dynamic conception of life as violent struggle is equally fundamental
in Malraux (and later will become one of the key ideas in his art
philosophy). This conception is constantly affirmed throughout
the novel: affirmed, not argued rationally. Men who do not gird
themselves for the fight against destiny are contemptuously referred to as *soumis*: in a long passage Claude justifies his choice of
life to himself:

> Aucune envie de vendre des autos, des valeurs ou des discours,
> comme ceux de ses camarades dont les cheveux collés signifiaient la dis-
> tinction; ni de construire des ponts, comme ceux dont les cheveux mal
> coupés signifiaient la science. Pourquoi travaillaient-ils, eux? Pour
> gagner en considération. Il haïssait cette considération qu'ils recher-
> chaient. La soumission à l'ordre de l'homme sans enfants et sans dieu est
> la plus profonde des soumissions à la mort. (p. 37)

And yet his apparently positive aims—'Arracher ses propres
images au monde stagnant qui les possède . . .' (p. 37), 'Posséder
plus que lui-même, échapper à la vie de poussière des hommes
qu'il voyaient chaque jour . . .' (p. 38)—scarcely defend themselves against careful analysis. Claude's primary purpose in searching for the statues is to become rich by selling them; it is never
made clear precisely what he wants the money for, but the distinction between his aim and that of the acquaintances he despises
is far from clear, perhaps no more than the difference between
attaining 'considération' in his own eyes, rather than in others'.
Again, Perken's notorious desire to 'laisser une cicatrice sur cette
terre' (it is vaguely hinted that his ultimate wish is to emulate
Brooke of Sarawak and become ruler of the whole of Siam) is not
self-evidently desirable, even to Perken himself; above all, it must
imply that the scar is noticed by others, which is surely only
another form of 'considération', or recognition by 'autrui'.
Malraux's heroes do not really stand alone: Perken and Claude

need, at the very least, each other, and domination is impossible without the people who are to be dominated.

The moral aspects of the novel are, indeed, distinctly dubious; and though Perken is a 'Nietzschean' hero one may doubt whether Nietzsche himself would have recognized his disciple in him. But certainly there is no question here of respect for the dignity of man, as in *Les Conquérants*. In *La Voie royale* the Cambodian peasants no less than the 'uncivilized' tribesmen are described, mostly, in entirely impersonal terms, as hardly more human than the insects which are so often made to symbolize the hostility of nature; while the *soumis* are also likened to termites, equally slaves to the rhythm of their existence. This attitude of contempt for all men who do not share the ethic of constantly renewed attacks by will against all obstacles is perhaps the clearest internal sign that the novel is conceived in very different—and earlier—social terms from the 'political' novels.

Since dependence is contemptible, sexual bonds are equally undesirable, unless they imply the subjection of another: sex, for Perken, must be domination rather than partnership, eroticism rather than emotional exchange. Eroticism is, indeed, one of the major themes in the novel, which opens with Claude's first meeting with Perken, brought about through a visit to a Djibouti brothel; Perken's first act when he realizes that he is dying is to ask for a woman. Eroticism is perhaps best defined as sexual pleasure experienced not primarily in the body, but in the brain, or through the imagination: only thus can it be put to the service of will, since as a bodily urge it is degrading, weakening pure volition. Eroticism is, indeed, treated almost in terms of masochistic experience: Perken speaks of 'Le besoin maniaque, le besoin d'aller jusqu'au bout de ses nerfs' (p. 8). Mythomania, too, enters into the theme; in the same discussion Perken also points out the role of imagination in transforming sexual memories—'Elle compense toujours.' Sexuality is in this way turned into a metaphysical concept, an integral part of the general ethic of will; love in any normal sense, and even comradeship is excluded: 'L'essentiel est de *ne pas connaître* la partenaire. Qu'elle soit: l'autre sexe' (p. 10).

Grabot, too, sees sex in similar terms—'le pouvoir doit se définir pour lui par la possibilité d'en abuser' (p. 96)—and eroticism has been one of his main motives in coming to Siam—to obtain power for its sexual privileges. Yet eroticism, too, is ultimately unsuccessful; in Perken's last experience—a scene presenting a quite daring, yet careful and dispassionate analysis of sexual intercourse —he is forced to realize, at the very instant of orgasm, that 'jamais, jamais, il ne connaîtrait les sensations de cette femme, jamais il ne trouverait dans cette frénésie qui le secouait autre chose que la pire des séparations. On ne possède que ce qu'on aime' (pp. 157–8). His final feeling, far from erotic satisfaction, is a desire to 'anéantir, à force de violence, ce visage anonyme qui le chassait vers la mort' (p. 158). Here we have, perhaps, a hint that Perken's ideal of eroticism is basically inadequate, not so much a magnificent failure as a pursuit flawed from its inception; but this remains just a hint, only developed fully in La Condition humaine.

It is impossible to give unreserved approval to La Voie royale. The novel illustrates Malraux's basic theme, man's violent struggle with destiny, and, in my view at least, is greatly superior to the 'Surrealist 'works. Yet it suffers in comparison with Les Conquérants: Malraux is not yet in full control of his material, nor are his treatment of his themes and his technique completely adequate to communicate his experience to the reader. Primarily, the plot of the novel does not give him the vehicle he requires to convey his vision. This may in part be due to the autobiographical basis of the novel, which is probably greater than in the later works—without, however, being at all a close transcription of lived experience. There are, of course, episodes that seem genuinely autobiographical: Claude's fruitless interview with Ramèges, the Director of the French Institute in Saigon, probably gave Malraux his revenge on an unco-operative official, since otherwise it is not essential to the plot (although the discussion between the two men also includes several ideas developed in the later art philosophy, this too is scarcely relevant to the immediate action). The character of Claude Vannec appears to be deliberately based on the author— the parallel is obvious, and is reinforced by the later use of some of the same material in drawing the background of Vincent Berger in *Les Noyers*. But Perken too is probably constructed round Malraux's own feelings and ideas, and the author seems to identify too closely with his protagonists for a clear individual impression of them to carry across. The basis of the characterization is, in fact, a simple *dédoublement*—the technique used by Rolland in *Jean-Christophe* or Martin du Gard in *Jean Barois*; and it is a commonplace of Malraux criticism that his characters are all very much of the same kind—all spring in fact from what might be called the same 'syndrome'. It is tempting to think that Malraux used two heroes chiefly as a means of overcoming the difficulties of dramatizing his themes. If this were so it would go far to explain the general imbalance of the novel. Although the search for the statues occupies most of the early part of the novel, once will has achieved this particular object, Malraux seems to lose interest in them completely, and finally they are simply left at the small town in Siam with no indication of their ultimate fate. Perken has become the centre of the novelist's attention, and Claude is reduced from protagonist to little more than an observer.[1] But Claude in any case appears as a less forceful personality than Malraux intended: in particular in his attitude to the jungle, from which he exhibits a semi-hysterical revulsion. This ultra-self-consciousness may, indeed, have been experienced by Malraux himself, but it clashes both with the conception of Claude as the metaphysical hero, struggling against Nature, and with the use of insect and other symbols. These symbols, foreshadowing the imagery which gives such a personal mark to the later novels, mark an attempt to lend an epic note to the fundamental metaphysical struggle. But, if we take Claude as the victim of a psychological allergy to insects, what is clearly intended to be metaphysical tends to dissolve into no more than the neurotic. The presentation of Claude thus weakens the impact of the novel; and we find in fact a recurrence of the common Romantic confusion between genuine experience and introspective fantasy. This confusion will be avoided in the later novels by the adoption of a more effective narrative technique.

[1] This break might possibly indicate that Malraux's intentions changed when, having dropped the novel for a time, he took it up again.

In any case the symbolism is often strained. The discovery of Grabot, not as a chief but as a blinded slave, is dramatically impressive;[1] but the use of him as a symbol of the absurd, of utter defeat, becomes somewhat forced when Grabot makes the often-quoted answer, on being asked who he is: '... Rien. ....' He is then made perhaps too obvious a foil for Perken's bravery—the affirmation of the positive values of courage even in the face of this meaninglessness—when the Dane faces and dominates the tribesmen. Grabot, in fact, suffers from inadequate presentation: first he is described by Perken, entirely at second hand, and when he is met in the flesh he is more or less incoherent, filled only with a thirst for cruel vengeance. Although certain aspects of his character, such as the equation of power with the erotic, and his enormous 'orgueil primitif', foreshadow Ferral, he remains an unsatisfactory, rather melodramatic character, a crude symbol of failure, of degeneration of will—'la conscience de la plus atroce déchéance' (p. 124). All in all he cannot really bear the weight of meaning placed upon him.

Melodrama is of the essence of the thriller, and certainly *La Voie royale* can be read as a pure adventure story; though towards the end the plot is too confused. Perken's final, vain attempt to regain his own territory, his conflict with a chief whom he once could easily have cowed, and the movements of the Siamese punitive column, are far from easy to follow. But naturally the book is intended as far more than a mere thriller—despite the wide popularity of much of Malraux's work on the thriller level—and many incidents and episodes tend to have this melodramatic, even adolescent, quality about them. Perken, dying, accomplishes the brilliant feat of shooting dead two natives through his pocket; earlier he had filled a bullet with blood from his injured knee in order to impress the Moïs when he put the bullet through an animal skull. Other images, such as the native chief thrown alive into a cask of vipers, add to this impression, and throughout the novel there is a certain exaggeration, perhaps glamorization, of the

[1] The whole search for Grabot is somewhat reminiscent of the search for Kurtz in Conrad's *Heart of Darkness*, a work which had considerably impressed Malraux shortly before leaving for Cambodia (C. Malraux, *Nos vingt ans*, p. 114).

danger and mystery; even the epigraph, 'Celui qui regarde long-
temps les songes devient semblable à son ombre', whether or not
it is a 'proverbe malabar', appears to contain an element of deliberate mystification; while the novel is studded with such lines as
'sa vie valût le prix d'une balle' (p. 71). This 'Gothic' element can
only damage the novel. Similarly the obsession with violence is
perhaps unfortunate; in the later political novels violence is
necessary, implied by the very choice of subject-matter, but here
it is gratuitous, betraying indulgence in personal obsessions in the
author rather than illuminating essential aspects of experience. A
certain immaturity is also revealed occasionally in dialogues such
as that between Perken and the European doctor, an opium addict,
who pronounced on him: here Malraux clearly intends to indicate
the 'haine des vieux intoxiquées [sic] pour l'action' (p. 150), but
Perken's comment—'Il y a entre la mort et moi un vieux contact'
—raises a smile.

Yet the novel has undoubted qualities. In the first place it holds
the reader's interest firmly. Although the story-line may at times
be confused, Malraux succeeds in building up suspense, first about
the discovery of the statues, then about the whereabouts of
Grabot, and finally about the fate of Perken; in fact, it might even
be argued that, once the introductory section on the ship is over,
the pitch becomes keyed too high, and there is little variation from
the intensity and nervous strain of the comparatively few dramatic
scenes presented. The long introductory section itself, if containing incidental material, such as anecdotes about Claude's grandfather, which are not strictly relevant, is more important in that it
contains, in the dialogue between Perken and Claude, the intellectual basis of the book. The theory outlined here is translated
into action in the later part of the novel. And as a philosophical
novel, an embodiment of certain ethical values, the novel is certainly reasonably effective; the drawback here is that these values
are tied much more loosely to the general human situation than in
the political novels, and it is correspondingly difficult for the
reader to identify himself with their projection in the figures of
Claude and Perken—let alone Grabot. Whereas it is perhaps a fair
claim that the characters in La Condition humaine are typical of

twentieth-century man, the protagonists here are clearly exceptional and unrepresentative—deliberately so. Whether or not Malraux later succeeds in resolving the contradiction between the hero as outstanding individual and the hero as typical man, here the problem is not yet formulated. To judge the ethic itself is not necessarily to judge the novel; but it is a reasonable criticism that matters are made too simple here, since both heroes are entirely devoid of any kind of family or even social tie, acting in a moral vacuum. Their pursuit of unrestricted will may or may not provoke admiration, but it can hardly serve as a model for more ordinary men.

Possibly some of the strongest features of the novel are its poetic qualities. Ordinary passages of descriptive local colour are not common, although the sense of the jungle, proliferating, impervious to human desires, is well communicated in several places, and the spirit of Cambodia is briefly sketched in a lyrical passage recalling *La Tentation* (pp. 48–9). But imagery is perhaps Malraux's best-developed feature: images are used to evoke atmosphere throughout the novel, particularly the smell of jungle vegetation—Nature, everywhere in decay, symbolizes death—and the punctuating of dialogue with sounds or silence outside. The whole struggle of the two men to detach the statues is summed up in a short passage studded with imagery like a prose poem:

Un immobile frémissement, une vibration sans fin animait les dernières feuilles, bien qu'aucun vent ne se fût levé: la chaleur. . . .
Une pierre détachée tomba, retentit deux fois, sourdement d'abord puis avec un son clair, appelant dans l'esprit de Claude le mot: in-so-lite. Plus que ces pierres mortes à peine animées par le cheminement des grenouilles qui n'avaient jamais vu d'hommes, que ce temple écrasé sous un si décisif abandon, que la violence clandestine de la vie végétale, quelque chose d'inhumain faisait peser sur les décombres et les plantes voraces fixées comme des êtres terrifiés une angoisse qui protégeait avec une force de cadavre ces figures dont le geste séculaire régnait sur une cour de mille-pattes et de bêtes des ruines. Perken le dépassa: ce monde d'abîme sous-marin perdit sa vie comme une méduse jetée sur une grève, sans force tout à coup contre deux hommes blancs. (pp. 76–7)

The identification here of insects with 'l'inhumain', the 'other', is complete; while a little later in the novel death itself is seen as 'la forme d'un petit tas grouillant d'insectes' (p. 93). This use of imagery, alternating with a high level of dramatization and clipped, elliptical dialogue, will characterize all Malraux's novels.

Taken as a whole, *La Voie royale* is only a partial success; and, published after *Les Conquérants* as it was, appeared to indicate a falling-off in Malraux's creative abilities. If he had produced no other novels, however, it would no doubt have found a niche for him in the history of the twentieth-century novel: an exotic novel of adventure with its distinctly personal, poetic tone, and containing many original ideas. These, it is true, are more fully and successfully treated in later novels; but the metaphysical problems such as the destructive effect of time, obsession with death, suicide, destiny, *angoisse*, *déchéance*, humiliation, sexuality and eroticism, mythomania and the psychology of the adventurer, and the absurd—these are all existentialist themes touched on here, and lend considerable depth to the plot. Even if the discussion of these perhaps raises more ethical problems than Malraux at that time realized, and even if it was impossible to give them full treatment without unbalancing the aesthetic unity of the novel, they do, together with the poetic imagery, lend the novel its more lasting qualities.

3

LES CONQUÉRANTS

L ES CONQUÉRANTS came out under Grasset's imprint in 1928, after being serialized in the *N.R.F.* from March to July of the same year; a *version définitive*, containing hundreds of minor changes, together with several deletions and insertions of some length, and a *postface* by the author, was published in 1949.[1] The title of the novel is significant: it is, like *La Condition humaine*, primarily symbolical. The idea of the *conquistador* must have been in Malraux's mind: the psychology of the twentieth-century political adventurer is his main theme, and in the *postface* Malraux states that the principal value of the work consists in his having 'montré un type de héros en qui s'unissent l'aptitude à l'action, la culture, et la lucidité', not in any possible documentary value (p. 230). Whereas in *La Voie royale* the adventurer was battling against Nature, Malraux now puts him in a political setting. The result is not only that he can be seen in violent action, carving out his destiny from the raw material of life, but also that his consciousness can be explored more deeply by showing him in his relationship with those to whom he is pledged in the political struggle.

The novel is told in the first person, which avoids some of the confusion of viewpoint in *La Voie royale*: the narrator, never identified by name, is looked through, rather than at, and cannot therefore obscure the reader's view of Garine, the adventurer who is the real centre of dramatic interest. Moreover, the tense used is the present; the narrator relates events directly, so that an impression of eye-witness veracity is created. The novel is divided into three parts: *Les Approches*, *Puissances*, and *L'Homme*, the middle section being rather longer than the other two. In the first section the narrator is sailing to the East across the Indian Ocean;

[1] Quotations are from the *Livre de Poche* edition of this version.

the centre of interest is the fate of the Chinese Nationalist government in Canton, and the associated general strike against the British in Hong Kong: Malraux selects actual political events of 1925. As the ship moves to Singapore, then Saigon, and finally to Hong Kong, where the narrator disembarks, the exposition of the revolutionary situation takes place; and through the use of radio flashes, pinned to the ship's notice-board, we can follow the progress of events, together with the narrator's thoughts. Interest is primarily directed to Garine, a commissar working under Borodine, the (historical) Soviet adviser to the Nationalists in Canton; and tension gradually mounts as the ship moves eastwards. In revising the novel Malraux seems to have felt that the first section was over-long and not sufficiently dramatic: certain episodes were sharply pruned, as, for example, ten pages of largely local colour and description of Singapore—where the narrator meets a Russian art connoisseur, a *fantaisiste* called Rensky, who foreshadows Clappique in *La Condition humaine*—, a few pages at Saigon, and nearly ten pages again on Hong Kong and the perhaps slightly exaggerated effects of the strike there. In this way attention is concentrated more powerfully on Garine and Canton—the centre of the real action. In the second section the narrator has joined Garine, and events—largely the successful fight against the forces of General Tang, a warlord in British pay—are seen at first hand; this is the political centre of the novel. In the final section the interest narrows down to Garine's personality and his relationship with the Communist movement, and the progress of the purely political developments fades rather into the background. Finally Garine, a sick and probably dying man, leaves China, at odds with his superiors. The novel ends on a rather indeterminate note:

Lentement, mordant sa lèvre inférieure, il [Garine] sort de l'écharpe son bras blessé, et le lève. Nous nous étreignons. Une tristesse inconnue naît en moi, profonde, désespérée, appelée par tout ce qu'il y a là de vain, par la mort présente. . . . Lorsque la lumière, de nouveau, frappe nos visages, il me regarde. Je cherche dans ses yeux la joie que j'ai cru voir; mais il n'y a rien de semblable, rien qu'une dure et pourtant fraternelle gravité. (p. 228)

The similarity to the ending of *La Voie royale* is clear. There is another parallel: both novels appear to switch themes to some extent in mid-course. In *La Voie royale* Claude's search for the statues had given place to Perken's psychological struggle; here again, after the initial impression that we are reading a kind of political epic, the focus narrows down to Garine alone. Tension thus drops sharply, and the effect of the ending is somewhat muffled. One reason for this may lie in the historical events themselves. Despite the victory of the Nationalist forces over Tang, their efforts to destroy British mercantile power in China by means of the Hong Kong strike and an economic blockade ended historically in complete failure; yet Malraux evidently wished to contrast political success against personal failure in Garine, and no doubt this obliged him to drop the political story at the point where he did. However, this switch of interest, leaving the final outcome of affairs in Canton in uncertainty, seems a weakness, possibly reflecting an unsureness in Malraux as to which subject he really wished to treat; the contrast with *La Condition humaine*, where the line of events is clear-cut, is marked.

The character of Garine is thus at the centre of the novel. The narrator is a rather shadowy figure, whose functions in Canton as an assistant to Garine are very vague; indeed, his real role is to provide an eye-witness account of Garine's actions, proving that Malraux intended to solve the problem of the narrative viewpoint by using a first-person observer as a 'central intelligence'. Occasionally the narrator's presence at a scene of great importance, like Garine's confrontation with Tcheng-Daï (pp. 105–11), is a little clumsy and improbable; at other times, as when he describes Rebecci, the 'accoucheur' of Hong, the terrorist, it is clear that the narrator shows much more knowledge of background than he would in fact have had—he is really a transposed third-person, 'omniscient' narrator; while again, some of the descriptive passages—of Saigon, Hong Kong, or Canton—are distinctly 'literary'—if at the same time fine pieces of evocative writing. But on the whole the narrator succeeds very well in directing attention to Garine and his actions with a note of immediacy, even urgency, and compelling authenticity.

Garine has often been taken as a projection of Malraux himself.

There clearly are parallels: Garine's suspended condemnation to six months' imprisonment for—quixotically—financing abortions in Switzerland, recalls Malraux's own difficulties in Cambodia. This episode is given over four pages in the novel, and forms a crucial stage in Garine's formation. Humiliation is often given the concrete form of imprisonment in Malraux's novels; while Garine's trial is described in terms of the absurd: 'Pendant toute la durée du procès, il eut l'impression d'un spectacle irréel; non d'un rêve, mais d'une comédie étrange, un peu ignoble et tout à fait lunaire' (p. 60). Above all, this episode was one not chosen by Garine himself, and was therefore an affront to his will. Although this court scene is one which has little bearing upon the plot in Canton, it provides an interesting analysis of the ritual of justice: Garine frames the paradox, 'Juger, c'est, de toute évidence, ne pas comprendre, puisque si l'on comprenait, on ne pourrait plus juger', and wearily is forced to assume 'ce même sentiment d'impuissance navrante, de mépris et de dégoût que l'on éprouve devant une multitude fanatique, devant toutes les grandes manifestations de l'absurdité humaine' (p. 61).[1]

It is this experience that has made Garine a revolutionary, but not a Communist by conviction: in a letter to the narrator he states:

Je ne tiens pas la société pour mauvaise, pour susceptible d'être améliorée; je la tiens pour absurde. C'est bien autre chose. . . . Qu'on la transforme, cette société, ne m'intéresse pas. Ce n'est pas l'absence de justice en elle qui m'atteint, mais quelque chose de plus profond, l'impossibilité de donner à une forme sociale, quelle qu'elle soit, mon adhésion. Je suis a-social comme je suis athée, et de la même façon. (p. 62)

Revolutionary attitudes therefore primarily imply a means to action, his real ambition. Literary studies had merely led him to the rhetorical question, 'quels livres valent d'être écrits hormis les Mémoires', and his first steps in extreme socialist circles had been in quest of 'un temps de troubles' (p. 57), rather than to improve social conditions. Action, however, is morally neutral, and Garine

[1] There is an obvious parallel between this episode and the trial of Meursault in Camus's L'Étranger.

at this point had only scorn for many of his comrades: 'Ces crétins-là veulent avoir raison. En l'occurrence, il n'y a qu'une raison qui ne soit pas une parodie: l'emploi le plus efficace de sa force' (p. 57). And later, 'je n'aime pas les hommes', he states categorically (p. 68). In view of this we may presume that his political affiliations provide little more than a cause in which to exercise his will and to affirm his personal values against the existing society; but in other circumstances he could just as easily have become a fascist. It might in fact have been much more logical if he had: pure individualism sits more easily on opportunists and activists of the extreme Right than on those of the Left, whose entire social and political philosophy is devoted to the suppression of individual values in favour of collective discipline. The heart of Garine's later difficulties with his fellow Communists lies here, as do, no doubt, Malraux's own reasons for never extending his support of the Communist cause to party membership. Indeed, Garine's political development seems to correspond fairly closely to Malraux's own (without for that being directly autobiographical); while it also recalls Lawrence, whose relationship to the Hashemite kingdom resembles Garine's to the Communists. Garine's decision, at the end of the novel, to leave Canton, is similar to Lawrence's sudden resolve to quit Damascus and the Arabs at the apogee of his success in 1918: neither man allowed the cause for which he fought to dominate him, turning it instead into a field for the exercise of his own will and energy, the means by which he could 'leave his scar on the map'.[1]

Politics, then, is not so much the subject of the novel as the pretext and the setting, while of course it helps to unify the material as a whole. Use of politics reunites Malraux's novel with a traditional theme by providing a dramatic basis for development of ambition; just as political events supplied the opportunity for Sturel to exercise his ambitions in Barrès's *Roman de l'énergie nationale*. What is new is Malraux's idiom: the constant stressing of such key terms as *volonté, absurde,* and *révolte*—and, to a lesser

---

[1] Langlois has also suggested that Garine is, physically, modelled on Paul Monin, a French lawyer who was Malraux's associate in his journalistic activities in Saigon (*André Malraux: The Indo-China Adventure*, p. 240).

extent, the atmosphere of violence in which the whole novel is
bathed. The choice of Canton and the events of 1925 is, certainly,
far from irrelevant and arbitrary; but at the same time the basis of
the novel proves to be certain attitudes of the Western intellectual,
attitudes which are largely prior to experience. Perhaps the best instance is the description of Garine's effect on the Canton coolies, in
terms of human dignity:

> Les coolies sont en train de découvrir qu'ils existent, simplement
> qu'ils existent. . . . La propagande nationaliste, celle de Garine, . . . a agi
> sur eux d'une façon trouble, profonde — et imprévue, — avec une ex-
> traordinaire violence, en leur donnant la possibilité de croire à leur
> propre dignité, à leur importance, si vous préférez. . . . La révolution
> française, la révolution russe ont été fortes parce qu'elles ont donné à
> chacun sa terre; cette révolution-ci est en train de donner à chacun sa
> vie. (pp. 19–20)

This explanation in terms of idealism, or an awakening of individualism, quite apart from its contradiction with the cynicism
shown in fact by both Garine and Borodine, for whom the end
amply justifies the means, is very much a cerebral one. In *La
Condition humaine* the concept of human dignity and its denial will
be used to great effect in motivating the revolutionary action of
Kyo and the counter-revolutionary one of König; but here it remains more at the level of an intellectual generalization of the type
common in *La Tentation de l'Occident*, wished on the Canton
coolies rather than arising naturally from their observed behaviour
(which in the event shows them just as easily manipulated by the
Communist leadership as formerly by the imperialist and capitalist
exploiters).

Nearly all the characters are, in fact, intellectual types; and the
Chinese point of view is largely passed over. Even Tcheng-Daï
and Hong can scarcely be called representative Chinese. The former is introduced and described at considerable length, but he is
fundamentally a transposition on to the Chinese scene of Gandhi,
an exemplary exponent of non-violence and ideal justice, whose
death becomes necessary for the advance of the Communist cause.
(There seems to have been no historical figure in Canton at the
time occupying any remotely similar position.) Hong, on the

other hand, is the pure terrorist, the forerunner of Tchen in *La Condition humaine* and the Spanish anarchists in *L'Espoir*—again an international rather than purely Chinese figure. First brought to the reader's attention during the long description of the Genoese, Rebecci, whom the narrator meets in Saigon, Hong represents pure fanaticism, hate of any kind of privilege, not for any kind of humanitarian reason, but for its own sake. As he expresses himself, intensity of emotion getting the better of coherence:

> La torture — moi je pense — est, là, une chose juste. Parce que la vie d'un homme de la misère est une torture longue. Et ceux qui enseignent aux hommes de la misère à supporter cela doivent être punis, prêtres chrétiens ou autres hommes. Ils ne savent pas. Ils ne savent pas. Il faudrait — je pense — les obliger (il souligne le mot d'un geste, comme s'il frappait) à comprendre. Ne pas lâcher sur eux les soldats. Non. Les lépreux. Le bras d'un homme se transforme en boue, et coule; l'homme, il vient me parler de résignation, alors c'est bien. Mais cet homme-là, lui, il dit autre chose. (p. 140)

In his subsequent discussion of Hong, Garine sees him as fundamentally Chinese under his veneer of Western ideas acquired from Rebecci (who stands in the same relationship to Hong as Gisors to Tchen); but nevertheless this philosophy of hate recurs in *La Condition humaine* in the character not of another Chinese, but of Hemmelrich, a Belgian. Both automatically hate 'avant tout l'homme qui se respecte'; both wish to engage in violent action, at whatever personal cost, to satisfy their thirst for revenge. Specifically, idealism is completely lacking: Hong 'juge que trop d'hommes se sont laissé détourner de leur seule vocation par l'ombre d'un idéal quelconque'. He has far outgrown his mentor, whose early revolutionary ardour has grown feeble as he sits in his shop in Canton, selling cheap toys. Hong 'entend ne pas terminer sa vie en louant des oiseaux mécaniques, ne pas laisser l'âge s'imposer à lui' (p. 145). His chief *bête noire* is Tcheng-Daï, the supreme idealist and epitome of 'générosité' and 'noblesse de caractère', a man with enormous moral authority in the Kuomintang movement; against Tcheng-Daï's burning desire for absolute justice, Hong 'haït les idéalistes parce qu'ils prétendent "arranger les choses". Il ne veut point que les choses soient arrangées. Il ne veut point abandonner, au bénéfice d'un avenir incertain, sa haine présente' (pp. 144–5). Like Tchen, Hong finds himself on a different plane from other men, although in his case there develops a peculiarly revolting sadism in addition: after assassinating Tcheng-Daï, he kills Klein, one of Garine's associates, and mutilates the corpse by slitting the mouth with a razor and cutting off the eyelids, before being arrested and executed himself by the Kuomintang authorities.

It is perhaps because of this gratuitous cruelty that Hong, if as powerfully drawn as Tchen, never in any way attracts the reader's sympathy. Indeed, on reading the novel, an uneasy feeling remains that at least some of the various scenes of violence with which it is filled are really extraneous to the action. In fact, Malraux himself seems somewhat attracted by the sadistic for its own sake. Garine initially criticizes Hong, not for his thirst for blood, but for his unreliability: 'Ah! qu'il y aurait avantage à faire remplacer le Comité de Sept par un comité dictatorial plus sûr, à créer une Tchéka, à n'avoir pas à compter sur des gens comme Hong!' (pp. 151–2). Again, at the end of the novel, interrogating two suspected well-poisoners, he simply shoots one and thus coerces his companion into confession; this act also appears to be held up by Malraux for admiration, as fulfilling Garine's ideal of efficiency. Moreover, several episodes described at second hand, such as Garine's obsession by the memory of a young soldier who, during the war in France, had been raped by his comrades after an elaborate mock marriage ceremony, seem barely relevant at all; and since this must have been a scene of which Malraux had learnt at second-hand—like various violent, if colourful, episodes during the Russian revolution related here and in *La Condition humaine*—it is difficult to see why he should introduce it into his novel, unless it represented some kind of personal obsession. Another scene, in which Klein described how he had earlier killed a man called Kaminsky, was in fact removed by Malraux from the revised edition; partly, no doubt, because it was again dramatically unnecessary, and partly because it bore too great a similarity to the murder committed by Tchen at the opening of *La Condition humaine*.

There is also a certain irony that Klein should have become one of Hong's victims. Klein too anticipates Hemmelrich in his hate of the bourgeois, and is not far from Hong's position when he says that the very sight of a group of European clerks on the Canton boat makes him want to shoot them, and when he describes how, in prison, his constant dream was of wiping out the entire population of a town by poisoning its water-supply. Klein is, however, rather thinly drawn, and has little function in the novel except to be murdered by Hong later. In Nicolaïeff, the Canton police chief, we are shown an even more complicated character. A former Czarist police-informer, he had sunk to a low level of indignity before ending the war in Vladivostok, moving down to China, and gaining Sun Yat-Sen's confidence, and was thus able to re-adopt his old profession of policeman—but on the other side. Nicolaïeff prefigures König in *La Condition humaine*; again, in his association of cruelty with eroticism, he is tinged with a sadism not essential to the action of the novel. Both these characters are more important as types—obsessed with violence—than as individuals, though they add considerably to the general creation of atmosphere, the imaginative vision of the world which Malraux is concerned with projecting. It is this which provides the justification for such scenes as the peculiarly horrible, yet almost unforgettable, discovery of Klein's corpse by Garine and the narrator.

A character also worthy of close examination is Borodine, the Soviet commissar in Canton. Indeed, initially Malraux seems to have attached considerable importance to Borodine, the representative of party discipline: a ten-page section dealing with him was deleted from the original edition of the novel, and published separately in 1929.[1] Evidently Malraux, on second thoughts, considered that, however valuable the analysis of the Communist functionary—treated again as a type—might be in itself, it would have weighed the novel down and held up the action without obvious gain. It might too have created special difficulties, since Borodine was still alive and active; and indeed forms a special case among the characters of the novel, since Malraux could use his knowledge of him, possibly at first, and certainly at second, hand.

[1] 'Fragments inédits des *Conquérants*', in *Bifur*, 31 Dec. 1929, pp. 5–15.

The professional revolutionary Borodine stands in direct contrast to the adventurer Garine, as an early speech by Gérard to the narrator in Saigon makes clear:

> ... vous trouverez à Canton deux sortes de gens. Ceux qui sont venus au temps de Sun, en 1921, en 1922, pour courir leur chance ou jouer leur vie, et qu'il faut bien appeler des aventuriers; pour eux, la Chine est un spectacle auquel ils sont plus ou moins liés. Ce sont des gens en qui les sentiments révolutionnaires tiennent la place que le goût de l'armée tient chez les légionnaires, des gens qui n'ont jamais pu accepter la vie sociale, qui ont beaucoup demandé à l'existence, qui auraient voulu donner un sens à leur vie, et qui, maintenant, revenus de tout cela, *servent*. Et ceux qui sont venus avec Borodine, révolutionnaires professionnels, pour qui la Chine est une matière première. . . . Garine représente—et dirige—les premiers, qui sont moins forts mais beaucoup plus intelligents. . . . (p. 21)

This important passage, which clearly illustrates the development from Perken to Garine, marks a fundamental difference between the latter and Borodine, which will grow larger as the novel moves to its end. Borodine is—and remains—the practical man, who never needs to question the premisses of his actions. Gérard continues:

> Borodine, c'est un grand homme d'affaires. Extrêmement travailleur, brave, audacieux à l'occasion, très simple, possédé par son action. . . . Un homme qui a besoin de penser de chaque chose: 'Peut-elle être utilisée par moi, et comment?' Borodine, c'est cela. Tous les bolchéviks de sa génération ont été marqués par leur lutte contre les anarchistes: tous pensent qu'il faut d'abord être un homme préoccupé par le réel, par les difficultés de l'exercice du pouvoir. (p. 22)

But, whereas Borodine never changes his attitude, Garine, shocked into a new degree of self-awareness by the sight of Klein's corpse, begins to doubt the value of his presence in Canton, of his whole life: 'Quand je pense que toute ma vie j'ai cherché la liberté! . . . Qui donc est libre ici, de l'Internationale, du peuple, de moi, des autres?' He has, precisely, become an instrument of the machine, just as much as Borodine: 'Servir, c'est une chose que j'ai toujours eue en haine. . . . Ici, qui a servi plus que moi, et mieux?' (p. 194). And the scene concludes with Garine grimly muttering to himself: 'Il y a tout de même une chose qui compte, dans la vie: c'est de ne pas être vaincu . . . ' (p. 197). At this point he doubts the value of his action more than any other of Malraux's heroes until *Les Noyers de l'Altenburg*, and in fact his disillusionment is very close to that of Vincent Berger when he abandoned his Turan adventure in Central Asia.

From this point Garine detaches himself mentally from the revolutionary cause; the episode in which he shoots the well-poisoner is as much to convince himself that his energies and abilities are unabated as to serve the movement. He now sees himself as a gambler first and foremost:

> Si je me suis lié si facilement à la Révolution, c'est que ses résultats sont lointains et toujours en changement. Au fond, je suis un joueur. Comme tous les joueurs, je ne pense qu'à mon jeu, avec entêtement et avec force. Je joue aujourd'hui une partie plus grande qu'autrefois, et j'ai appris à jouer: mais c'est toujours le même jeu. Et je le connais bien; il y a dans ma vie un certain rythme, une fatalité personnelle, si tu veux, à quoi je n'échappe pas. Je m'attache à tout ce qui lui donne de la force. . . . (J'ai appris aussi qu'une vie ne vaut rien, mais que rien ne vaut une vie. . . .) (p. 201)

The last words, taken up from *La Voie royale*, link Garine to Perken. The parallel becomes closer, since Garine too is now seriously, probably fatally, ill; as the narrator puts it, 'il semble se séparer de son action, la laisser s'écarter de lui avec la santé, avec la certitude de vivre' (p. 203). Yet he is not afraid; death does not obsess him at anywhere near the same level of intensity as the Dane, and he can still say 'Le souvenir d'un certain degré de misère met à leur place les choses humaines, comme l'idée de la mort' (p. 204). The tension due to Garine's realization that he is not fundamentally a party man is increased when Borodine has Hong executed, and obliges Garine to pronounce a funeral oration at Klein's grave. Nicolaïeff expresses Borodine's attitude to Garine, the commissar now insisting on complete party discipline: 'Borodine est logique: il n'y a pas de place dans le communisme pour celui qui veut d'abord . . . être lui-même, enfin, exister séparé des autres. . . . — Le communisme s'oppose à une conscience individuelle? — Il exige davantage. . . . L'individualisme est une maladie

bourgeoise....' (p. 210). The point is deliberately driven home by
Malraux, who added an extra page in the revised version of the
novel at this point (and perhaps also in his mind was his experience
of collaborating with Communists during the Spanish Civil War):

> Garine ne croit qu'à l'énergie. Il n'est pas anti-marxiste, mais le
> marxisme n'est nullement pour lui un 'socialisme scientifique'; c'est
> une méthode d'organisation des passions ouvrières, un moyen de
> recruter chez les ouvriers des troupes de choc. . . . Et il découvre (c'est
> bien tard . . .) que le communisme, comme toutes les doctrines
> puissantes, est une franc-maçonnerie. Qu'au nom de sa discipline,
> Borodine n'hésitera pas à le remplacer, dès que lui, Garine, ne sera plus
> indispensable, par quelqu'un de moins efficace, peut-être, mais de plus
> obéissant. (pp. 207–8)

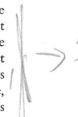

Nevertheless, although this passage was written after Malraux's
break with the Communist movement, the problem of Garine's
relationship with party discipline was already clearly defined in
the original version; Malraux's thought on this issue moves more
or less in a circle in the next fifteen or twenty years. But it is in this
analysis of Garine that the main interest of the novel must lie: and
the final point in his development is his consciousness of the absurdity of the Communist cause, which is just as pointless as everything else in the world except personal affirmation. His deepest
perceptions are of this: 'Pas de force, même pas de *vraie vie* sans la
certitude, sans la hantise de la vanité du monde' (p. 213). Beside
this his revolutionary activity itself must pale: 'La souffrance ren-
force l'absurdité de la vie, elle ne l'attaque pas; elle la rend
dérisoire' (p. 214). And in the end Garine expresses the surprising
wish to go to England, such has become his admiration for effective imperialism: 'Maintenant je sais ce qu'est l'Empire. Une
tenace, une constante violence. Diriger. Déterminer. Contraindre.
La vie est là . . . ' (p. 226). Although the narrator tells us that
Garine is trying primarily to convince himself, the idea of power
revealed by the three verbs underlies the whole of Garine's
activity (and points forward to Ferral in *La Condition humaine*).

The use of the first-person narrator, despite occasional lapses
from complete plausibility, allows many striking effects in the
novel, above all the ability to dramatize. The narrator acts not

only as a 'central intelligence', but also as a 'camera eye', and by using the present tense throughout the novel (except, of course, for historical explanation) can sharply highlight episodes such as the visit to the dead Klein, or the street battle between the Whampoa cadets and the anti-revolutionary troops of General Tang. The technique is not particularly original: quite apart from Martin du Gard's *Jean Barois* (1913)—which, with a very different theme, uses the present tense throughout, with a 'cinematographic' unseen narrator and brief, often verbless, descriptive traits—models could also be found in a good deal of writing, even journalism, during the First World War. But Malraux makes confident use of this method; tension remains high, on the whole, with great immediacy of sensation and impression, thus heightening the sense of realism (which is no doubt why so many readers initially accepted the novel as an autobiographical account), and enabling full emphasis to be laid on the carefully selected 'significant detail'. The main drawback of the first-person narrator is that the author reduces his ability to analyse the psychological make-up of his characters. As a friend of Garine, the narrator could perhaps know as much as he does about him; but in other cases he adopts the expedient of introducing anecdotes about their earlier life—as with Rebecci and Nicolaïeff—and these flashbacks tend to break up the action to some extent. Sometimes it becomes evident that the narrator is merely a device—as when he introduces Tcheng-Daï with extensive background detail, whereas only a week or two previously, in Saigon, he had heard Tcheng's name for the first time. Apart from Garine the characters do not develop much beyond types, and even here they are not greatly differentiated. Klein's attitude to violence is, as we have seen, very close to Hong's; while his comment, 'Au fond de la misère, il y a un homme, souvent . . . ' (p. 53), echoes Garine's own belief in awakening the dignity of the coolies. The psychological examination of the adventurer seems to spread over from Garine to the other characters—perhaps because all derive from Malraux's perception of certain aspects of his own character; and most seem to be conceived skeletally, very much in terms of acute self-awareness, with physical details and biographies added later.

In addition to the combination of action and dialogue which forms the bulk of the novel, there are many long passages which are more purely descriptive: often composed of simple enumeration of details observed by the narrator, and with the normal elliptical style amplified somewhat. The result is that often there is an alternation between episodes of action and static description, but even here the impression of action is to some extent maintained through the tension in the narrator and in his reactions to what he sees. A good instance is his walk through the streets of Hong Kong during the general strike:

Voici la rue principale. Limite du roc et de la mer, la ville, édifiée sur l'une, accrochée à l'autre, est un croissant dans lequel cette rue, coupée perpendiculairement par toutes les rampes qui joignent le quai au Pic, dessine en creux une grande palme. Toute l'activité de l'île, d'ordinaire, s'y concentre. Aujourd'hui, elle est déserte et silencieuse. De loin en loin, unis et méfiants, deux volontaires anglais vêtus en boy-scouts se rendent au marché pour y distribuer les légumes ou la viande. Des socques sonnent dans l'éloignement. Aucune femme blanche. Pas d'automobiles.

Voici des magasins chinois: bijouteries, marchands de jades, commerces de luxe; je rencontre moins de maisons anglaises; et, la rue décrivant brusquement un coude, je cesse d'en voir. Ce coude est double et la rue semble fermée comme une cour. Partout, à tous les étages, des caractères: noirs, rouges, dorés, peints sur des tablettes verticales ou fixés au-dessus des portes, énormes ou minuscules, fixés à hauteur des yeux ou suspendus là-haut, sur le rectangle du ciel, ils m'entourent comme un vol d'insectes. Au fond de grands trous sombres limités par trois murs, les marchands aux longues blouses, assis sur un comptoir, regardent la rue. Dès que je parais, ils tournent leurs petits yeux vers des objets pendus au plafond depuis des millénaires: seiches tapées, calmars, poissons, saucisses noires, canards laqués couleur de jambon, ou vers les sacs de grains et les caisses d'œufs enrobés de terre noire posés sur le sol. Des rayons de soleil denses, minces, pleins d'une poussière fauve, tombent sur eux. Si, après les avoir dépassés, je me retourne, je rencontre leur regard qui me suit, pesant, haineux. (pp. 41–2)

This passage, besides being an admirable description of one of Hong Kong's main streets—and one in most ways still accurate today—contains Malraux's other main stylistic device: his use of sensory imagery, in the alternation of elements of sound and silence, and of light and darkness. The sound images have been extensively treated by critics:[1] their function has been shown to be highly important in the creation of atmosphere, and at times takes on almost a structural significance. The light images are similar in nature, and, indeed, the two types are frequently used together. The result is that intellectual description goes together with dramatic immediacy and creation of atmosphere, while the ultimate interpretation is left to the reader.

Malraux also makes use of other types of imagery. Insects symbolize the non-human, as in *La Voie royale*: the flies buzzing around the corpses of Klein and his fellow victims, or, earlier, in the hospital where the narrator visits Garine, 'cet hôpital où semblent seuls vivants les insectes qui bourdonnent, en masses agitées, autour des ampoules . . .' (p. 158). Frequently people and things are described in religious terms, as if to identify the Communist movement with a new religious force: Nicolaïeff, with his 'voix de prêtre' (p. 164), or the mass meeting, where the crowd's replies to the orator alternate with the muffled sounds of gongs, 'comme des répons de litanies' (p. 152), while Tcheng-Daï too, perhaps less surprisingly, has priest-like mannerisms. Other images derive from Malraux's reading, and are more intellectual in content, as when we are told of Hong's development in terms of his distancing himself from the 'cour des Miracles' (p. 144); or, again, the lights of Hong Kong at night remind the narrator of 'un spectacle polynésien, l'une de ces fêtes dans lesquelles les dieux peints sont honorés par de grandes libérations de lucioles lancées dans la nuit, comme des graines . . .' (p. 40)—clearly an image taken from ethnological reading, rather than personal observation. This tendency to use intellectual images is one which will increase in the later novels, and marks Malraux's interest in the history and philosophy of culture: at times he seems to be taking up again the dialogue of East and West from *La Tentation de l'Occident*, though on a much

---

[1] W. M. Frohock, 'Notes on Malraux's Symbols', *Romanic Review*, xlii (1951), pp. 274–81; and G. O. Rees, 'Sound and Silence in Malraux's Novels', *French Review*, xxxi, pp. 223–30.

more politically conscious level, and with a much keener interest in the sights and sounds of the East, often covered at some length, almost for their own sakes as set-pieces of description. The lyrical tone of the early works is greatly subdued, and the result is a great increase in coherence and striking effect. Malraux also is developing here a gift for pithy formulae, often expressed in dialogue, as when Garine cuts short a discussion with the terse remark, 'La mort ne se manie pas comme un balai' (p. 80).

Les Conquérants marks a great step forward from *La Voie royale*, both in content and in expressive ability. Yet it is in some ways flawed, and, above all, suffers by comparison with *La Condition humaine*, where many of the same themes are taken up again and treated more incisively and dramatically. One might instance the distant yet pervading rumbling noise, in the closing pages of the novel, which in fact marks the emergence of the Kuomintang army as an effective fighting force: the same image is introduced, and more strikingly, during the episode of the destruction of the armoured train in the later novel, and the scene here tends to pale by comparison. In general, it would seem that Malraux has still not found a completely adequate vehicle for his themes, nor has his technique reached full maturity. Neither his characters nor his plot are really strong enough to carry the necessary weight; and above all the 'tragic' conception of the individual's struggle with destiny is unsatisfactorily married to the train of events in Canton. Yet the themes are there: almost all the elements of the later 'political' novels are clearly present. Not only do we meet the themes of time, age, and death, ubiquitous in Malraux's work, which are accentuated by the individual's obsession with violent action— here shown first in Rebecci before reaching full treatment in Garine; but especially the analysis of the revolutionary mentality, the problem of discipline, and the relationship between the individual and the collective group for whom he is fighting. This, indeed, points forward more to *Le Temps du mépris* and *L'Espoir* than to *La Condition humaine*, where emphasis is more metaphysical.[1] In Garine's engagement, too, we look forward to *fraternité*

---

[1] It can also be compared with Roger Martin du Gard's similar analysis in *L'Été 1914*; here Martin du Gard appears to have profited from Malraux.

virile; while Klein's discussion of suicide, at the death of Tcheng-Daï, foreshadows the same theme in *Les Noyers de l'Altenburg*. Hong, as an intellectual conception, is possibly even more interesting than Tchen; but as a character in the novel he appears less successful because he tends to remain no more than an intellectual conception, whereas Tchen's actions are more dramatic, being seen at first hand, a technique impossible in *Les Conquérants* with its first-person narrator. Similarly the two scenes of street-fighting, among the most powerful in *La Condition humaine*, obviously derive from the episode here of General Tang's attack on Canton, where the narration is hampered by the narrator's inability to see things as a whole.

The most serious weakness in the novel is probably the excessive and rather immature fascination with thriller elements. These were removed, or modified, to a considerable extent in the revised 1949 edition; and it may well be to them that Malraux was referring when in his *Postface 1949* he described the novel as 'ce livre d'adolescent' (p. 229). Above all there is what one can only call Malraux's keen interest in secret police methods, if not admiration for them: Garine shooting the well-poisoner, or his decision to obtain information by the torture of slow strangulation (p. 176). The moral issues involved are completely ignored, and these episodes scarcely rise above the exoticism of schoolboy magazines. The novel also betrays an utter contempt for all democratic values, which has perhaps not been sufficiently noted: as when the narrator, in Saigon, listens to 'le verbiage démocratique du dîner, ces formules, dérisoires en Europe, recueillies ici comme les vieux vapeurs couverts de rouille' (p. 29). Throughout the novel the emphasis is on violent action rather than words, and it is difficult not to conclude that Garine's contempt for liberal democracy was shared by his creator. This aspect of Garine goes together with a misogynistic contempt for women: the only sexual scene of the novel, where the narrator finds Garine together with two young Chinese prostitutes, is in the same tone as *La Voie royale*; not until *La Condition humaine* will Malraux attempt to treat sexual relationships on a more profound level.

The revised version of the novel also plays down another

intrusive element of the earlier text: the narrator's rather naïve anti-European enthusiasm about events in the Hong Kong strike, together with the undue attention given to the nefarious machinations of the British 'Intelligence Service', seen as the villains of the political plot. Originally there was almost a hysterical note of delight in the narrator's description of how the British in Hong Kong, servantless through the strike, were obliged to do their own housework in the enervating humidity of the tropical summer; and although this was perfectly true it contrasts rather grotesquely with the world-shaking nature of happenings in Canton.[1] The drawback of all this is that the political struggle is over-simplified to a simple contest between black and white. It is also arguable that nationalism, rather than Communism, provided the chief dynamic of the northern campaign of the Kuomintang, and this aspect is very much neglected. The narrator's violent anti-European feelings—although they no doubt indicate a normal attitude of the sensitive intellectual to the arrogant way of life of settlers in the East—might have been better transposed into the Nationalist attitude to the Europeans (of whom, of course, he was himself one). As things stand the political struggle tends to be seen more as a conflict between British interests, on the one hand, and Soviet ones, on the other—both equally foreign to China.

Nevertheless, these weaknesses do not fatally damage the novel, irritating at times though they may be. With it Malraux succeeded in finding the field which best suited his talents, and in projecting a personal vision of contemporary life which has been passionately accepted by a wide readership. One may, it is true, object that Garine's devotion to revolutionary activity is in essence no more than a symptom of over-prolonged adolescence, rather than an indication of real greatness, that his life represents not so much modern heroism as barren heroics. Certainly Malraux, at this stage of his career, had nowhere near the experience of war and revolution that he attributed to his hero, and may to some extent

---

[1] On the other hand, Malraux considerably distorts actual events when he makes Garine responsible, just as much as Chiang Kai-shek, for the organization of the Whampoa military cadet school, and, even more, when in the original edition he ascribes the British general strike of 1926 to Garine's planning of the Hong Kong strike!

have been merely projecting his own fantasies into a suitably exotic setting; and the suspicion remains that Garine's contempt for Western society is fundamentally neurotic—if not psychotic— and that the gesture of scarring the map is no more than a destructive reaction to frustration. Cannot destiny be fought, the absurd be challenged, on a level where the taste for violence and blood is less prominent? We may note, in this connexion, that the *Postface* of 1949 has comparatively little to say about the original novel, however much it provides an opportunity for Malraux to express some of his basic ideas on art, and a backing for his post-war Gaullist policies. He had in fact so outgrown the enthusiasms of his twenties that in many ways the *Postface* is a refutation of the premisses of Garine's actions. But against all this there stands the powerful argument that it is the task of the novelist to pose problems, not to solve them. *Les Conquérants* is a vivid and passionate expression of the central dilemma in revolutionary action; a more judicious attempt to evaluate Garine's action might well have destroyed the qualities of vigour and colour which so characterize the novel. Ultimately we have to take it as it stands.

4

LA CONDITION HUMAINE

ALRAUX'S early work did not attract anywhere near as much attention at the time as it has in retrospect. *Les Conquérants* came in for some acclaim; *La Voie royale* for less. Only with *La Condition humaine* in 1933 did he first reach a really wide audience; the award of the Goncourt Prize in that year was both one of the most popular, and the most justified by subsequent events, in its history. It also meant a decisive change in publisher, to Gallimard, at the same time his employers. After serialization, like *Les Conquérants*, in the *N.R.F.*, from January to June 1933, Gallimard brought the new novel out the same year. A new edition, *revue et corrigée*, replaced the original one in 1946.[1]

La Condition humaine: the novel's title indicates both its central theme and its universal claims. Whether or not Malraux took his title from Montaigne's phrase, 'l'humaine condition', or from Pascal, its implications are clear. The characters and events in the novel are intended to be typical of human life at all times, not merely of their setting, Shanghai in civil war in 1927. This means that the novel is primarily 'metaphysical' rather than political, despite first appearances. The characters' antagonist is still destiny; and not all of them are revolutionaries. It is merely that the revolutionary situation, the intrigue, anxiety, and above all violence, which Malraux visualized in Shanghai make the setting and action a suitable allegory of human experience as a whole. Dr. Jenkins has pointed out in his essay on Malraux that each of the main characters represents an attempt to escape from the human condition, 'his useless, elected idiom, his Pascalian *divertissement*';[2] yet possibly the word *divertissement* gives a slightly false colour to the book. Malraux's first premiss is, certainly, Nietzsche's claim

[1] Textual references are to this 1946 revised edition.
[2] C. Jenkins, in J. Cruickshank (ed.), *The Novelist as Philosopher*, p. 65.

that 'God is dead'; the characters' strivings are not only an attempt to cheat the wait before death, but also a struggle to create their own transcendental values, to justify their own lives. In this it is not clear that all fail equally hopelessly; indeed, if they did, all Malraux's own later work would be unnecessary and irrelevant.

As in his earlier novels, the time span is only a few months: March to July 1927. And, as in *Les Conquérants*, an actual sequence of events is used to provide a basis to the plot: the Communist-sponsored uprising in Shanghai as Chiang Kai-shek's Northern Expedition nears the city, the defeat of the Whites, followed a fortnight later by Chiang's decision to break with the Communists and to suppress their militants. Since many of Malraux's characters are members of the Communist leadership, the events chosen give the novel a characteristic rhythm: triumph, followed by defeat. This is, in fact, very much the same development as in the earlier novels, but here it is much more marked, and the symmetry of the parabola is emphasized by the two episodes of street-fighting round which each phase of the curve is constructed.[1] This triumph and defeat are not merely political: even Trotsky was not tempted into print to complain that the book misses the Communist target. From the start it is clear that Malraux is not interested in events so much as in his characters, and in this novel as many characters are set outside the Communist group as inside it, including some of the highest importance. Nor are they divided rather crudely, as in *Les Conquérants*, into good and bad: in their search for a transcendental replacement for religious belief all are equal.

La Condition humaine is an international novel. Although it is set in the Far East, the action takes place in Shanghai, perhaps the most cosmopolitan city in the world at that time; while the characters, as Henri Peyre has commented, are for the most part Europeans,[2] albeit exiles and expatriates. There is also no definite hero,

---

[1] Even details of the fighting are paralleled: the last desperate fight of the doomed armoured train is equalled by the final hopeless struggle of Katow and his men, besieged in their headquarters: 'condamnés, tuer était le seul sens qu'il pussent donner à leurs dernières heures' (p. 321). A careful analysis of the sequence of events is given in Frohock, *André Malraux and the Tragic Imagination*, pp. 61–5.

[2] H. Peyre, *The Contemporary French Novel*, p. 194.

although Kyo Gisors, the son of old Gisors, a former professor of sociology, expelled for left-wing activities from the University of Peking, is the figure for whose ethical values Malraux has the most personal predilection, while the epilogue is based on his memory.

It is in narrative technique that Malraux has moved furthest away from his earlier novels; there is no question of a privileged narrator here, such as Claude Vannec or the unnamed narrator in *Les Conquérants*. Instead, the events are narrated, in the past tense, by the ordinary third-person technique, with knowledge of the characters' thoughts and feelings as well as of their actions and words. This suits Malraux's purpose much better; he can switch freely from character to character, from scene to scene, and thus show the influence of sudden events on a number of individuals or groups at the same time, gaining depth by a comparison of perspectives without sacrificing immediacy of description.[1] The main narrative problem becomes one of imposing unity on the different elements in the material—a unity imposed automatically by the privileged narrator of the earlier novels—and of striking a balance between the different characters and groups. Malraux solves this problem in several ways. Above all, unity tends to be imposed very largely by the sequence of events itself, because of the rise and fall of the parabola curve already mentioned. Then again, the character of Gisors holds the various strands together, since he acts very much as a father-figure, respected and consulted not only by his son and his son's comrades, but by such widely different figures as Ferral, the Western capitalist, Clappique, the mythomaniac, or Kama, the Japanese painter. There is also—as in *Les Conquérants*—a certain schematic symmetry, with at the one extreme complete party discipline (Borodine, Vologuine), at the other individualist fanaticism (Hong, Tchen), with the central figure (Garine, Kyo) balanced between them.[2] And finally, linking of the political and

---

[1] A parallel may be drawn with Jules Romains's *Verdun*. Clearly Romains had developed his own technique of narrating 'collective' events, yet he may also have profited from Malraux's signal success, which took place before *Les Hommes de bonne volonté* was properly under way.

[2] Cf. M. Krieger, *The Tragic Vision*, pp. 51–2. Professor Krieger also suggests that Kyo stands at the mid-point between pure action (Tchen) and pure thought (Gisors).

metaphysical aspects of the novel, or rather the binding of the metaphysical implications on to the framework of violent action, is achieved by a systematic alternation of scenes of action and meditation, description and dialogue, so that, for example, the initial highly dramatic murder by Tchen is immediately followed by a group dialogue by the various revolutionaries, this again by a description of the mythomaniac Clappique in full spate sitting between two whores in a night-club, then more revolutionary dialogue in a philosophical discussion between Kyo and his father, another between Kyo and his wife, and so on. In this way Malraux achieves not only the integration of his different characters, but a constant variation in tension, so that suspense is not kept at too high a level, and above all so that there is time for reflection on the metaphysical implications of events immediately after they happen. This being said, however, it must also be stated that *La Condition humaine* is not, at first reading, a particularly easy book: it shares the modern tendency for the serious novel to make demands on the reader unknown in the traditional chronological narrative. Yet Malraux is not indulging in virtuosity for its own sake; and his technique undoubtedly permits him a communication of insights and a feeling for texture that would not otherwise be possible.

Characterization in *La Condition humaine* is much superior to anything in Malraux's earlier work; there is both a wider range and more variation in peculiarities and in environment. At the same time, all characters are unmistakably Malraux's; but this is because each one is seeking to escape the human condition by the creation of his own set of transcendental values, and, though the values they seek may differ, the search for them is common to all. This idea is put explicitly into the words of Gisors, whose own particular escape is through opium, and who therefore equates all others—except Kyo—with his own undeniable escapism:

— Il faut toujours s'intoxiquer: ce pays a l'opium, l'Islam le haschich, l'Occident la femme. . . . Peut-être l'amour est-il surtout le moyen qu'emploie l'Occident pour s'affranchir de sa condition d'homme. . . .
Sous ses paroles, un contre-courant confus et caché de figures glissait: Tchen et le meurtre, Clappique et sa folie, Katow et la révolution, May

et l'amour, lui-même et l'opium . . . Kyo seul, pour lui, résistait à ces domaines. (p. 271)

This list could be supplemented: König and torture, Ferral and power, Kama and art. And even Kyo is not exempt, despite his father's belief, since his vision of human dignity is itself an escape, if a more complex one.

Gisors, though his part in the novel is largely functional, is by no means a hollow, ideal figure, bereft of living human qualities.[1] This is partly because his position is able to put him into personal relationships to many characters, without any straining of plausibility: he is at the same time Kyo's father, Tchen's former teacher, and a long-standing acquaintance of Ferral and Clappique. Again, his escape, or vice—opium (although there is a touch of the cliché of the gentle, opium-smoking Wise Man of the Orient about him)—removes him from the sphere of action to that of thought and meditation, so that he would be a logical person for them to talk to and thus attempt to break out of their isolation and solitude. For one of the key elements in the human condition, alongside old age and death, and the tyranny of time, is metaphysical solitude: the inability to escape from the bounds of one's ego and make real, lasting contact with others. This theme is repeated again and again in the novel: Tchen finds murder separates him still more from his fellows; Kyo suddenly realizes that, despite their love, his wife May is a person he does not know, since she can go to bed, on impulse, with another man; even Ferral, alone in his pride, constantly needs other people, since he cannot inflict humiliation and demonstrate his power when alone. Finally Gisors's relationship with Kyo, the love between father and son, is finely treated; enabling Malraux to make the final scene of the novel a conversation, in Japan, between Gisors and May, who is precious to Gisors simply because Kyo had loved her. Gisors represents an ideal of human love without violence, and cannot really understand the 'amour intellectuel et ravagé' between his son and May; his own love for Kyo's mother had been

---

[1] He might be compared in this respect with Luce in Martin du Gard's *Jean Barois*. Luce plays a somewhat similar functional role, but always remains on the ideal plane, never achieving full plausibility.

of an entirely different kind: 'Lui avait aimé une Japonaise parce qu'il aimait la tendresse, parce que l'amour à ses yeux n'était pas un conflit mais la contemplation confiante d'un visage aimé, l'incarnation de la plus sereine musique, — une poignante douceur' (p. 398). Gisors respects ideas more than he does fellow men, so much so that Kyo's death cuts his only real tie with them, throwing him back on his own solitude and making him indifferent to the prospect of death. Though he is theoretically a Marxist, the vanity of all human life has come to vanquish any belief in the virtues of revolution, and his only solace is to listen to Kama's music. In a fine passage he sums up one basic attitude to human existence, Schopenhauer's view that thought can only lead to unhappiness:

'Tous souffrent, songea-t-il, et chacun souffre parce qu'il pense. Tout au fond, l'esprit ne pense l'homme que dans l'éternel, et la conscience de la vie ne peut être qu'angoisse. Il ne faut pas penser la vie avec l'esprit, mais avec l'opium. Que de souffrances éparses dans cette lumière disparaîtraient, si disparaissait la pensée. . . . ' Libéré de tout, même d'être homme, il caressait avec reconnaissance le tuyau de sa pipe, contemplant l'agitation de tous ces êtres inconnus qui marchaient vers la mort dans l'éblouissant soleil, chacun choyant au plus secret de soi-même son parasite meurtrier. 'Tout homme est fou, pensa-t-il encore, mais qu'est une destinée humaine sinon une vie d'efforts pour unir ce fou et l'univers. . . . ' Il revit Ferral, éclairé par la lampe basse sur la nuit pleine de brume, écoutant: 'Tout homme rêve d'être dieu. . . . ' (pp. 400–1)

Gisors, a naturally meditative character, provides an excellent means of introducing, plausibly, the intellectual, cerebral element into a novel of violent action. But he is not alone in permitting intellectual overtones; practically all the characters in the novel share in an extreme self-consciousness and self-awareness—again one of the distinguishing marks of the Malraux hero.

Gisors's son, Kyo, was, it has been tentatively claimed, based on the figure of the future Chinese Prime Minister, Chou En-Lai.[1] Although Chou played the leading part in the real Shanghai uprising, before escaping the subsequent repression and joining the main body of the Chinese Communists under Mao, this seems unlikely. It has also been suggested, with possibly more plausibility,

[1] Frohock, op. cit., pp. 17–18.

since the suggestion originated from the person himself, that Kyo was modelled on the Japanese writer—and Malraux's translator—Kiyoshi (Kyo) Komatsu, who died in 1963.[1] There is, however, little point in tracking down possible models for Malraux's characters, since, whatever his works are, they are not *romans à clef*; but the suggestions made in connexion with *La Condition humaine* do have some interest. Frohock has also commented that Malraux may have had the French writer and thinker, Bernard Groethuysen, in mind when he portrayed Gisors, and that Clappique may be a composite of two other men known to Malraux. It is significant that neither of these, nor Kiyoshi Komatsu, were in Shanghai at the time of the events concerned: Malraux had known them primarily, if not entirely, in France.[2] The novel is, undoubtedly, not an autobiographical account of Malraux's own experiences and revolutionary comrades in Shanghai; and, indeed, it is doubtful if he himself was ever there before 1931, well after the events narrated. Instead Malraux is basically concerned with using the events in Shanghai as a vehicle for more metaphysical preoccupations; and the result is the lurid combination of violent action and intellectual meditation which forms his typical vision of the world.

Kyo Gisors stands out from the other revolutionaries in one major respect: he is, essentially, a bourgeois. This has functional consequences in the novel apart from differentiating him from the others psychologically. In the first place, he can move around in different social spheres, closed to the others—such as the 'Black Cat' night-club—while as a Eurasian he is equally at home with—or alienated from—both Orientals and Occidentals. More important, he is the character with whom the reader (it seems likely that, at least in the West, all novels, including revolutionary ones, are read largely by bourgeois readers) can most easily identify himself

[1] D. J. Enright, *The World of Dew*, London, 1955, p. 46; and in a personal communication to the present writer.

[2] Frohock, op. cit., p. 78. The same argument applies to Hoffmann's suggestions (op. cit., pp. 166, 176) that Ferral may be based on André Berthelot, and Gisors possibly on Gide. In giving the name Martial to the Shanghai police chief, Malraux seems possibly to have intended a dig at Martial Merlin, a reactionary Governor of Indo-China in the early 1920s.

—and, probably, not only the reader, but also the author. In this way Kyo becomes a privileged character, of whom we see more, and more aspects, than the others—and who is *récupérable* even for König and the right-wing police, so that when he refuses to save his life by betraying his comrades his death takes on added significance and poignancy.

Malraux, in *Les Voix du silence*, has stated that in *La Condition humaine* he wrote the story of a man who did not recognize the sound of his own voice.[1] This remark, referring to the well-known scene where Kyo, having recorded his own voice, cannot recognize it when played back, may be taken as an example of Malraux's liking for *mystification*. Yet it is true that this episode (pp. 24–6), where the revolutionary group are passing instructions to other groups by means of gramophone records, has nothing to do with the rest of the political action of the novel, and clearly was only introduced by the author to bring out the theme of metaphysical solitude, to illustrate the idea that man, far from being able to establish true contact with others, cannot even recognize himself. Revolutionary activity, for Kyo, has a psychological origin—it is an attempt to conquer his solitude and alienation, as well as a result of Marxist political beliefs.

The fundamental element in Kyo's intellectual beliefs is his conception of human dignity. This conception had already been used in *Les Conquérants*, where dignity, rather than hunger and material need, is seen as the dynamic of the revolutionary coolies, but now it is developed at much greater length. Whereas Tchen is naturally drawn towards political action (like most of the others) for 'la satisfaction de ses haines, de sa pensée, de son caractère. Elle donnait un sens à sa solitude' (p. 80), for Kyo things are different. More simple, his father muses, though one might equally well claim more subtle:

Le sens héroïque lui avait été donné comme une discipline, non comme une justification de la vie. Il n'était pas inquiet. Sa vie avait un sens, et il le connaissait: donner à chacun de ces hommes que la famine, en ce moment même, faisait mourir comme une peste lente, la possession de sa propre dignité. (p. 80)

[1] *Les Voix du silence*, Paris, 1951, p. 628.

Kyo's belief in revolution, therefore, does not spring naturally from his own social position, but is a kind of altruism from the start; he both lives and dies not so much for his fellow men as for an idea. At the same time, he can be no orthodox Marxist, since his conception of dignity is at bottom a personal and individual value rather than a collective one. Dignity is seen by Malraux as at the opposite pole from humiliation: not only in Kyo, but also in Ferral's relations with women. But the direct confrontation between the two is most clearly shown after Kyo's arrest, when his fate lies in the hands of the police-chief König. First Clappique goes to see König, in an attempt to do something for Kyo, but the very mention of Kyo's reason for becoming a Communist—'par volonté de dignité'—immediately rouses the policeman to fury. He describes how, when a prisoner of the Reds in Sibera, long nails had been driven through the stars on his epaulettes into his shoulders. Humiliation and the desire for revenge make him hate the very word of dignity. This scene, like several others about the Russian civil war in Malraux's work, has the ring of authenticity: we may assume that they were probably based on genuine anecdotes. At the same time, this story, on which the whole conception of König's character as a killer is centred—'A coup sûr il racontait cette histoire — ou se la racontait — chaque fois qu'il pouvait tuer, comme si ce récit eût pu gratter jusqu'au sang l'humiliation sans limites qui le torturait' (p. 317)—is also closely linked with the sexual: König has been impotent for over a year. No less than Tchen, König lives in complete metaphysical solitude; the analysis of the brutal police-chief is taken much further than with Nicolaïeff in *Les Conquérants*, to an almost Dostoevskyan intensity:

cette intoxication totale, que le sang seul assouvissait: il [Clappique] avait vu assez d'épaves des guerres civiles de Chine et de Sibérie pour savoir quelle négation du monde appelle l'humiliation intense; seuls le sang opiniâtrement versé, la drogue et la névrose nourrissent de telles solitudes. Il comprenait maintenant pourquoi König avait aimé sa compagnie, n'ignorant pas combien, auprès de lui, s'affaiblissait toute réalité. (p. 319)

The theme of humiliation is taken up again when the narrative moves to Kyo in prison, facing his jailer: 'il ressentait jusqu'à l'envie de vomir l'humiliation que ressent tout homme devant un homme dont il dépend: impuissant contre cette immonde ombre à fouet, — dépouillé de lui-même' (p. 334). It is pointed by the further episode where the lunatic is whipped by the guard, who finally desists when paid to do so by Kyo: here the concept of dignity succeeds in overcoming—temporarily—brutality and humiliation, yet by a neat irony it is only by the negation of Kyo's ideas—private possession of money—that this result is achieved. Ultimately Kyo manages to maintain his personal dignity, refusing the offer of his life if he betrays his comrades, even at the risk of torture; and his meditation before poisoning himself is a fine passage:

Allongé sur le dos, les bras ramenés sur la poitrine, Kyo ferma les yeux: c'était précisément la position des morts. Il s'imagina, allongé, immobile, les yeux fermés, le visage apaisé par la sérénité que dispense la mort un jour à presque tous les cadavres, comme si devait être exprimée la dignité même des plus misérables. Il avait beaucoup vu mourir, et, aidé par son éducation japonaise, il avait toujours pensé qu'il est beau de mourir de *sa* mort, d'une mort qui ressemble à sa vie. Et mourir est passivité, mais se tuer est acte. (p. 360)

Behind Kyo's conception of dignity, at this ultimate point, we find again the idea of will, one of Malraux's fundamental *données* in the creation of character, and perhaps the most powerful psychological link between his characters, all of whom are to some extent obsessed by will, even if, like Gisors, their main efforts go towards its suppression.

One further aspect of Kyo deserves attention. This is his relationship with his wife May. In *Les Conquérants* and especially in *La Voie royale* sexual relationships had taken the form of eroticism, mixed with a certain sadism; and this aspect is also very evident in the present work. But Malraux seems to have made a deliberate attempt to treat a non-erotic love relationship, based on emotional equality, in portraying Kyo and his wife. At the same time this relationship is far from simple; like all Malraux's imaginative attempts, it is intellectually conceived, and at times perhaps it is implausibly cerebral. Above all, the initial incident when the two characters are brought together, and May confesses her infidelity with Lenglen earlier that day, has nothing to do with the rest of the action of the novel, and, indeed, is somewhat artificial at this point; it must therefore have been inserted by Malraux for the light it casts on this relationship. Despite Kyo's belief in sexual equality, his intellectual principles cannot withstand his natural emotional reaction: one of deep humiliation, not so much jealousy as loss of identification, being thrown back on his own solitude. The result is that his own weakness makes him want to lose himself completely in her embrace, to conquer his humiliation and solitude:

Elle lui échappait complètement. Et, à cause de cela peut-être, l'appel enragé d'un contact intense avec elle l'aveuglait, quel qu'il fût, épouvante, cris, coups. Il se leva, s'approcha d'elle. Il savait qu'il était dans un état de crise, que demain peut-être il ne comprendrait plus rien à ce qu'il éprouvait, mais il était en face d'elle comme d'une agonie; et comme vers une agonie, l'instinct le jetait vers elle: toucher, palper, retenir ceux qui vous quittent, s'accrocher à eux. . . . Avec quelle angoisse elle le regardait, arrêté à deux pas d'elle. . . . La révélation de ce qu'il voulait tomba enfin sur lui; coucher avec elle, se réfugier là contre ce vertige dans lequel il la perdait tout entière; ils n'avaient pas à se connaître quand ils employaient toutes leurs forces à serrer leurs bras sur leurs corps. (pp. 64-5)

The vocabulary used by Malraux in this passage—'enragé', 'aveuglait', 'épouvante', 'agonie', 'angoisse', 'vertige'—marks this episode as one of the most emotionally powerful in the whole novel, and goes some way to explain why sex takes the form of eroticism in most of his other work. Here genuine love is shown as producing pain (quite apart from Kyo's death, which naturally does so); whereas through the erotic the individual can indulge in sexual pleasure without weakness and damage to the ego. Once more, when May insists on accompanying Kyo on the night when he is to be arrested, a remark is made, which may be May's reported thought, or, more probably, a psychological generalization by Malraux: 'Les blessures du plus profond amour suffisent à faire une assez belle haine' (p. 239). Or again, on the previous page, Kyo comments: 'Reconnaître la liberté d'un autre, c'est lui donner raison contre sa propre souffrance.' This discussion on sexual liberty, although it marks a distinct progress since the earlier episode, seems perhaps a little strained at this crucial point of the political action, but it is designed to lead to Kyo's conclusion, again rather cerebral: 'Il comprenait maintenant qu'accepter d'entraîner l'être qu'on aime dans la mort est peut-être la forme totale de l'amour, celle qui ne peut pas être dépassée' (p. 244). Malraux's view of love is, therefore, distinctly pessimistic; he will attempt a somewhat similar relationship between Kassner and Anna in *Le Temps du mépris*, but thereafter love—and the erotic—disappear from his work. As a satisfactory escape from the human condition, love is evidently to be dismissed.

Already in this novel it is arguable that the concept of *fraternité virile*, seen above all in Katow, is one that is shown as superior to love. Katow, as a revolutionary, is, in fact, an embodiment of the idea of virile fraternity, and it forms his own means to self-transcendence. This feeling of brotherhood in action, indeed, acts as a direct challenge to metaphysical solitude. (It is also an important element in Kyo's relationship with May.) And it is the cement which Malraux sees as uniting the different revolutionaries: in the first insurrection, when a young Kuomintang cadet comes to take command, Tchen thinks: 'Il était brave, sans aucun doute, mais il n'était pas lié à ses hommes.' Tchen too, since his murder, had begun to lose his feeling of fraternity, and the passage continues: 'Tchen était lié aux siens, mais pas assez' (p. 124). Katow, however, is undisturbed by intellectual complications, and his whole life, from going to the salt mines as a volunteer after the unsuccessful 1905 revolution in Russia to his final heroic death, is dedicated to the ideal of self-sacrifice so that he can build a better world for his fellows. One may suspect, in fact, that his role in the novel—a comparatively minor one, since any other of the revolutionaries could have led the seizure of the weapons on the *Shan-Tung*—is largely a preparation for his bravery and self-abnegation later. And it must be said that, although Malraux tries to individualize all his characters, both by means of a brief biographical sketch and by giving them a characteristic mode of speech, such as Katow's swallowing his 'e's—'L'interm'diaire avait p't-être pris un rend'-

vous' (p. 26)—Katow does not come to life as much as many other
characters. Sometimes, as well, heroism seems likely to spill over
into heroics: as when, having given his cyanide to two comrades
more afraid than he of being burnt to death in a locomotive fire-
box, he says to himself: 'supposons que je sois mort dans un
incendie' (p. 368). Yet a moment earlier a genuine emotional
climax had been achieved: after passing the cyanide over, it
dropped to the floor, and Katow's searching hand touched, then
was gripped by, another:

> Katow, lui aussi, serrait la main, à la limite des larmes, pris par cette
> pauvre fraternité sans visage, presque sans vraie voix (tous les chuchote-
> ments se ressemblent) qui lui était donnée dans cette obscurité contre le
> plus grand don qu'il eût jamais fait, et qui était peut-être fait en vain.
> (p. 366)

For Katow, indeed, the ideal of virile fraternity assumes the
passion of the religious ascetic and martyr, and he becomes perhaps the most exemplary figure in the novel.

Of the other revolutionaries Hemmelrich is worthy of attention.
He too feels, perhaps unknown to himself, some of the same
sense of human comradeship; but hate of those more fortunate
than himself is the real mainspring of his revolutionary action.
'Quand je vois des gens qui ont l'air de s'aimer, j'ai envie de leur
casser la gueule', he exclaims, referring to the rich (p. 247); the
Kuomintang officer whom he kills before escaping 'n'était plus un
homme, il était tout ce dont Hemmelrich avait souffert jusque-là'
(p. 327). Having married a Chinese woman out of pity, their child
suffering deeply, he is inhibited from taking an active part in the
insurrection, merely lending his shop as a headquarters. Then,
with a profound but deliberate irony, in the repression by Chiang's
troops, his wife and child are killed, and at last he is free to act and
to take over from Tchen the *anti-destin* of violence—a feeling
which Malraux describes, typically, in sexual terms:

> une exaltation intense bouleversait son esprit, la plus puissante qu'il eût
> jamais connue; il s'abandonnait à cette effroyable ivresse avec un con-
> sentement entier. 'On peut tuer avec amour. Avec amour, nom de
> Dieu!' répéta-t-il frappant le comptoir du poing — contre l'univers
> peut-être. . . . (p. 303)

76 LA CONDITION HUMAINE

Hemmelrich's life of misery has deprived him of all fear of death, but there is a double irony: 'cette fois, la destinée avait mal joué: en lui arrachant tout ce qu'il possédait encore, elle le libérait' (p. 302); then, as the revolutionary group are overcome by the Kuomintang troops, Hemmelrich, by killing an officer and putting on his uniform, is the only one to escape, and at the end of the novel is in Moscow. This irony is not merely an intellectual conceit: it marks the appearance of the absurd in human, even revolutionary, affairs. There is no historical inevitability in the events of the novel, which are ruled much more by pure chance or contingency.

The character of Tchen is one of the most striking in the novel; he is a development of the political terrorist and assassin, and grows organically out of Hong in *Les Conquérants*. It is not for nothing that Malraux begins his novel with the account, a typical alternation between violent action and meditation, of Tchen's act of murder in the hotel. This scene seems to set the note of the novel as an intellectual thriller, built round Tchen, and it is only later that his apparent importance is superseded by other characters such as Kyo, Ferral, and Clappique. For Tchen, murder and terrorism become his means of self-transcendence: before his attempt on Chiang's life his conversation with Souen makes this explicit:

— Tu veux faire du terrorisme une espèce de religion?

Les mots étaient creux, absurdes, trop faibles pour exprimer ce que Tchen voulait d'eux.

— Pas une religion. Le sens de la vie. La . . .

Il faisait de la main le geste convulsif de pétrir, et sa pensée semblait haleter comme une respiration.

' . . . La possession complète de soi-même.' (p. 221).

He feels deeply that his initial act of killing has separated him from his fellows, even the other revolutionaries; the description of his visit to Gisors, immediately after the murder, is largely to drive this point home. Malraux combines the idea of killing with that of sexual possession—as with König—and Tchen describes his contempt, greater even than for his victim, for those who have not killed: 'les puceaux' (p. 73). Tchen's complex feelings at this point, further confused by his background, his Confucianist uncle, his education by Smithson, the Protestant missionary, and his sexual development, are already recognized by Gisors as a kind of death wish, or urge for self-destruction:

— Je serai bientôt tué.

N'est-ce pas cela surtout qu'il veut? se demandait Gisors. Il n'aspire à aucune gloire, à aucun bonheur. Capable de vaincre mais non de vivre dans sa victoire, que peut-il appeler, sinon la mort? Sans doute veut-il lui donner le sens que d'autres donnent à la vie. Mourir le plus haut possible. Âme d'ambiteux, assez lucide, assez séparé des hommes ou assez malade pour mépriser tous les objets de son ambition, et son ambition même? (p. 75)

Before his first, frustrated attempt on Chiang, Tchen is made to meet Smithson again in the street; this encounter, not very plausible, is clearly designed to show that Tchen has now gone far beyond the solace of Christian religion, and leads up to Tchen's brutal interruption of the missionary's pious words: 'Écoutez bien. Dans deux heures, je tuerai' (p. 201). This episode is the only one in which religion is introduced at all: for Malraux's characters complete rejection of religion is the first premiss of their search for a means of self-transcendence, and, in the earlier novels at least, religion as a serious theme is therefore ruled out.

Tchen's death, in his second, equally unsuccessful, attempt on Chiang, is an exercise in the absurd. At the very moment when he has developed his ideas on terrorism, which is to become a *mystique*, based on solitude and the need to give an aim to the lives of the workers, an aim depending on the dynamic of martyrdom rather than political organization, Tchen dies, stupidly, without killing Chiang, and without even knowing whether he has killed him or not. Even his final suicide is not an act of will, despite his enormous efforts; when he is kicked by a policeman, it is the automatic muscular reaction which makes him pull the trigger, not his own volition. And as a final irony, his death is no martyrdom; it is scarcely even noticed in the hundreds of deaths which follow the repression of the whole Communist movement in Shanghai.

The other revolutionary figures are much less significant. Souen is little more than a foil for Tchen. Peï, apart from being one of the few survivors, is sketched slightly more extensively, as a nationalist first and foremost and a Communist only because 'pour lui, le communisme était seulement le vrai moyen de faire revivre la Chine' (p. 218). More, indeed, might have been made of this character; certainly, in the light of subsequent events, it seems clear that nationalism has played at least as large a part as Marxism in providing the dynamic to clear much of Asia of European domination. Vologuine, the commissar at Hankow, is described (like several other characters in the present novel and *Les Conquérants*) in almost religious terms: 'ses mains ecclésiastiques' (p. 169). He is not a man of action, but a missionary of the new Communist religion, bound to absolute obedience. Malraux makes this aspect of him more explicit in a passage inserted later in the 1946 edition:

Vologuine était beaucoup plus mal à l'aise qu'il ne le laissait paraître. La discipline du parti sortait furieusement renforcée de la lutte contre les trotzkistes. Vologuine était là pour faire exécuter des décisions prises par des camarades plus qualifiés, mieux informés que lui — et que Kyo. En Russie, il n'eût pas discuté. (p. 165)

The whole episode of Kyo and Tchen visiting Hankow, highly undramatic, bears little organic relationship to the remainder of the novel, and, together with the closing scenes in France and Japan, it breaks the unity of place, otherwise maintained throughout. This episode is necessary to explain the political action, however, and also to give Kyo's analysis of Marxism, and his affirmation of will as its real basis, not blind belief in historical inevitability: 'il y a dans le marxisme le sens d'une fatalité, et l'exaltation d'une volonté. Chaque fois que la fatalité passe avant la volonté, je me méfie' (p. 166). This statement accords well with Malraux's own relationship with, and qualified support of, the international Communist movement in the 1930s.

Of the other characters Ferral and Clappique are the most important; and they are two of the most convincingly drawn. The conception of Ferral owes much to Nietzsche: he is practically an embodiment of the will to power. But he also owes something to a popular view of Adler's psychology: the scenes with his mistress

Valérie show that sex is, for him, channelled into the single outlet of eroticism, and ultimately depends on his need for power. Sexual pleasure is therefore subordinated to the need to dominate his partner; as he passes a superb White Russian woman on the stairs to Martial's office, he thinks to himself: 'Je voudrais bien savoir la tête que tu fais quand tu jouis, toi' (p. 103). In addition, there is probably much of Malraux himself in Ferral; as Frohock has commented, he is much more clearly an adventurer than either Kyo or Tchen,[1] and with his bourgeois intellectual background is much more easily assimilable to Malraux's own career. Thirst for power goes together with a lucid realism, and leads inevitably to political intrigue; while Ferral's recipe for political power, brute force, and cynical manipulation of public opinion is clearly Fascist in conception. Even intelligence, for him, is not something abstract, but to be applied to the ends of power: as he defines it to Gisors it means 'la possession des moyens de contraindre les choses ou les hommes' (p. 268).

Ferral's role in the action is to buy off Chiang: but it is not really necessary to bring him into the foreground of the story merely for this purpose. We may assume, therefore, that Malraux introduces him into the novel partly because he wishes to achieve a better balance than in Les Conquérants and so wishes to show the 'capitalist' side of events, and partly because he is interested in Ferral for his own sake. Again, Ferral's sexual relationship plays no more intrinsic part in the development of the political action than does Kyo's; but his character would be inadequately portrayed if it were not described. Ferral is, in this sexual respect, the development of Perken in La Voie royale; the importance of the two episodes with Valérie can perhaps be gauged by the fact that these were two of the scenes most changed by Malraux in the revised 1946 edition of the novel,[2] where Ferral's self-analysis (inappropriate for a devotee of will) is reduced and the eroto-sadistic action in the scenes given more chance to speak for itself. There is no tenderness, for Ferral, in sexual relations; he sees his own attraction

[1] Frohock, op. cit., p. 76.
[2] Cf. my article, 'Malraux—a Note on Editions', AUMLA, no. 21, p. 82. In the revised version the role of Tchen and terrorism is also played down.

to Valérie as being the flattery to her vanity of having as lover one of the most powerful men in the Far East, while his own enjoyment of intercourse depends on his domination of her body, so that her orgasm depends entirely on his will. It might be claimed that the relationship with Valérie is, once again, too cerebral, something of an intellectual conceit; but in fact the first scene between the two (pp. 139–45) contains one of the most lucid analyses of the sexual 'affair' in the whole of French literature, one which can stand comparison with similar passages in Proust. The basis of Malraux's analysis is egoism, and it is the temporary coinciding of two egoisms that provides the spark that touches off the relationship; when Valérie's egoism—as much a product of her will as Ferral's—is damaged by his deliberate humiliation of her, the relationship turns into a battle of wills, and she immediately breaks off to humiliate him in his turn. They are not interested in each other as independent human beings, but only as functions of their own egoism: Ferral thinks, as Valérie lies sleeping, 'elle n'était rien que l'autre pôle de son propre plaisir. Jamais elle n'avait vécu: elle n'avait jamais été une petite fille' (p. 145). And, humiliated himself by the ridiculous scene with the birds, Ferral's automatic reaction is to humiliate someone else—the unfortunate Chinese courtesan.[1]

Frohock has commented that the ultimate ruin of Ferral, defeated by the Paris bankers as Kyo was by the Hankow hierarchy, lengthily described in what might easily have become an anticlimax at the end of the novel, is the embodiment of the absurd.[2] Clearly Ferral's attempt at escape from the human condition takes the form of this will to power, but it is no more successful, ultimately, than Kyo's search for human dignity or Katow's yearning for brotherhood, since it ends in humiliation just as theirs do in death. No more successful, but no less; Ferral's development runs parallel to theirs, and it is not for nothing that the two episodes with Valérie are placed contemporaneously with the two crucial

[1] It is perhaps worthy of note that Malraux describes Ferral's humiliation in terms reminiscent of Sartre's La Nausée: 'Il se sentit entouré de la vraie bêtise humaine, celle qui colle, qui pèse aux épaules' (p. 256).
[2] Frohock, op. cit., p. 77.

scenes of revolutionary violence, the first of apparent success, the second of defeat. This juxtaposition represents another aspect of the absurd, and, just as much as it gives metaphysical significance to events in Ferral's life which might otherwise seem to be purely comical, it leads to a certain relief from the high emotional tension of the revolutionary scenes.

If Ferral's career terminates in the absurd, Clappique *is* the absurd personified. His attempt at self-transcendence is both the most ambitious—he wishes to escape from himself by actually becoming someone else—and the most certain of ultimate failure. At the same time, Malraux does not overstress these metaphysical aspects, but allows Clappique to provide relief from high seriousness and tension with his tall stories and ridiculous exploits, and constant identification with something other than himself. 'De quelque façon qu'il fût habillé', we early learn, 'le baron de Clappique avait l'air déguisé' (p. 35), and the final result is that his individual personality has almost disintegrated completely; Kyo watches him leave, 'nez baissé, dos voûté, tête nue, les mains dans les poches du smoking, semblable à sa propre caricature' (p. 44). As often, it is Gisors who is given the key to Clappique's character: 'Sa mythomanie est un moyen de nier la vie, n'est-ce pas, de nier, et non pas d'oublier' (p. 53). A strong interest in mythomania has been a constant feature in Malraux's career, but this is not to identify Clappique with himself to anything like the same degree as Ferral. In Clappique he has created probably the most original character in any of his novels, the buffoon who, as Frohock rightly comments, is in some danger of running away with the story.[1] At one time or another we see him play the part of an open-handed Hungarian aristocrat, when in fact he is handing out his last dollars; of a would-be suicide; and, immediately after escaping with his life, suitably disguised, on to a steamer, of an experienced sailor and traveller. A scene to which Malraux devotes

[1] Ibid., p. 75. Frohock cites the episode, excised from the published novel and printed separately in *Marianne*, 13 Dec. 1933, where Clappique, after failing to warn Kyo, is enticed by a nude woman into a hotel room, only to find subsequently that he is performing the sexual act for a group of hidden voyeurs. But it seems more probable that this episode was not simply cut out, but *replaced* by the section (pp. 292-6) which now follows his departure from the 'Black Cat'.

a good deal of space and trouble is that of Clappique in the 'Black Cat', where, captured by the excitement of roulette, he lets the moments slip by until it is too late for Kyo to be warned. Nominally Clappique is responsible for the downfall of the Communists, since the warning he should have given them would have enabled them to hide; but there is no moral condemnation of him, merely an analysis of the psychology of gambling, linked closely with his desire for self-escape, so that he identifies himself with the roulette ball itself: 'Cette boule dont le mouvement allait faiblir était un destin, et d'abord *son* destin. Il ne luttait pas contre une créature, mais contre une espèce de dieu; et ce dieu, en même temps, était lui-même' (p. 289). In Clappique, Malraux to some extent recaptures the fantastic imaginative world of his earliest, Surrealist, works, but one allied to the central intellectual conception of self-transcendence. Leaving the 'Black Cat', Clappique picks up a prostitute, and convinces her that he is about to commit suicide; as always, Malraux selects action for its metaphysical overtones:

Bien qu'il eût à peine bu, il était ivre de ce mensonge, de cette chaleur, de l'univers fictif qu'il créait. Quand il disait qu'il se tuerait, il ne se croyait pas; mais, puisqu'elle le croyait, il entrait dans un monde où la vérité n'existait plus. Ce n'était ni vrai, ni faux, mais vécu. Et puisque n'existaient ni son passé qu'il venait d'inventer, ni le geste élémentaire et supposé si proche sur quoi se fondait son rapport avec cette femme, rien n'existait. Le monde avait cessé de peser sur lui. Délivré, il ne vivait plus que dans l'univers romanesque qu'il venait de créer, fort du lien qu'établit toute pitié humaine devant la mort. La sensation d'ivresse était telle que sa main trembla. La femme le sentit et crut que c'était d'angoisse. . . . (p. 295)

Yet Clappique's attempt to escape is, again, only temporarily successful; once back in his hotel, with a bottle of whisky and the *Tales of Hoffmann*, his *livre de chevet*, his destiny retakes possession of him: 'Il était parvenu à échapper à presque tout ce sur quoi les hommes fondent leur vie: amour, famille, travail; non à la peur' (p. 307); despite his further success in embarking on the ship disguised as a sailor, Malraux wisely leaves his future open.

In all Malraux's characterization the one constant factor is intellectual conception. He does not achieve such richly human characters as Proust, or even Martin du Gard; but to some extent this is compensated by intellectual analysis, itself a means of giving density to a novel. This often borders on the traditional French technique in the novel of extracting psychological generalizations from the action, the novelist becoming simultaneously a *moraliste*. Thus, after Clappique has gained the ship, his thoughts verge on the generalization, 'Non, les hommes n'existaient pas, puisqu'il suffit d'un costume pour échapper à soi-même, pour trouver une autre vie dans les yeux des autres' (p. 350); or, in his conversation with Gisors, come to ask him to intercede with König for Kyo's life, when a whole series of psychological insights are introduced (pp. 311–12). Even the very minor characters, such as the police inspector Chpilewski, are used for similar purposes; Chpilewski is given his own means of attempting self-transcendence, in stealing toys from shops. One minor character, Kama, the Japanese painter, who appears only briefly in the novel, deserves special attention, since he foreshadows Malraux's art philosophy of the 1940s and 1950s. For Kama art itself is the means of fighting the human condition: 's'il ne peignait plus, il lui semblerait qu'il est devenu aveugle. Et plus qu'aveugle: seul' (p. 226); art, together with music, his *shamisen*, which he has found, enables him to achieve at any time and in any place his 'silence intérieur' (p. 229). Kama's point of view is put forward in a dialogue with Clappique; but his only role in the action is to provide a refuge for Gisors in Japan after the defeat of the Shanghai Communists. We may assume therefore that Malraux introduced him primarily for metaphysical purposes; and we might further suppose that, although Malraux was already interested in art at this time, he did not consider it as of the same importance as the other *anti-destins* developed by his various characters.

Malraux's style in *La Condition humaine* shows a firm development from that in his earlier work, a development shown most clearly in his greater virtuosity and confidence in tackling scenes requiring high technical ability. This virtuosity is expressed above

X

all in variation and alternation, both from scene to scene—switching from insurrectionary fighting to Ferral's bedroom, then on to the expiry of the armoured train—and within each scene—from meditation to action and back again, from description to dialogue, from dialogue to analysis. Such frequent changes of scene or tone demand strict discipline from the novelist, who cannot afford to indulge in scenes of excessive length lest they break the rhythm of the narrative; occasionally, indeed, the need for exposition does slow Malraux's pace, as in the long explanatory passages dealing with Ferral's financial situation (pp. 252–4), but on the whole he keeps up a crisp tempo. It is perhaps in the devising of scene and episode that the creative imagination shows itself to best effect; certain scenes here are compelling in the extreme. Not so much the initial murder by Tchen, which, although providing a highly dramatic opening to the novel, borders on the melodramatic; but certainly the two scenes of street-fighting—despite hundreds of minor changes made by Malraux in his 1946 edition, these two episodes were left practically untouched. Another scene verging on melodrama is that where König offers Kyo his life at the price of the betrayal of his comrades; this was substantially toned down in the 1946 edition. Juxtaposition of incongruous scenes is also a means of expressing the absurd; a technique especially used in the scenes covering Ferral, which move from important political moves (buying off Chiang) immediately to sexual episodes not far removed from the comical. Or again, the absurd appears when Tchen is prevented from carrying out his first attempt on Chiang's life by his ridiculous conversation with the curio-dealer.

Style, too, has reached heights only dimly foreshadowed in the earlier novels, and each episode is narrated in the appropriate style. The scenes of action and violence are presented in brisk dialogue, interspersed with longer passages of reported thought—Malraux indulges in these latter perhaps all the more vigorously for having voluntarily deprived himself of them in his earlier novels. Occasionally he breaks into the lyrico-Romantic tone of *La Tentation de l'Occident*, as when he describes Gisors smoking opium; the change is not gratuitous, but expresses the drug-induced feeling of beatitude in the old man:

Il se souvint d'un après-midi de septembre où le gris parfait du ciel rendait laiteuse l'eau d'un lac, dans les failles de vastes champs de nénuphars; depuis les cornes vermoulues d'un pavillon abandonné jusqu'à l'horizon magnifique et morne, ne lui parvenait plus qu'un monde pénétré d'une mélancolie solennelle. Sans agiter sa sonnette, un bonze s'était accoudé à la rampe du pavillon, abandonnant son sanctuaire à la poussière, au parfum des bois odorants qui brûlaient; les paysans qui recueillaient les graines des nénuphars passaient en barque, sans le moindre son; près des dernières fleurs, deux longs plis d'eau naquirent du gouvernail, allèrent se perdre avec nonchalance dans l'eau grise. Elles se perdaient maintenant en lui-même, ramassant dans leur éventail tout l'accablement du monde, un accablement sans amertume, amené par l'opium à une pureté suprême. Les yeux fermés, porté par de grandes ailes immobiles, Gisors contemplait sa solitude: une désolation qui rejoignait le divin en même temps que s'élargissait jusqu'à l'infini ce sillage de sérénité qui recouvrait doucement les profondeurs de la mort. (pp. 84–5)

Malraux's most striking individual technique is his use of images, already essayed in his earlier novels but now brought to a new pitch of effectiveness. Although some of these, particularly those of light and darkness, clearly have symbolical significance—such as the darkness inside the prison, or the evening mist descending immediately before Tchen's death—there is no need to search for a symbolical counterpart to every individual image. Often the sound images are used merely to emphasize the dialogue at important moments; as with Clappique's reaction to Chpilewski's warning that he must leave Shanghai within forty-eight hours or die: 'Ah! ah! ah! dit Clappique, montant la gamme. Comme un écho, la trompe d'une auto, dehors, sonna en arpège' (p. 195). Malraux's imagination leads him to four main types of images. First there are the images seen in the contrast between light and darkness, the latter often having a sinister quality—'la nuit menaçante' (p. 138). Kyo's arrest, the destruction of the armoured train, and the defeat of the Communists all take place in gloom and semi-darkness, lit up only by brief and ghostly flashes, as of hope. This type of image, a development of the 'pathetic fallacy', is very common, and almost every scene is touched with light and darkness, with the latter predominating. The total effect of these

images is to reinforce the tone of the book, as in Tchen's discussion
with Souen and Peï on the afternoon of his death:

> Il commença à marcher de long en large. L'arrière-boutique n'était
> éclairée que par le jour qui pénétrait à travers le magasin. Le ciel étant
> gris, il régnait là une lumière plombée comme celle qui précède les
> orages; dans cette brume sale brillaient sur les panses des lampes-
> tempête des effets de lumière, points d'interrogation renversés et paral-
> lèles. L'ombre de Tchen, trop confuse pour être une silhouette, avançait
> au-dessus des yeux inquiets des autres. (p. 220)

The next type of image is that seen in the contrast between sound
and silence. Naturally the scenes of insurrection lend themselves
to, in fact compel, description in terms of sound: rifle or pistol
shots, the explosion of grenades, the cries of the wounded; and
these same sounds carried on the wind can also be used to punctuate scenes, such as that between Ferral and Valérie, taking place
simultaneously elsewhere in the city. The most striking use of
sound in the novel is the well-known episode of the armoured
train, when the gunners, convinced of their fate when Chiang's
troops appear—their arrival heralded, fittingly, by sounds, cries,
and shouts—fire off all their remaining ammunition in one huge
broadside. In the relative silence following, the Communist group,
their headquarters in a clockmaker's shop, hear, above the tramp-
ing of feet and ticking of innumerable clocks, a rumbling in the
distance: the nationalist artillery. The episode, throughout narrated principally in terms of sound, ends with a direct equation
of this sound with their forthcoming death: 'Derrière chaque
blindage, un homme du train écoutait ce bruit comme la voix
même de la mort' (p. 156). Again, when Kyo and Tchen are at
Hankow, seeking instructions from Vologuine, just at the moment
when the two men realize that no help is forthcoming and that
they and their comrades are doomed, Vologuine's words are as it
were echoed by the mighty pounding of the printing presses in the
building: 'Kyo ne pouvait se délivrer de cet ébranlement de
machines transmis à ses muscles par le sol—comme si ces machines
à fabriquer la vérité eussent rejoint en lui les hésitations et les
affirmations de Vologuine' (p. 176). Less appeal is made to the

other senses; although sometimes Malraux refers to odours, this is usually in direct description, rather than imagery. The third kind of image frequently employed is that of insects and animals. As in the earlier novels these images symbolize the unpleasant and non-human, the ultimate obstacle to will; or at the very least what is seen as hostile and distasteful, as when Ferral, forcing his way through the crowds in the first insurrection, feels their essential hostility, in a passage where sound and silence are also introduced: 'Les enfants, cessant de jouer, filaient entre les jambes, à travers l'activité pullulante des trottoirs. Silence plein de vies à la fois lointaines et très proches, comme celui d'une forêt saturée d'insectes; l'appel d'un croiseur monta puis se perdit' (p. 107).[1] The same idea of dehumanization is presented in the prison scenes, when Kyo thinks that 'Ces êtres obscurs qui grouillaient derrière les barreaux, inquiétants comme les crustacés et les insectes colossaux des rêves de son enfance, n'étaient pas davantage des hommes. Solitude et humiliation totales' (p. 336); or where Hemmelrich awaits the Kuomintang officer, whose murder will save his life, and sees him as an 'énorme insecte', 'monstrueux insecte', and 'monstre composé d'ours, d'homme et d'araignée', in the space of a few lines (pp. 325–6). That the ultimate origin of images like these lies in some childhood obsession of Malraux's, like Tchen's 'pieuvres' (or Sartre's crabs and crayfish), is probably beyond doubt; but Malraux has succeeded here, as he did not in *La Voie royale*, in integrating them into their context, so that they cast light on character and feeling, rather than purely on private obsession.

The fourth type of image is much more common than in the earlier novels; it is the reference to art or to history. It is this which marks Malraux as the literary intellectual, prior to his status as a man of action; references to the burial of Attila (p. 40), once more the 'Cour des Miracles' (p. 108), or Roman history (p. 130); to Kyo's father's 'Bouddha de la dynastie Wei, d'un style presque roman' (p. 51), to Kyo's 'bouche d'estampe japonaise' (p. 21). In these, as in the character of Kama, gleams of Malraux's later

---

[1] The image here recalls, incidentally, a line in Leconte de Lisle's *Rêve du iaguar*: 'Dans l'air lourd, immobile et saturé de mouches'.

fascination with art can be seen, although he may not be entirely free of a certain desire to parade his knowledge. So far art has not developed to its full status as the crucial symbol of man's fight against destiny and of his essential humanism; and the imagery taken from art and history, unlike that in Proust, does not go much further than the decorative.

One of the counterparts of high seriousness or an extreme degree of intensity is that detachment, and its most usual corollary, irony, tend to be lacking. This is true of *La Condition humaine*, although occasionally we do find an ironical observation, such as the remark, *à propos* of Ferral's financial problems: 'L'approche de la faillite apporte aux groupes financiers une conscience intense de la nation à laquelle ils appartiennent' (p. 253). On the other hand, Malraux excels in neat formulations of psychological truth, almost aphorisms: 'la charité ne suffit pas toujours à épuiser l'angoisse' (p. 77); 'l'extrême densité d'un homme prend quelque chose d'inhumain' (p. 170); 'on ne possède d'un être que ce qu'on change en lui' (p. 67); 'tout homme rêve d'être dieu' (p. 272). This gift of the striking formula is one which Malraux will subsequently use to the full in his art philosophy. Another technique frequently used is the single sentence at the end of an episode, bringing one aspect of the novel back into relation with the other elements; a technique developed and exploited by Flaubert and Maupassant. Malraux usually lacks the irony of these predecessors; but he achieves the sudden change in focus aimed at. Perhaps the most striking example occurs after the sexual scene between Ferral and Valérie; one line brings the main line of action in the novel back to the forefront of attention: 'Le canon, de nouveau: le train blindé recommençait à tirer' (p. 145).

Although the novel is not direct *reportage*, it is undeniable that a strong sense of authenticity emerges from it, one which derives more from action and dialogue than from conventional passages of local colour. Atmosphere is Malraux's first aim in this respect; and a few well-chosen details combined with epithets of mood can produce this as well as any lengthy pieces of meticulous observation. The quality of Malraux's writing emerges from a passage such as the following, describing Kyo's arrival at Hankow and his walk around while awaiting the transporter bridge:

Il lui fallait attendre vingt minutes. Il marcha au hasard. Les lampes à pétrole s'allumaient au fond des boutiques; çà et là, quelques silhouettes d'arbres et de cornes de maisons montaient sur le ciel de l'Ouest où demeurait une lumière sans source qui semblait émaner de la douceur même du ciel et rejoindre très haut l'apaisement de la nuit. Malgré les soldats et les Unions ouvrières, au fond d'échoppes, les médecins aux crapauds-enseignes, les marchands d'herbes et de monstres, les écrivains publics, les jeteurs de sorts, les astrologues, les diseurs de bonne aventure, continuaient leurs métiers lunaires dans la lumière trouble où disparaissaient les taches de sang. Les ombres se perdaient sur le sol plus qu'elles ne s'y allongeaient, baignées d'une phosphorescence bleuâtre; le dernier éclat de ce soir unique qui se passait très loin, quelque part dans les mondes, et dont seul un reflet venait baigner la terre, luisait faiblement au fond d'une arche énorme que surmontait une pagode rongée de lierre déja noir. Au delà, un bataillon se perdait dans la nuit accumulée en brouillard au ras du fleuve, au delà d'un chahut de clochettes, de phonographes, et criblé de toute une illumination. Kyo descendit, lui aussi, jusqu'à un chantier de blocs énormes: ceux des murailles, rasées en signe de libération de la Chine. Le transbordeur était tout près.

Encore un quart d'heure sur le fleuve, à voir la ville monter dans le soir. Enfin, Han-Kéou. (pp. 160–1)

The mood here can only be called poetic: evocation rather than precision. In this concentration on atmosphere rather than on careful description of setting, Malraux is, of course, only following in what has become almost a twentieth-century tradition. Again, in Hemingway and the American novelists of violence, swift narration of action precludes time-consuming portrayal of setting in the nineteenth-century style; instead of trying to bring out the individuality of physical details, writers concentrate on creating a general impression in a few selected traits, an impression which the reader can recognize and identify himself with. Malraux does precisely this, as for instance in the description of the 'Black Cat' near the beginning of the novel (pp. 33–4).

By any standards *La Condition humaine* is a considerable novel.

In it Malraux achieved what had been denied to almost all the novelists of the First World War—the underpinning of violent action by profound intellectual themes. Whereas in *La Voie royale* he developed the *anti-destin* of pure action, and in *Les Conquérants* attached it, though somewhat arbitrarily and uneasily, to episodes of political action, now he brings the theme of man's struggle against destiny to its full fruition by showing the many widely different, though parallel, forms which it may take. The political side thus moves into perspective; although there is no doubt that Malraux has political bias, siding ultimately with the Communists, there is none of the naïve black-and-white treatment, and exultation at the—temporary—discomfiture of the capitalists, which had marred *Les Conquérants*. If there is a political lesson in the novel it is surely that the social condition mirrors the human condition, that revolutionary action is politically futile, since the revolutionaries gain none of their political aims and merely bring about their own destruction. A few survive, but this is cold comfort. And the folly of the initial rising is redoubled, since it is precisely this which both frightens Ferral and the Western capitalists into buying off Chiang, and fills Chiang with fears about his own power as long as the revolutionaries remain intact with their arms. The political action in the novel is far from exemplary, as it might be claimed to be in *Les Conquérants*; it leads only to the absurd.

The concept of the 'human condition' in the novel is not quite so original as it might at first seem; a passage from *War and Peace* shows that Tolstoy was preoccupied with a similar view of life:

Sometimes he remembered having heard how soldiers under fire in the trenches, and having nothing to do, try hard to find some occupation the more easily to bear the danger. And it seemed to Pierre that all men were like those soldiers, seeking refuge from life: some in ambition, some in cards, some in framing laws, some in women, some in playthings, some in horses, some in politics, some in sport, some in wine, and some in government service. 'Nothing is without consequence, and nothing is important: it's all the same in the end. The thing to do is to save myself from it all as best I can,' thought Pierre. 'Not to see *it*, that terrible *it*.'[1]

[1] L. Tolstoy, *War and Peace*, Penguin edn. 1957, p. 636.

But Tolstoy does not develop the concept further; Malraux's real
originality lies in having united the idea of the human condition
with, first, the idea of the struggle against destiny, tragic in its
inevitable failure but man's only way of affirming himself, and,
secondly, the idea of the absurd. In this way he can escape—
illogically it may be true—from pure pessimism; although Kyo
comments, sadly, that 'La souffrance ne peut avoir de sens que
quand elle ne mène pas à la mort, et elle y mène presque toujours'
(p. 59), he is prepared, in full lucidity, to sacrifice his life in a vain
attempt to prevent that same suffering, in the name of an abstract
conception of human dignity. His final suicide is seen not as pure
waste, but as necessary and even beautiful, on an emotional,
rather than rational, level. Even more this is true of Katow, for
whom a horrible death comes as the culmination of a life devoted
to his fellow men; by risking his life man can at least choose his
own death, and thus in one sense escape the absurdity of an acci-
dental, contingent, and metaphysically meaningless end.

The basis of Malraux's thought, already fully conceived and
which he does little more than develop in his subsequent works, is
an attempt to escape from the ethical consequence of pure
atheistic determinism, which is of course metaphysical pessimism,
since nothing can matter in the face of a meaningless death. In this
obsession with death and meaning, despite superficial divergences,
he rejoins the great tradition of the French novel, that of Flaubert
and Proust; like them he refuses to accept any religious solution,
but will fall back ultimately on art as the most powerful, if still inadequate, form of anti-destiny. Yet he does not break away from
religious ideas completely; an interesting thought of Kyo's, looking at Tchen in Hankow, foreshadows the idea of the *sacré* developed in Malraux's art philosophy: 'Ce camarade maintenant
silencieux, rêvassant à ses familières visions d'épouvante, avait
quelque chose de fou, mais aussi quelque chose de sacré — ce qu'a
toujours de sacré la présence de l'inhumain' (p. 180). The closing
scene of the novel has been somewhat neglected; but it cannot
have been without purpose that Malraux ended it in this way, with
a scene between Gisors and May. Gisors, who loves his son far
more than most fathers, attempts to comfort May; after depicting

the absurdity of the human condition in all its fullness, 'il faut soixante ans pour faire un homme. . . . Et quand cet homme est fait, quand il n'y a plus en lui rien de l'enfance, ni de l'adolescence, quand, vraiment, il est un homme, il n'est plus bon qu'à mourir'; Gisors nevertheless comes down firmly on the side of life: 'il faut aimer les vivants et non les morts' (p. 403). Despite the failure of the revolution in Shanghai, life goes on and is still uniquely valuable, itself the strongest anti-destiny. The last words of the novel, from May, again undoubtedly carefully pondered, provide a fine stoical ending: 'Je ne pleure plus guère, maintenant, dit-elle avec un orgueil amer' (p. 404).

The novel is, perhaps naturally, not without faults. Above all, often into the heroic note creeps a touch of exaggeration, the false heroics also evident in the earlier novels. Katow is perhaps too ideal a character, virile fraternity personified, not to stretch our credulity; the bravery of the entire revolutionary group is too much emphasized: we read that Katow, inspecting his militants, 'n'avait pas rencontré la peur' (p. 48). Again, the group is too self-conscious: all of them share the extreme self-awareness, no doubt Malraux's own, which is only really fitting in certain cases like Kyo and Tchen; and all are too convinced of the world-shaking nature of their action. 'Victoire ou défaite, le destin du monde, cette nuit, hésitait près d'ici', thinks Kyo (p. 56) as he lies waiting for May; and the same idea is running through Ferral's mind the next day: 'Voici un des instants où le destin du monde tourne . . . ' (p. 136). (This is one of the occasions where subsequent history has played Malraux false; the events in Shanghai in 1927, if far from irrelevant, have not, either, been among the most crucial of modern Chinese history.) One may also detect a tendency towards slightly swollen rhetoric in these and other passages, particularly in the prison scene, which is in places overwritten: 'O prison, lieu où s'arrête le temps, — qui continue ailleurs . . . ' (p. 361). But on the whole these are minor blemishes, perhaps due to Malraux's inadequate experience—he only really began to know war and violence at first hand in Spain in 1936—, in a work which embodied the ethos and feelings of millions of readers in the 1930s. *La Condition humaine*, though a best-seller, was not a popular novel in the pejorative sense, since its admirers included many, if not most, of the shrewdest and most sensitive critics of the period.

The key to its success is, surely, to be found in the wideness of its appeal, owing to the different levels of readers who can all find something to their taste. This question of reader-appeal, of course, is as much a matter of sociology as of literature; Taine's formula of *race*, *moment*, and *milieu*, if inadequately explaining the genesis of literary works, is much more useful when used to explain the success or failure of a book. Possibly, above all, the taste for the novel of violence was at its height in the early 1930s. It is well known that until about 1928 or so books dealing with the First World War were shunned by publishers on the ground that the public had had enough of war; this may indeed be one of the reasons why the First World War ultimately produced so few books, either fiction or testimony, which satisfactorily deal with this—then—cataclysmic experience. But by about 1928 a new generation had grown up to enjoy, vicariously, the experience of war; and in the ex-soldiers themselves horror was turning to nostalgia—not, indeed, for the experience of war, as much as for their own past and youth. A succession of books, all over Europe, had profited from this new attitude: for example, *Goodbye to All That*, *All Quiet on the Western Front*, and *A Farewell to Arms*. Malraux provided a similar experience, one which was even more up to date. The novel can, in fact, be read strictly for the plot, the series of violent events ending in the virtual annihilation of the Communist movement in Shanghai at the hands of Chiang and his forces. But Malraux has more trumps in his hand. Shanghai— leaving aside the question of exactly how much of the description in the novel is observation and how much imagination—gives him an exotic setting, with its rickshaws, opium, bar-girls, and so on, quite apart from the course of revolutionary action; and, as in so many 'exotic' novels, the exotic is closely linked with the erotic. As a conventional thriller set in strange and brilliant surroundings, or equally as a factual record of revolutionary events, *La Condition humaine* could find an abundance of readers, without recourse to its intellectual qualities in the least.

These intellectual qualities are, however, on what the novel's fame must ultimately depend. Primarily the theme of the novel is metaphysical: the theme of death, man's inevitable destiny, and the defence he creates against it. *La Condition humaine* is, in fact, a metaphysical epic in the purest sense of the term. The characters are all larger than life, in their intensity and preoccupation with destiny, will, and transcendence; the narrative follows the epic curve of victory and defeat; the style and moral lessons are—despite 'journalistic' narrative—both lofty and elevated. Whether the novel will stand the test of time one cannot at present say; there is no doubt that Malraux's vision of a world twisted and torn by violence was immediately identifiable to his readers, and subsequent events—the world of the extermination camp and the threatening atomic holocaust—have done nothing to remove the belief that violence and sudden death are an integral part of the human condition. In this Malraux seems to depart most clearly from the nineteenth-century tradition of the novel, which, whether its author's general philosophy was optimistic or pessimistic, was usually set in a secure, peaceful world where adultery or bankruptcy were the most powerful events likely to be encountered. Yet this view of the nineteenth-century tradition only shows one of its aspects; even in Balzac and Flaubert there are undercurrents of violence, while one need only cite, again, *War and Peace* to see that Tolstoy's characters are, at times, as anguished as Malraux's in their search for values amidst a world of futile and meaningless bloodshed. The contrast with Tolstoy's novel is, indeed, revelatory; just as much as that with Dostoevsky, to whom Malraux has frequently claimed affiliation. The principal difference between Tolstoy and Dostoevsky is one of sweep, of detachment as against intensity; Malraux has chosen intensity, and has followed Dostoevsky in cutting down the narrative time of the novel, in order to concentrate more exclusively on his key scenes. The consequence of this is that character is shown by sudden revelation rather than by development over a long period of time. Not that Tolstoy did not dramatize; the different drafts of *War and Peace* indicate a constant effort to make his narrative more dramatic; but both Dostoevsky and Malraux, in the present work, rely almost exclusively on dramatic techniques, particularly dialogues and the monologues of reported thought. And their attitude to character is also closely similar; they are sufficiently involved with the characters they present for them all to be unmistakably their work, all sharing their own metaphysical preoccupations. One further temptation besets both: of confusing the metaphysical with the abstract, of not satisfactorily objectivizing their themes, and covering the bare bones of theory with the flesh of creation. In *La Condition humaine* Malraux, like the Russian, avoids this pitfall created by his own technique; in later work, especially in *Les Noyers de l'Altenburg*, it is arguable that he falls into it. But a certain tendency towards incoherence remains; as if materials were not completely assimilated, or intellectual positions fully worked out. Intellectual artistry, as we know it in Tolstoy, was still outside Malraux's range; however, this is small criticism to make of a novel which has, more than any other, captured both the atmosphere and the philosophical implications of the institutionalized violence of our age.

5

LE TEMPS DU MÉPRIS

ALRAUX'S two main problems in the early years of his literary career were both technical: to find a suitable vehicle for what he wanted to say, and to develop the means of expressing these themes once the vehicle was there. In the early novels the themes are clear; but his technique was insufficiently mature to make fullest use of them. In *La Condition humaine* he achieved the necessary synthesis, and the artistic success of the novel was paralleled, even surpassed, by its popular appeal. Since 1933 technique has presented Malraux, an experienced writer fully in control of his means of expression, with few further problems. But his other initial problem, to find the vehicle for his ideas, has remained with him; he had to depend on contemporary events for the setting of his three further novels, and we may surmise that the difficulties encountered while wrestling with this problem—fundamentally one of creative imagination—had much to do with his abandonment of the novel form after *Les Noyers de l'Altenburg*.

All this goes some way to explain the failure of the work which followed *La Condition humaine: Le Temps du mépris* (1935). Practically all critics agree that *Le Temps du mépris* is Malraux's weakest novel; he himself, by excluding it from the *Pléiade* collected edition of his novels, gives support to this opinion. The very success of the previous book made it difficult for him to write another: he had made full use of his themes, and to carry on in the same vein would mean the risk of repeating himself. In the meantime he gave himself over, much more than for some years previously, to political action. The rise of Hitler gave a stimulus to writers of left-wing sympathies to band together in what might be called an anti-Fascist popular front, two or three years before the emergence of the actual political grouping of 1936; and Malraux was a leading spirit in this 'virile fraternity' of anti-Fascist writers, helping to organize the defence of Dimitrov and his co-defendants in the Reichstag Fire trial, to found the Ligue Mondiale contre l'Anti-sémitisme, and to launch the Congrès International des Écrivains pour la Défense de la Culture. In view of this activity it is not surprising that his immediate literary interests should have moved away from the metaphysical to the more pressing political questions of the day. At the same time, however, the pure adventurer in Malraux had not been inactive. In February 1934 his air-exploration, with Corniglion-Molinier, of the Arabian desert took place; and, with great publicity from the newspaper financing the flight, he made the claim (not subsequently accepted) that he had discovered the lost city of the Queen of Sheba. This rather bizarre episode makes it clear that Malraux had by no means lost his youthful zest for gratuitous adventure, and was not too busy with anti-Fascism to take time off.

Criticism of Le Temps du mépris has to some extent been confused by Malraux's preface to the work, in which he discusses it in terms of Greek tragedy. Now, although the ideas he expresses in this preface are of interest as indications of his general aesthetic theory, they need not compel the reader to accept his book as a Greek tragedy. Authors' prefaces are notoriously unreliable as evidence of their real intentions, since they are usually written after the works themselves, and thus in justification. In this case, indeed, the preface was written, on Malraux's own statement, after the book had been published in serial form. To arrive at a valid judgement the work must be examined without any preconceptions; only afterwards should it be viewed in the context of the literature of the day and of the author's general ideas.

Le Temps du mépris differs fundamentally from Malraux's other works: it is not a novel, but a nouvelle. This is not merely a matter of length (about 170 small pages of large print, probably not more than 30,000 words), but also of limited theme, event, and character. It is, in fact, almost a classical example of the genre: with only one character, Kassner, a Communist organizer, at all fully drawn, it consists of a subjective third-person account of his arrest by Nazi police, his interrogation, imprisonment, subsequent release, flight through a storm over the frontier, and reunion with his wife.

Nothing extraneous to this chain of happenings is included, and most of the characters never achieve even the individuality of a name. The use of the *nouvelle* form is of course perfectly legitimate, but it entails several consequences unhappy for the work if it is to be taken as a contribution to literature and not to propaganda. In the first place Malraux is forced, through limitations of space, to treat the hero and his opponents in terms of black and white: a treatment which had already marred *Les Conquérants* and the avoidance of which had been one of the major gains in *La Condition humaine*. The Nazi police and prison staff are seen entirely as not very intelligent bullies, and the Communists as heroes; yet to the dispassionate observer the psychological make-up of both sides seems very similar. Thus the subtle psychological motivation of the reactionaries in *La Condition humaine* is lost, replaced only by a simplistic black versus white. And above all there is no place for individual values of any kind between the two opposed camps; although Prague is seen as a haven from torture and oppression, the impression is given that this is because of its Communist militants, not because of its democratic government and way of life. In this way the whole feeling of *angoisse*, of metaphysical uncertainty about all human activities, which dominates the Shanghai novel, has been swept away, and the over-simplified heroics of a struggle between good and bad are put in its place. Kassner lives in the security of a system of thought which amounts to religious faith; never at any point in the book is there any questioning of values.

Then again, although the book is a *nouvelle*, it is not a unity. Indeed, it falls into three distinct sections—each of which can be related to one of Malraux's own preoccupations at this period. The first section, covering Kassner's imprisonment and the disintegration of his mind until the tapping of messages through the walls provides him, at the point of madness, with the full moral support of the virile fraternity of Communist prisoners, corresponds to Malraux's general anti-Fascist political preoccupations; it is in fact the kernel of the book, and the remaining episodes are in the nature of anti-climaxes. The first of these is the flight across the mountains, through a storm so violent that only one in three has a

chance of survival. This flight has no real organic connexion with
the political struggle, and its introduction in the book can possibly
be put down to Malraux's desire to make literary use of his experience in flying across Arabia with Corniglion-Molinier. It
shows, admittedly, a movement from the psychological to the
physical, but this in itself helps to damage the general balance,
since the bravery of the pilot and Kassner verges on heroics, with
their unhesitating courage against heavy odds. Possibly Malraux
felt that Kassner's descent to the confines of insanity while in
prison needed counterbalancing by a display of positive courage;
possibly he wished to present another example of virile fraternity
in the pilot's selfless devotion to the cause; but, whatever Malraux's motive, the episode remains aesthetically unsatisfying.

The same is true of the last section of the book, in which
Kassner, safely back in Prague, returns to his flat, finds his wife out
at a monster anti-Fascist meeting, looks for her there, fails to find
her, but is swept up in the passion of fraternity once more, and
finally is reunited with her at his home. This part of the book is
somewhat incoherent, and the theme of the love of two party
militants is very thinly treated, at times even sinking into senti-
mentality, as when Kassner listens outside the door to his wife
comforting their child. Whereas Kyo's relationship with May in
La Condition humaine had been extensively treated, the conflict between the individual value of sexual love and the collective value
of loyalty to the party cause is never properly analysed here, let
alone resolved. The impression remains here that Kassner and his
wife, rather than typical human beings with their individual faults
and weaknesses, are exemplary figures of self-sacrifice to the cause.
Boisdeffre has commented that May is perhaps more a soldier in
disguise than a real woman,[1] and, again in this novel, the note on
which the nouvelle ends, far from indicating an interlude of sexual
tenderness, as might be expected, is one rather of masculine comradeship: 'J'ai envie de marcher, de sortir avec toi, n'importe où'
is all that Kassner says, (p. 184). The relationship is above all lacking in emotional warmth; and the idea, constantly stressed, of
virile fraternity, is insufficiently attractive to take its place.

[1] P. de Boisdeffre, Des Vivants et des morts, p. 156.

The narrative technique employed by Malraux can also be considered a regression. Although the story is told in the third person, the narrator is not omniscient, but follows Kassner's movements and thoughts throughout. This is one of the reasons why all other characters, including Kassner's wife, receive such sketchy treatment; but it also means that Kassner is looked through, rather than at. The subjective manner of narration is notoriously difficult to execute successfully, unless the narrator is an observer rather than a participant in events, and Malraux had already fallen between two stools in *La Voie royale*. One of the chief factors in the success of *La Condition humaine* is the normal third-person narrative, which allows diversity of viewpoint and variation of focus much more liberally than in Malraux's earlier novels; but in the present case Kassner never properly comes to life. This is partly because, like others of Malraux's characters, he has been inadequately conceived as a human being detached from his creator. We are given a 'potted biography' of Kassner (p. 28), from which we learn that he is not only a Communist agent and organizer, but also a writer. Why a writer? The only answer would seem to be that Malraux identified himself, imaginatively, with his character; and an important passage seems to show that Malraux was thinking of his own career in describing Kassner:

Il semblait que Kassner, chroniqueur de la guerre civile sibérienne, fort d'un pittoresque plastique intense développé par ses rapports avec la scène, et d'un âpre don de l'émotion virile, dût traîner avec lui les drames qu'il avait vécus et décrits, et sa vie se confondait dans la mémoire avec l'épopée haillonneuse de la Sibérie. . . . Pour ses ennemis mêmes, il participait de ce qu'il avait vu, comme le voyageur du pays qu'il a traversé, comme le passant de la catastrophe à laquelle il vient d'échapper. (pp. 29–30)[1]

If we substitute China for Siberia the passage fits Malraux—or at least the Malraux legend—almost like a glove.[2]

---

[1] Quotations are taken from the Paris, 1935, edition.

[2] There are a number of anecdotes about the Russian civil war in Siberia in various of Malraux's novels, and we can conclude that he was keenly interested in it; but he can only have heard them at second-hand. They are mostly accounts of gratuitous cruelty and brutality; very different from the anecdotes of the Spanish civil war presented later in *L'Espoir*, when Malraux was much closer to events.

Again, it can be claimed that the portrayal of Kassner is not only blurred, but also lacks plausibility. In the first place Kassner's arrest is entirely his own fault: hearing that a comrade, Wolf, is wanted by the police, that his flat is being watched, and that a compromising list of names may be found there, Kassner, in a grandiose gesture, goes to the flat, finds the list, swallows it, and is promptly arrested by a squad of S.A. men. This particular episode seems to belong to the melodramatic thriller—like one or two of the weaker scenes in *Les Conquérants* or *La Voie royale*—rather than the psychological novel of action. Kassner's action is false heroics: as he well knows, his own arrest, as a leader, and possible breakdown under torture are much more dangerous to the Communist movement than any list in the possession of Wolf, a minor figure; yet he virtually gives himself into the hands of the Nazis. No doubt Malraux was faced with the problem of how a senior and experienced agent like Kassner should have been captured and later released when another comrade has himself arrested in Kassner's name; but the solution he selects leaves much to be desired. Perhaps more important is the speed with which the imprisoned Kassner mentally disintegrates. It is true that we know—or think we know—a good deal more about the process of brain-washing today than thirty years ago; but for a hardened militant Kassner seems to go to pieces much faster than one would expect. He is only imprisoned for a period of eight days all told, and suffers one beating-up, solitary confinement, and the completely unmotivated delusion that his wife is dead. To the detached reader, indeed, there seems to be a hysterical streak in Kassner, perhaps comparable to Claude and his over-taut nerves in *La Voie royale*.

The basic cause of these implausibilities is perhaps to be found in Malraux's lack of experience of the type of events he is using. Although the book is dedicated to the 'camarades allemands qui ont tenu à me faire transmettre ce qu'ils avaient souffert et ce qu'ils avaient *maintenu*' (p. 15), it seems unlikely that much first-hand knowledge of either Nazi prisons or concentration camps was available in 1935; few if any detainees had regained their freedom. In any case, the details Malraux gives are often wrong: his secret police officers are called S.A. men, yet the S.A. had had little political importance after the assassination of Roehm in 1934, and it was the Gestapo who were responsible for security arrests and interrogation. Nor is Kassner in a concentration camp at all: with the cells and corridors, he is obviously in a simple prison, despite the references to 'le camp'. It seems most probable that Malraux had to rely on his imagination above all—and after all there are many prison scenes in his earlier work, which indicate a psychological obsession with the idea of captivity. Again, the theme of torture as a prime cause of the humiliation of man is taken up once more here: 'Au fond de l'humiliation, comme au fond de la douleur, le bourreau a bien des chances d'être plus fort que la victime' (p. 35). But ideas are here much more difficult to integrate into the texture of the narrative, since there are no characters, apart from Kassner, in whom to embody them, and his own thoughts, in the prison sequence, are often incoherent.

The only idea which is conveyed perfectly clearly is, in fact, that of *fraternité virile*; the attempt to break the metaphysical solitude in which the individual was seen, in *La Condition humaine*, to be immured, by shared experience at the service of some higher goal —in this case, communism. Or, put another way, virile fraternity is seen as providing a means of uniting individual and collective values. It is present throughout the book: in Kassner's act in destroying Wolf's list; in the message, 'camarade, prends courage', slowly tapped through the cell wall; in the pilot's fearless flight through the storm—'ils étaient suspendus avec leur fraternité quelque part dans les mondes' (p. 134); in the mass anti-Nazi meeting in Prague: 'Aucune parole humaine n'était aussi profonde que la cruauté, mais la fraternité virile la rejoignait jusqu'au plus profond du sang, jusqu'aux lieux interdits du cœur où sont accroupies la torture et la mort . . . ' (p. 165). Yet again, it is arguable that this virile fraternity is not properly integrated into characterization, but remains a mere element of Kassner's consciousness. The whole concept of virile fraternity, since it is not dramatically demonstrated as much as stated, remains abstract; and at the same time it is open to serious challenge. Ideally, virile fraternity is the individual's means of escaping from his metaphysical solitude, and is free choice; in practice it means complete subservience of the self to the Communist movement, to the point where free choice no longer is relevant. The pilot who flies Kassner across the mountains to Prague does not do so out of love for his fellow men, but because he is prepared to serve the Party in whatever it may require of him; and after dropping Kassner he immediately has to set off to Vienna with another Party member. Similarly the man who gives himself up so that Kassner may be freed has directly political, not metaphysical, motives. Why, indeed, should virile fraternity be an exclusively Communist attribute? Since it does not imply love for all men (Nazis are irrevocably *other*), Malraux is merely imputing to all Communists a special kind of virtue; but to the non-Communist and non-Nazi there seems little reason why such a similar type of militant brotherhood should not exist among other political (or religious) groups, such as the Nazis themselves, as a prime example. Virile fraternity is, in fact, a quality which Malraux affirms to be one of the foremost characteristics of Communists, and it is never developed here beyond the stage of simple affirmation.

Malraux's style shows no great development from that of *La Condition humaine*, although there is the same range of versatility. Since the action is seen throughout from Kassner's point of view, the basic technique is that of reported thought, or often hallucination rather than thought, broken by dialogue when others are present. This dialogue is of the same clipped, elliptical nature as that of the earlier novels; while Kassner's chain of thoughts as he imagines he is listening to the revolutionary songs rises to poetic heights (p. 59). At times this lyrical note degenerates into rhetoric: 'O dérision, appeler frères ceux qui ne sont que du même sang!' (p. 151). At times we find the crisp formula: 'Son courage avait pris la forme de la mort' (p. 84). This occasionally verges on the incomprehensible or the exaggerated: when Kassner is attempting to make out the inscriptions left on the cell wall by previous prisoners he thinks, 'le mur suait des destinées' (p. 38). Technically, perhaps the most interesting feature is the use of *monologue intérieur* to show Kassner's descent into near insanity, his nightmares and delusions, from which he is saved partly by his neighbour's tapped message, and partly by the use of music as a defence:

'La musique, avec lenteur, repoussait la folie de sa poitrine, de ses bras, de ses doigts, du cachot' (p. 51).

After this analysis Malraux's preface can be seen in better perspective. 'Le monde d'une œuvre comme celle-ci, le monde de la tragédie, est toujours le monde antique; l'homme, la foule, les éléments, la femme, le destin. Il se réduit à deux personnages, le héros et son sens de la vie; les antagonismes personnels, qui permettent au roman sa complexité n'y figurent pas' (p. 8). This theory of modern tragedy is perfectly legitimate, but it cannot prevent critics judging Malraux's own *nouvelle* by the same criteria as they do other books. *Le Temps du mépris* confines itself to the features Malraux lists above; yet it is nevertheless too elliptical, at times too intense, hysterical even, to be fully coherent. And throughout it is pervaded with special pleading: again Malraux formulates his ideas in the preface: 'Il est difficile d'être un homme. Mais pas plus en approfondissant sa communion qu'en cultivant sa différence, — et la première nourrit avec autant de force au moins que la seconde ce par quoi l'homme est homme, ce par quoi il se dépasse, crée, invente ou se conçoit' (pp. 12–13). As a basis for a humanist attitude this may be admirable—but it is better illustrated by Malraux's later work, after he had withdrawn his support from the Communists, in *Les Noyers* and his art philosophy, than by the present book. The temptation to political propaganda is too strong, and today it is glaring that the underground Communist struggle in Nazi Germany was politically completely irrelevant, and its portrayal in terms of black and white ends by failing to elucidate the psychological motivation of the Communists no less than the Nazis. The book contains some interesting ideas—the use of music as a defence against the 'other', here represented by madness—and some episodes which Malraux will use later—Kassner's return to Prague prefigures the well-known scene where Vincent Berger returns to Marseilles, and feels similarly *dépaysé*. As a study of prison psychology it may have had some influence: in *Darkness at Noon* there are similarities with Malraux's book, which Koestler may have used as well as his own experiences as a prisoner in Franco Spain. But there can be little doubt that the greatest value of *Le Temps du mépris* to Malraux was

to show him that this was a blind alley: his best work has needed
a wide canvas, numerous characters, and above all space for
physical as well as psychological action, rather than the narrow
focus and concentration he aimed at here. Above all, the book is a
strident reminder, if one is needed, that political partisanship and
good novels rarely mix.

6

L'ESPOIR

ALRAUX'S next novel, *L'Espoir*, although its central
theme is once again the struggle against Fascism, is in
other ways very different from *Le Temps du mépris*.
Above all, the attempt at concentration on a single protagonist is
abandoned, and instead Malraux takes a broad canvas and essays
an epic sweep. *Le Temps du mépris* is the shortest of his novels;
L'Espoir is almost double the length of the longest previous one,
La Condition humaine. If, after completion of this latter book,
Malraux had been casting round for a suitable subject, a search
which was only partly satisfied by the underground Communist
struggle in Germany, the outbreak of the Spanish Civil War in
July 1936 provided him with exactly what he required. And not
only a subject, but also a field for personal action; a good deal of
the material in the novel is probably first-hand, for the first time.
Malraux's own role in the war is fairly well known; in the initial
stages he apparently bought planes abroad on behalf of the Republican Government, and later organized an International Air Squadron, flying numerous missions (but not as a pilot) at Alcantarilla
and elsewhere.[1] Although *L'Espoir* is dedicated to 'mes camarades
de la bataille de Teruel', by summer 1937 Malraux was evidently
taking no further part in the actual fighting, but was a central
figure in the Writers' Congress in Madrid, a propaganda assembly
attended by Hemingway, Spender, Chamson, and others;[2] later
he made speeches and raised funds for the loyalists, besides writing
his novel and directing, in Spain, the film based on it. Clearly
Malraux was more use to the Republican cause in the capacity of
publicist than of airman, despite his courage and organizing ability;

[1] Cf. H. Thomas, *The Spanish Civil War*, pp. 225, 301.
[2] See above, p. 17, n. 1.

but the exact details of Malraux's activities, especially during the second half of the war, and the extent to which they were governed by party directives, must remain obscure until an adequate biography is available.

One of the strangest features of *L'Espoir* is that it was completed in 1937, although not actually published until early 1938: that is, while the war was still at its height, long before international cynicism and the hypocrisy of 'non-intervention' had made its final outcome inevitable. This means that Malraux was writing extremely fast, concerned essentially with the impact of his book on the public, his intention being to influence the outcome of the war itself. This marks a sharp break from the Asian novels, but not with *Le Temps du mépris*. Whereas in *La Condition humaine* six years separated the events from the novel, during which time Malraux had been able to reflect on their wider meaning in terms of human history, writing his novel, as his title implies, in that light,[1] he now had to make a rapid synthesis of the course of the war as far as the battle of Teruel, with neither a clearly marked point at which to end his novel, nor any knowledge of the final outcome. We might, indeed, hazard a guess that Malraux considered a sequel might be possible, once that outcome was known; but that its unsatisfactory nature, or the general European war supervening in 1939, deflected him from attempting this; certainly the 'open' nature of the novel's ending does not preclude, but in fact invites, such a sequel.

In these circumstances Malraux was obliged to adopt a much looser framework for his novel than in his earlier works.[2] The

[1] Actually the German Communist playwright, Friedrich Wolf (1888–1953), had already in 1931 written a play, *Tai Yang erwacht*, dealing with the 1927 uprising in Shanghai. Although Malraux, with his many close contacts in the Communist movement, probably knew of this play, it is unlikely that it had much influence on the composition of his novel. Cf. H. F. Garten, *Modern German Drama*, p. 190.

[2] Frohock, op. cit., pp. 104–11, gives a detailed analysis of the formal pattern of the novel, with its 146 scene-units and 58 chapters. I would only perhaps question how far in fact these groupings were based on 'an intricate and not always clear plan' (Frohock, p. 105). It seems more probable that only the general lines of the novel were established prior to writing, and that episodes were simply fitted in 'au fur et à mesure'.

time-structure is roughly chronological, with occasional simul-
taneity, though with big jumps between the principal events, such
as the fall of Toledo, which are narrated *in extenso*; but the scene
moves about all over Spain (to follow the exact course of events a
map, except for specialists, is almost obligatory), from Madrid to
Barcelona, Toledo to the Sierra, the Malaga–Almeria road to
Teruel. And at the same time this diffusion in space implies a
diffusion in characters, most of whom do not know each other, or
are brought together only at the cost of a certain number of co-
incidences. All this is in strong contrast with *La Condition humaine*,
its characters all either members of the small Communist cadre or
brought together by the figure of Gisors, nearly all the principal
events taking place within the city of Shanghai, and with its
symmetry of action, the parabola of rise and fall.

   The main formal problem of the novel is, then, to impose a
sense of unity on the multiplicity of events in the first nine months
of the war. This Malraux does by treating them, as it were, from
the point of view of a Republican leader or general, whose overriding aim is the strictly practical one of defeating the Fascist insurrection. *Être et faire* is the title of the first section of the second of
the three parts of the novel; but it might stand as the epigraph of
the whole work. The first part, *L'Illusion lyrique*, covers the initial
events of the uprising, and the victory of the workers in Madrid
and Barcelona; but bare hands and enthusiasm alone are not
enough to win the war—hence the *illusion*. This part of the novel
ends in defeat, as the militia flees from Toledo and the Moors
without even making a proper fight; the rhythm of this first part
alone is in fact the same parabola as in *La Condition humaine*, the
rise to apparent victory and the fall to defeat, all the more poignant because of smashed hopes. But here the direction of the novel
changes, and the tone rises, gradually this time, not in one single
'lyrical' burst, towards optimism. In *Le Manzanarès* the key phrase
is 'organiser l'Apocalypse': the militia is reformed, and the first
troops of the International Brigade arrive just in time to save
Madrid. The city survives extensive bombing and shelling, and
finally the Republican forces are built up until they can not only
repel the Fascists but take the offensive themselves. The third and

final part of the novel gives the book its title: *L'Espoir*. This part is much shorter than the two earlier ones, and covers the plane crash near Malaga, and the escape of the crew; the defeat of the Italians on the Guadalajara; the well-known episode of the bombing of the hidden airfield, the second crash, and the 'descent from the mountain'. The novel ends on a lyrical note once again; but this time the optimism is more soundly based on an organized war machine.

Authenticity is one of Malraux's principal considerations in *L'Espoir*; whereas in his Eastern novels he had been dealing with events already several years in the past and little known in Europe in any case, now he had to handle material which had provided the headlines in newspapers for months. Not only does he follow fairly exactly the sequence of events from the beginning of the Fascist uprising onwards;[1] genuine historical events are also integrated, such as Unamuno's courageous speech at Salamanca, interrupted by the crippled General Millan Astray's shouts of 'A mort l'intelligence, vive la mort!'[2] At the same time, and for the same reason, documentation could provide few difficulties, since Malraux had vast quantities of newspapers to draw on, quite apart from his own experiences and the first-hand accounts of those with whom he came into contact. It can be presumed that many of the minor events in the novel actually took place, or at least were reported to Malraux as fact; since they are largely reported through dialogue, they are less important in themselves than for the effect they produce on the listeners. Sometimes Malraux uses radio announcements to link up the various episodes in the total struggle; again, he could draw these from any newspaper.

At the same time Malraux's intention is not historical, nor even to present a simple *reportage* of events in the war. He has to keep within the bounds of the acceptably realistic, but within those limits he can invent whole episodes, or model on the structure of a factual occurrence the clay of significance. It is impossible,

---

[1] With occasional exceptions: e.g. in the telephone exchanges which open the novel, Malraux made Avila rise before it actually did, on 19 July 1936. Cf. Thomas, op. cit., p. 139.

[2] Ibid., p. 354.

therefore, to know whether either of the two plane crashes actually took place; the reader accepts that if these individual ones did not other similar ones did, and that the significance Malraux draws from these is as genuine as if he were never stepping outside the factual. The novel is, in fact, constructed round what Malraux considers significant, rather than merely authentic, and the interpretation is his alone. In this way he can give his novel greater value than the merely journalistic, and above all relate the sequence of violent events which it chronicles to the ideas and themes he had treated in his earlier novels. Although *L'Espoir* is still one of the best factual books on the Spanish Civil War, comparable, in its descriptions, to Orwell's *Homage to Catalonia* or Koestler's *Spanish Testament*, it is much more profound, with its insights into what can be called the metaphysical meaning of events, their ultimate significance as part of the general human condition. The characters of the novel are, certainly, obsessed with metaphysical implications. It has been commented, perhaps somewhat unfairly, that there is far too much dialogue, too much talk, in the novel; which is to forget that most of war, quantitively speaking, consists of waiting, with talk the only possible occupation, between comparatively brief bursts of action. But it is true that the talk is on much too high a plane to be truly realistic, permanently oriented to the intellectual and philosophical; in fact much of the dialogue is more a dramatized form of Malraux himself reflecting than a record of what others may have said. But this insight into their thoughts, hopes, and fears is precisely what differentiates them from the incidental figures who appear in Orwell's and Koestler's works; Malraux has endowed his novel with another dimension, the metaphysical.

It is therefore not very illuminating to seek for models for his characters. Colonel Ximénès may have had, as his original model, the commander of the Barcelona Civil Guards, Colonel Escobar, or the anarchist Puig the real figure of Ascaso, killed in the Barcelona uprising;[1] but they are important for what Malraux makes them say and think, just as much as for what they do. Again, Manuel is said to have been based on Lister, now a leader of the

[1] Thomas, op. cit., pp. 145 and 158, respectively.

Spanish Communist Party in exile; but he is even more an expression of Malraux himself and a vehicle for the main lesson of the novel, that *être* is less important than *faire*, that victory will be on the side, not of the more just, but of the more efficient.[1] Magnin, also, has been taken to be Malraux himself, largely because their function as air commander is identical, but here too caution is needed. Magnin is a pilot with years of experience; Malraux's experience in the air was limited to a few flights as observer and possibly as navigator. Indeed, from Magnin's background, it would be as reasonable to assume that Malraux had Saint-Exupéry in mind, or even Rivière in *Vol de nuit*. In all his novels Malraux's characters are very close to himself, but in their thoughts and ideas, not their actions. And the amount of attention devoted to Magnin is in any case less than that given to Manuel, who is the most privileged figure in the novel in this respect; Magnin merely 'echoes' the same lesson that fraternity is not enough, that the apocalypse must be organized.

To repeat, the central theme of the novel can be summed up in the phrase *être et faire*. All the principal characters are conceived in terms of this antithesis, all the events narrated have their main significance in their relation to it, and probably many of the lasting qualities of the book derive from its implications, much more than from any degree of authenticity or effectiveness as propaganda. It also supplies the major link between the novel and Malraux's other works, in which action is also the major *anti-destin*; here the analysis is taken much further.

The most immediate application of the antithesis is, of course, in the matter of simple military efficiency. Right from the beginning of the revolt it is obvious that pure courage is inadequate to beat the well-trained and well-armed Fascists: General Goded's insurrection in Barcelona is not defeated by the anarchists as much as by the trained discipline of Ximénès's Civil Guards. The fraternity of the workers, however admirable as an emotion, is rapidly seen as a positive hindrance to the development of an efficient Republican army. The lack of an accepted leader and

[1] The ultimate outcome, the Republican débâcle in 1939, far from contradicting this lesson, simply confirms it.

unwillingness to take orders rob their fighting units of most of their efficiency; individual courage is not enough: 'Ils commençaient à comprendre qu'à la guerre, approcher est plus important, plus difficile que combattre; qu'il ne s'agit pas de se mesurer, mais de s'assassiner' (p. 51).[1] And in the early fighting on the Sierra the advantage is inevitably with the enemy: 'Les fascistes bombardaient, nettoyaient, puis envoyaient leurs hommes sur un terrain préparé. Le peuple, sans chefs et presque sans armes, se battait . . .' (p. 55). The necessity of training, of *Bildung*, is therefore central in the war, and is fully treated by Malraux. Manuel is the character to whom most attention is devoted; he exemplifies this theme of military education. At the opening, as Frohock has pointed out, his chief usefulness to the Republican cause is that he owns a small car (bought for the frivolous purpose of week-end skiing); at the end he is about to be promoted to the rank of general.[2] From the outbreak of the revolt, when his car, loaded with dynamite, crashes on its first run, Manuel's life is a constant process of learning, acceptance of responsibility, and subsequent isolation from his fellows: fraternity cannot be a reality for the leader. Above all, the leader has to accept the responsibility for death: after the capture, court-martial, and execution of three Civil Guards, Manuel sees a cat licking the pool of blood and a young peasant writing 'Death to Fascism' on a wall in letters of blood. This gives him his first intuition about the true meaning of responsibility, described, like Tchen's first experience of murder, as 'le pucelage du commandement' (p. 69). In other words, the means must be subordinate to the end: 'la guerre, c'est faire l'impossible pour que des morceaux de fer entrent dans la chair vivante' (p. 71).

In this practical problem of the creation of a disciplined force, with a satisfactory chain of command, there can be no doubt that Malraux accepts the necessity of discipline through Communist organization. The few regular officers on the Republican side are not sufficient to provide the nucleus of commanders of the militia; while they do not fully trust their men, or are not trusted by them. This is discussed by Garcia and Hernandez at Toledo; as if to

---

[1] Quotations from the novel are taken from the 89th impression, Paris, 1948.
[2] Frohock, op. cit., p. 122.

drive the point home, they go over to a barricade and try to give instructions as to necessary improvements. A picturesque anarchist with huge moustachios, a wide-brimmed Mexican hat, tattoos, and an aluminium skull on his sleeve, informs them curtly that if they are not C.N.T. members his barricade is none of their business (p. 94). Indeed, the whole Toledo episode, a sad defeat for the Republicans, can only have been chosen by Malraux as an example of how the war should not be fought, a contrast to the successful defence of Madrid and the battle on the Manzanarès, and the occasion for one of Manuel's organizational achievements, the restoration of morale and discipline after the disintegration and *sauve-qui-peut* of the militia. To drive the point home, the same development is described among the aviators: the contagion of fear, after Leclerc's cowardice in turning back from the flak. Magnin had already discussed the question of discipline with Enrique, a commissar; now his doubts are resolved. Although he himself is not prepared to join the Communist party, he sets about organizing his unit on Communist lines, cancelling all contracts with the mercenaries, enforcing the wearing of uniform, expelling all the inadequate and replacing them with men from the International Brigade, and appointing a political commissar. And again, the move is entirely successful in reconstituting the unit as an efficient fighting force.

In learning how to command Manuel is very much a pupil of Ximénès, who plays a double role in the novel, since he is both a fervent Catholic, whose spiritual and intellectual attitudes and reactions can be analysed, and an exemplary leader, an able and experienced officer. Ximénès has no illusions about war: the object is to win it. 'N'oubliez pas que celui qui nous contemple, je veux dire l'histoire, qui nous juge et nous jugera, a besoin du courage qui gagne et pas de celui qui console' (p. 122). He perceives in Manuel a born leader, although he does not realize that any 'militant communiste de quelque importance, . . . à la fois administrateur, agent d'exécution rigoureux et propagandiste, a beaucoup de chances d'être un excellent officier' (p. 122). But he sees that courage has to be organized, and that the major task is the institution of a 'discipline républicaine' (p. 127). After the Toledo débâcle, Manuel first realizes that he has succeeded in restoring discipline among the escaping rabble when certain militiamen voluntarily set up a sentry system, impressed by his speech to them: 'Pour la première fois, il était en face d'une fraternité qui prenait la forme de l'action' (p. 197).

The comment has been made that Manuel is a much more colourless character than others in the novel: in particular, than the luckless Hernandez. This may, however, be intentional: Malraux deliberately chooses Manuel to be a cinema sound-engineer by profession, and a technician he remains throughout the novel, occupied above all with practical, not ethical, problems. Indeed, when faced by a difficult moral problem, he can find no answer: two soldiers who had attempted to desert are condemned to death, and appeal to Manuel, clinging to his legs, as he walks past at night: 'il ne savait que faire, pris entre l'hypocrisie et l'odieux: fusiller est assez sans ajouter la morale' (p. 277). Doing nothing implies death for these men; but faced with the choice, Manuel cannot even find a word to say. The prime necessity is to win the war, and, immediately, to restore morale; common humanity has to be the loser:

La défense de ces hommes était dans ce que nul ne saurait jamais dire, dans ce visage ruisselant, bouche ouverte, qui avait fait comprendre à Manuel qu'il était en face de l'éternel visage de celui qui paie. Jamais il n'avait ressenti à ce point qu'il fallait choisir entre la victoire et la pitié. (pp. 277-8)

Thus responsibility automatically contradicts fraternity: Manuel is separated by it from the men he commands, forced to kill volunteers. 'Tout homme paye en ce dont il se sait responsable: pour lui, désormais, c'était en vies' (p. 288). Once again he points the moral to Ximénès: 'il n'est pas un des échelons que j'ai gravis dans le sens d'une efficacité plus grande, d'un commandement meilleur, qui ne m'écarte davantage des hommes. Je suis chaque jour un peu moins humain' (pp. 289-90). And Ximénès can only agree: 'Le vrai combat... commence lorsqu'on doit combattre une part de soi-même' (p. 290). This key episode in the psychology of the military leader ends with General Heinrich's words to Manuel, about to be raised to the command of a brigade, 'd'un ton tel que Manuel ne sut si

c'était celui de l'amertume, de l'expérience ou de la résolution:
— Maintenant, tu ne dois plus *jamais* avoir pitié d'un homme
perdu' (p. 292).

Manuel, therefore, exemplifies what is necessary in the training
of a Republican fighting leader; but there is no need for such a
leader to be either *sympathique*, or as complex as some of Malraux's
earlier heroes; on the contrary. There is nothing new in this, indeed; it is nothing more than a convincing repetition of Horace
Walpole's view that 'often a country in danger cannot be saved by
virtuous and scrupulous men, because a country in danger can
be saved only by measures far from virtuous and scrupulous'.
Malraux's treatment of Manuel, if it stood alone, might well be
regarded as characterization in the service of propaganda; and,
indeed, the antithesis of idealism and practicality is sometimes
stressed at perhaps excessive length. But on the other side we find
several characters who demand purity before success: the Négus,
Mercery, old Alvear, and above all Hernandez. In this way
balance is restored, and the novel becomes not merely a demonstration of how to win a war, but a serious discussion of the ethical
implications of all wars.

For Hernandez personal ideals are more important than winning
the war: in forwarding a letter from the besieged commander of
the Toledo Alcazar, Moscardo, to his wife, his reason is simple:
générosité, and we may detect a Cornelian, or rather traditional
Spanish, note, in his use of the word. Disillusioned by the collapse
of the defence of Toledo, he deliberately refuses the chance to
withdraw in time, like Manuel and Heinrich, but fights on until
captured by the Fascists. Shooting down the attacking Moors, his
ethical problems for the moment stilled, he feels at last 'heureux
avec plénitude' (p. 180).[1] Sentenced to death, he finds no will to
live left in him: his sense of justice had repelled him from joining
the Fascists, but now he is equally disgusted by the Republicans:
'Il en avait assez. Par-dessus la tête. Les hommes avec qui il eût
voulu vivre n'étaient bons qu'à mourir, et, avec les autres, il
n'avait plus envie de vivre' (p. 181). Again he refuses the chance of

_____
[1] There is perhaps a parallel here with Mathieu's feelings shortly before he dies,
in Sartre's *La Mort dans l'âme*.

escape, when the man to whom his hands are bound manages to produce a razor blade and cut the rope, then jumps an embankment and makes good his escape. Hernandez is too weary of life to follow his example. He can no longer think clearly, and is torn by doubts about whether he has acted correctly, or whether he is not in great measure responsible for the deaths of the men being shot with him. Like others of Malraux's heroes, Garine, Tchen, or Kyo before him, his death is almost a suicide: '[Il] regarde la glaise avec passion. O bonne terre inerte! Il n'y a de dégoût et d'angoisse que chez les vivants' (p. 187).

Hernandez is an extreme case, in preferring death to compromise with his ideals, since he is forced to make the choice. The Négus is more fortunate. He, like Puig, is an anarchist, and for him the height of endeavour is revolutionary action itself, not organization once the initial revolution has taken place. Human dignity, as exemplified by physical courage, is his highest ideal, and he thinks it better for revolution to be unsuccessful than for it never to have taken place at all. Defeat he can therefore face with equanimity: 'Si nous sommes écrasés ici et à Madrid, les hommes auront un jour vécu avec leur cœur' (p. 147). He wants no truck with dialectics or bureaucracy: revolution is a way of life fully satisfactory in itself. Garcia, as so often, the *raisonneur*, protests that this is a negative approach: 'quant on veut que la révolution soit une façon de vivre pour elle-même, elle devient presque toujours une façon de mourir. Dans ce cas-là, . . . on finit par s'arranger aussi bien du martyre que de la victoire' (p. 147). Here Malraux is finally dismissing Hong and Tchen, whose religion of terrorism is an earlier form of the Négus's anarchism. But the Négus is not to be deterred by argument. Again the antithesis between being and doing is before us; again the character who will not allow the end to justify the means is presented, both ethically and aesthetically, more favourably than the characters who want above all to win.

On the whole, the characters in *L'Espoir* are less important as individuals than for what they exemplify; principally they are vehicles for ideas and attitudes, rather than roundly drawn personalities in the traditional manner. Some, indeed, seem to have been introduced simply to present a certain point of view: such as

Moreno, the regular officer, a friend of Hernandez, who has been condemned to death by the Fascists and has escaped by a lucky chance. Moreno is able to add to the general intellectual dialogue of the novel—a dialogue constantly bearing on the same group of subjects implied by *être et faire*, whoever the actual speaker of the moment—the considerations of one who was not only risking his life, but believed it lost. Moreno comments that, living as he did in a community of men condemned to death for their political beliefs, there was no talk of politics. 'Celui qui aurait commencé aurait instantanément fait le vide autour de lui' (p. 164). Not only political convictions lose their meaning in the face of certain death; heroism too is impossible in solitude, but is a product of fraternity: 'il n'y a pas de héros sans auditoire. Dès qu'on est vraiment seul, on comprend ça' (p. 165). For Moreno there is no connexion between the outside world where men die together singing, and the lonely prison, formerly a convent—ironical setting—with its solitary executions by night. But the worst part, for him, is not so much the certainty of death, as the torture, irremediable and irrevocable, preceding it, which nothing will redeem (a feeling anticipated by Perken in *La Voie royale*). There is a deep irony in this scene, where Hernandez tries to reason with Moreno and dissuade him from his determination to escape from the whole 'comédie' of the war into France, since only shortly afterwards it will be he himself who undergoes a similar experience. In the end Moreno stays and survives to the end of the novel, but plays little further part: his importance is in this scene alone.

The introduction of old Alvear, the veteran Spanish art historian, visited by Scali, the comrade of his son, wounded and blind, and a professional colleague, again matters largely for the ideas embodied in their dialogue; and, again, the ideas are largely Malraux's own. Scali, although brave, is an intellectual, not a man of action; this is shown earlier the same day when he finds himself unable to dominate Leclerc, both more stupid and more cowardly: 'Bon intellectuel, il ne voulait pas seulement expliquer, mais encore convaincre; il avait le dégoût physique du pugilat' (p. 214). Yet Scali is of the world, compared to Alvear, who refuses to leave Madrid, since this would mean leaving his books and collection of paintings and sculptures. For Alvear art is life, or rather life is art. When Scali comments that in the south of Spain he has seen bloodstains alongside paintings, and that in these circumstances 'Les toiles . . . perdent leur force . . . ' (p. 229), Alvear replies simply, 'Il faudrait d'autres toiles, c'est tout.' Indeed, he goes on, art and music are the only things that can resist the sorrow and pain of war: 'Ni les romanciers ni les moralistes n'ont de son, cette nuit . . . : les gens de la vie ne valent rien pour la mort. La sagesse est plus vulnérable que la beauté; car la sagesse est un art impur. Mais la poésie et la musique valent pour la vie et la mort . . . ' (p. 230). Alvear has the same doubts about the absolute justification of the Republican cause which had weakened Hernandez; and Malraux, in an often-quoted passage, gives him the classic objection to revolution:

> Le gain que vous apporterait la libération économique, qui me dit qu'il sera plus grand que les pertes apportées par la société nouvelle, menacée de toutes parts, obligée par son angoisse à la contrainte, à la violence, peut-être à la délation? La servitude économique est lourde; mais si pour la détruire, on est obligé de renforcer la servitude politique, ou militaire, ou policière, alors que m'importe? (p. 231)

And, like Hernandez, Alvear puts personal ideals above political loyalties; which we may compare with Malraux's own essential individualism which kept him from pledging himself utterly to the Communist cause:

> Je veux avoir des relations avec un homme pour sa nature, et non pour ses idées. Je veux la fidélité dans l'amitié, et non l'amitié suspendue à une attitude politique. Je veux qu'un homme soit responsable devant lui-même—vous savez bien que c'est le plus difficile . . .—et non devant une cause, fût-elle celle des opprimés. (p. 232)

Revolution, as Alvear sees it, is a transcendental value, an *anti-destin* or a replacement for religion, and therefore carries with it fanaticism and intolerance; his scepticism leads him to think that revolutionary energies are misplaced: 'Si chacun appliquait à lui-même le tiers de l'effort qu'il fait aujourd'hui pour la forme du gouvernement, il deviendrait possible de vivre en Espagne'

(p. 232). And, although Scali replies that fraternity, 'les hommes unis à la fois par l'espoir et par l'action', is an even higher value than the individual, there is little doubt that Alvear has the more noble side of the dialogue. At the end of the conversation he twice repeats the statement, 'L'âge du fondamental recommence', a theme taken up again in *Les Noyers de l'Altenburg*, and which we may take to mean that the veneer of European civilization is now being stripped off, and basic human qualities underneath it are to be recognized and tested anew.

This chapter of dialogue between Scali and Alvear is important only as a vehicle for ideas, since it in no way advances the action of the novel. Nor is either of the two men an important character elsewhere; although Alvear is very reminiscent of old Gisors, in his passive wisdom and his anguished love for his son, Malraux does not attempt to give him any comparable position in the general balance of the narrative. Not all of his ideas are original, of course; indeed, only his view of art as the highest value of all, negating war and suffering—the view adopted by Malraux himself in his art philosophy—falls outside the realm of traditional and accepted arguments. But the episode indicates clearly the author's double preoccupation: simultaneously with his intention of writing a book to assist the Republicans in the war, he wished to extract from his theme every ounce of intellectual and metaphysical material, so that the significance is universal as well as particular.

Alvear exhibits a further quality, so typical in Malraux's heroes (like those of Hemingway) that it may perhaps be regarded as an obsession: stoical courage in face of death. In refusing to flee Madrid he risks death from Franco's Moors; as a bourgeois art dealer, perhaps also from the Communists. Yet he does not flinch. Physical courage is shown as one of the heights of human endeavour: Gonzalez, a dynamiter, feels this as he watches the enemy tanks approaching: 'Jamais il ne saura davantage ce que c'est qu'être un homme' (p. 171). Certainly, courage has always been regarded as the most manly virtue, and Malraux in his own life has shown himself amply possessed of it. Yet pure courage in battle is a quality which may be shared by both sides, whatever their other virtues: 'Pour Ximénès comme pour Puig, le courage aussi était une patrie' (p. 30); but love of one's country is morally neutral, and of the three Civil Guards captured and executed in the early stages of the novel, the one who openly and proudly admits his Fascist affiliations is as brave a man as Hernandez or any of his opponents. In his use of courage Malraux is certain of an appreciative response: but one which is, perhaps, stereotyped. Courage alone is also uncreative; and in his later work it will carry less emphasis.

In *L'Espoir*, more than any of its predecessors, Malraux is concerned with the full psychological analysis of his material, and this preoccupation gives the individual episodes their characteristic rhythm, swinging from action to reflection. The psychology of the leader is explored, as we have seen, in Manuel, and again in Magnin and Ximénès: 'être aimé sans séduire', which Manuel begins to see as 'un des beaux destins de l'homme' (p. 128). Ximénès's further comment is also revealing: 'Il y a plus de noblesse à être un chef qu'à être un individu, reprit le colonel: c'est plus difficile . . .' (p. 129). This remark we may well take as representative of Malraux's own views throughout his career: his belief in the individual implies a belief in the superior individual, just as his humanism is based on admiration for the exceptional and outstanding man, rather than compassion for the average or weak.

In the course of the novel Malraux deals not only with the psychology of the Communists—already extensively treated in *Les Conquérants* and *La Condition humaine*—from the viewpoint of military efficiency, but also with that of their opponents. Here he perhaps simplifies: on General Franco's side there were not only Fascists, but also straightforward conservatives, Royalist, Carlist, Catholic, or simply anti-Communist. But for Malraux's characters Fascism is the primary enemy and the psychology of the Fascist is therefore treated here. Contempt for their Republican opponents is a key element, as Scali notes while interrogating a captured aviator: 'L'idée, si commune parmi les fascistes, que leur ennemi est par définition une race inférieure et digne de mépris . . .' (p. 106). Later, we are shown a rather melodramatic episode, where Manuel takes a former Fascist deserter, Alba, suspected of being a spy, out towards the enemy lines, giving him his revolver as an act of trust. This episode is no doubt introduced because of the ensuing dialogue between the two men; and, in words which have, since his adherence to the Gaullist cause, often been used against Malraux, Manuel makes the statement: 'Un homme actif et pessimiste à la fois, c'est ou ce sera un fasciste, sauf s'il a une fidélité derrière lui' (p. 124). Manuel's argument is somewhat elliptical, but he is maintaining the view that Fascists believe in their authority by a kind of divine right, whereas the Communists draw theirs from their feeling of responsibility for the men they command, and it is the duty of the more able man to exchange the moral responsibility conferred on him by his ability for the concrete responsibility of command. Alba rather grudgingly accepts this line of argument, which marks a stage in Manuel's development of leadership. The real difference between the Communist and the Fascist which underlies the argument is that the Communist, ultimately, believes in the solidarity of man and in fraternity, while the Fascist does not; but this distinction is in practice slightly blurred. There seems no reason why Malraux could not have taken a young officer on the rebel side and shown his gradual development towards leadership at the cost of personal ideals; or a Fascist Hernandez, who dies executed by the Republicans, disillusioned both by his own comrades and by his enemy. Even fraternity, as we have seen in *Le Temps du mépris*, is not a satisfactory touchstone: a fraternity just as intense as anything felt by the Republicans no doubt existed among the rebel troops, while the very idea suggests the German—and Nazi—*Kameradschaft*. Fraternity is seen as, above all else, a feeling: 'le contraire d'être vexé', as Barca comments to Manuel (p. 75); feelings, too, are morally neutral. Manuel, indeed, in moving towards the values of hierarchy and discipline, without which courage is of little value, is doing no more than return to the traditional values of the Spanish military caste.

Another subject for intellectual discussion is the place of Christianity, and of the Church, in Spain and the war. Two characters in particular represent Catholic viewpoints, Ximénès and Guernico, and Malraux seems at pains to show that true Christianity is not

irrevocably opposed to the Republican cause, whatever the
position of the Spanish Church as an institution. In an early discussion at Barcelona, the anarchist Puig puts the traditional viewpoint of the Left in the epigram, 'On n'enseigne pas à tendre
l'autre joue à des gens qui depuis deux mille ans n'ont jamais reçu
que des gifles' (p. 31). Above all the hypocrisy of the clergy,
supporting political repression in the name of love, disgusts him.
This does not preclude sympathy for Christ, whom he sees as 'un
anarchiste qui a réussi. C'est le seul'. Ximénès has in this particular
dialogue no satisfactory answer, and the last word remains with
Puig. Earlier Ximénès protests that 'Il est mauvais de penser aux
hommes en fonction de leur bassesse', and that religion does not
originate in speeches or sermons, but in 'Les seules choses qu'un
homme entende vraiment dans sa vie: l'enfance, la mort, le
courage . . . ' (p. 30). This conversation is underlined later when
Manuel and Ximénès visit a burned church together, and hear the
comments of the peasants on religion. For the latter, matters are
simpler: priests are the enemy, and, indeed, their destruction is
essential to a true Christianity. The scene continues with a former
monk improvising parables of an 'amertume désolée' (p. 130); but
this time Ximénès does have the last word. Just as two hours after
the final shots in the unsuccessful Barcelona insurrection the
pigeons had settled again on the pavements where corpses were
still lying, human hatred will wear itself out and forget. 'Dieu, lui,
a le temps d'attendre'—but the colonel cannot withhold a further
sad question: 'Mais pourquoi faut-il donc que son attente soit
ceci?' (p. 134).

Guernico, the Catholic writer, shares in the belief of his friend
Garcia—and in the general theme of the novel—that 'la plus
grande force de la révolution, c'est l'espoir' (p. 39). He has set up
an ambulance service: his life is built upon the concept of help for
others—as Garcia thinks, 'il était le seul de ses amis chez qui
l'intelligence eût pris la forme de la Charité' (p. 220). With
Madrid threatened, Guernico, like old Alvear, risks his life by
remaining, and his convictions preclude any active resistance.
Christianity, for him, means duties and obligations, not privileges
or rites, or even the survival of the institution of the Church.

Guernico has, indeed, just advised Largo Caballero against the re-opening of churches, and comments, 'je fais appel à l'âme de l'Église contre le corps de l'Église' (p. 224). 'Orgueil' is what Guernico sees as the basis of all Fascist hopes; but this has nothing to do with true Christianity, which he equates—against the Spanish Church—with Faith, Hope, and Charity. Above all, the priesthood has become too easy, too comfortable, and he con-cludes: 'je crois qu'il *faut* que le sacerdoce redevienne difficile. . . . Comme peut-être la vie de chaque chrétien' (p. 226).

In this introduction of Christian viewpoints Malraux shows that his intellectual understanding has broadened: we have only to compare Guernico with the missionary Smithson in *La Condition humaine*, to see the substitution of a sympathetic figure for an almost comic caricature. It is clear that Guernico is introduced into the novel purely for his dialogue with Garcia. At the same time certain of Malraux's earlier themes are also presented again. Humiliation, in Spain as in Shanghai, is the gulf which separates the Left from the Right, as Garcia puts it to Manuel, 'Le besoin de la fraternité contre la passion de la hiérarchie' (p. 152). At this Manuel remembers Barca's formulation, so close to Kyo's defini-tion of dignity: 'Le contraire de l'humiliation, mon gars, c'est pas l'égalité, c'est la fraternité.'

The psychology of torture and atrocity is also treated. Scali in-terrogates a captured aviator, who refuses to believe that Repub-lican fliers have, when captured, had their eyes put out before execution, just as Scali himself had refused, even when faced with the evidence of photographs, to believe that anarchists on his side had committed atrocities. Malraux generalizes, 'les hommes ne croient pas sans peine à l'abjection de ceux avec qui ils combattent', while Scali comments grimly to his adversary, 'Vous avez encore à apprendre que ni vous ni moi ne connaissons grand'chose de la guerre. . . . Nous la faisons, ce n'est pas la même chose' (pp. 106–7). But atrocity is no longer seen as the exclusive property of the re-actionaries: Garcia, when Madrid is threatened, deliberately hushes up the activities of fifth columnist terrorists, since to make them public will spur the workers on towards atrocities, of which they are as capable as their enemies: 'Il savait qu'il ne faut pas tenter la bête en l'homme; que, si la torture apparaît souvent dans la guerre, c'est — aussi — parce qu'elle semble la seule réponse à la trahison et à la cruauté' (p. 220).[1]

The role of Garcia in the novel is privileged. As Daniels has commented, he acts in something of the same way as old Gisors in *La Condition humaine*;[2] indeed, with his lucidity and insight he verges on the *raisonneur*, since his understanding of the meaning of events is so complete, and his ability to draw the moral so automatic. If Manuel represents practicality as against the idealism of Hernandez, Garcia represents knowledge; it is as if he had drawn the lesson of the first year's fighting before the war had even begun. Less active than Manuel, he is equally less dramatic, and although he serves as a unifying element it is arguable that not much would be lost were he removed from the novel and his dialogues redistributed; and a certain didacticism, driving home the lesson of discipline and organization, could well be dispensed with. This lesson is quite adequately conveyed implicitly in the development of Manuel and Magnin, without requiring explicit reiteration by Garcia.

Other characters play only a minor role. Some, like the former French major who makes a brief irruption during the Manzanarès battle (pp. 239–41), appear only in order to die a heroic death. This is also the ultimate destiny of Mercery, a fire-brigade captain, who is earlier comically incompetent, both in Magnin's squadron and with the infantry at the front, but dies bravely fighting the fires of burning Madrid. Puig too dies heroically, leaving the Négus to continue the anarchist dialogue with the exponents of efficiency and technique, Garcia and Ximénès. At other times, introduction of new characters allows Malraux to describe nuances in motivation: in a short discussion Magnin compares his own

[1] Words which many Frenchmen might have pondered twenty years later, in connexion with the civil war in Algeria. Garcia's final question is still pertinent in Spain today: 'De quelque façon que finisse la guerre, à ce point de haine, quelle paix sera possible ici?' Indeed, the scar has not yet healed, and the country is still bitterly divided into partisans of the two sides, equally obsessed with either maintaining or reversing the final issue of the war.

[2] G. Daniels, 'The Sense of the Past in the Novels of Malraux', in L. J. Austin (ed.), *Studies in Modern French Literature presented to P. Mansell Jones*, p. 79.

reason for wanting the revolution, 'Je veux que les hommes sachent pourquoi ils travaillent', with those of Sembrano, the technician, who prefers to work for the factory as a collective unit rather than for an individual proprietor, and Vallado, a bourgeois nationalist, who wants to see Spain great once more and believes this rejuvenation only possible through revolution by the Left (p. 64). All these are fundamentally emotional grounds, not rational: 'Magnin admire les justifications que l'intelligence des hommes apporte à leurs passions.' This introduction of new figures in order to produce dialogue is the basis of Malraux's characterization: although he uses an omniscient narrator, he prefers to reveal attitudes and motivation through dialogue rather than through psychological description. Attitudes and motivation thus become explicit; at the cost perhaps of excessive self-awareness on the part of the individual characters. More important, dialogue is more dramatic than static description, and one of Malraux's main achievements in L'Espoir is to have assimilated so much intellectual material into a dramatic novel form. One further feature of Malraux's characterization is that the brief appearance of numbers of 'flat' subsidiary figures gives a certain 'body' to the novel. This of course since Tolstoy has been traditional in the novel of epic sweep, where the true protagonists are not so much individuals as a collectivity; the novelist is perfectly at liberty to bring in minor figures who play no organic part in the action, and may in fact even feel compelled to do so. Malraux follows this convention, exploiting it further for intellectual dialogue, and there are many brief episodes in the novel, such as the interview of Magnin's men by Nadal, the popular journalist (pp. 206–11), which carry out this function, at the same time adding to general verisimilitude.

Malraux's imagery in L'Espoir shows considerable development. Certain images from the earlier novels do in fact recur, such as those of the armoured train, like an enormous animal (p. 49); the fellow prisoners of Hernandez at Toledo, described as 'insectes menacés'; or anecdotes from the Russian revolution (p. 27). Sound and silence emphasize the conflict, as when hundreds of factory sirens in unison sound in Barcelona on the first day of the uprising: 'Jamais aucun des compagnons du Négus n'avait entendu plus de

cinq sirènes à la fois. Comme les villes menacées d'Espagne jadis
s'ébranlaient sous les cloches de toutes leurs églises, le prolétariat de
Barcelone répondait aux salves par le tocsin haletant des sirènes
d'usine' (p. 21). The same image is taken up again a few pages
later, when two anarchists drive Cadillacs 'dans un hurlement
haletant de trompes et de klaxons', and, at the cost of their lives,
knock out the Fascist guns (p. 25). Again the sirens hoot: 'Les
sirènes s'étaient remises à hurler, comme si le son des klaxons encore dans l'air, devenu immense, eût rempli la ville entière pour
les premières funérailles héroïques de la révolution' (p. 26).
Throughout this episode in Barcelona, Malraux uses the image of
pigeons flying up as shots are fired, and settling again in a lull.
Some of the birds themselves are killed; and later, Fascist leaflets
dropped from the windows of the Hotel Colon look like pigeons
themselves. This image again emphasizes the main action, and its
significance is thus heightened. (The sirens will again be heard
during the bombing of Madrid.) But the first of these quotations
illustrates a new development: Malraux is deliberately trying to
relate the events of the present to the tradition of Spanish history.
This technique is repeated again and again, with constant echoes of
Spanish history and art. Thus Guernico is 'long, blond pâle comme
tant de portraits de Velasquez' (p. 220); old Alvear like an El
Greco (p. 227); Hernandez 'ressemblait aux rois d'Espagne des
portraits célèbres, qui ressemblent tous à Charles-Quint jeune'
(p. 92); Puig, congratulating Ximénès on his courage, pleases the
veteran colonel by speaking in 'ce style dont tant d'Espagnols sont
capables et de lui répondre comme l'eût fait un capitaine de
Charles-Quint' (p. 29); Alvear, arguing with Scali about the
supremacy of art, immediately uses as an image the siege of
Saragossa by the French.

Malraux not only attempts to place the Civil War firmly in the
context of traditional Spanish history; many of his images show
that he conceives this particular struggle as an integral part of
human experience in general.[1] The peasants and militia standing

---

[1] Cf. Daniels, op. cit., and R. Girard, 'Malraux—Man and the Cosmos',
P.M.L.A., Mar. 1953, pp. 49–55. Both make perceptive comments on this aspect
of Malraux's work.

at the court-martial of the captured Civil Guards all possess 'la gravité de l'Islam guerrier' (p. 66): the Civil War is a holy war. The millennial and eternal are concepts frequently evoked: Hernandez, immediately before his death, looks back at Toledo, itself a city deeply impregnated with historical memories: 'Tolède rayonne dans l'air lumineux qui tremble au ras des monts du Tage: Hernandez est en train d'apprendre de quoi se fait l'histoire. Une fois de plus, dans ce pays de femmes en noir, se lève le peuple millénaire des veuves' (p. 187). Manuel, faced with the two men whom he has had to condemn to death, realizes that 'il était en face de l'éternel visage de celui qui paie'; the man who has been gripping his leg suddenly lets go: 'Il était au delà de la résignation; comme s'il eût compris — non seulement pour cette fois mais pour les siècles des siècles' (pp. 277-8). The siege of Madrid, burning under its bombs, is seen as the day of judgement; Malraux combines the visual image of the flames against the darkness with the sound image of the howling of stray dogs: 'Un troupeau de chiens abandonnés commença à hurler, absurde, dérisoire, exaspérant, comme s'il eût régné sur cette désolation de fin de monde' (p. 279). The choice of the word 'absurde' is significant, and relates events in Madrid to the human condition at all times. Again Magnin's plane, bombing the Alcazar at Toledo, is shown against a 'cosmic' background: 'L'avion qui tournait, comme une minuscule planète, perdu dans l'indifférente gravitation des mondes, attendait que passât sous lui Tolède, son Alcazar rebelle et ses assiégeants, entraînés dans le rythme absurde des choses terrestres' (p. 109). This type of imagery is perhaps Malraux's principal means of attempting to transform the novel from a topical work, with propaganda as its primary aim, into a transcendental work of art. Metaphysical detachment from the political events is thus achieved, the happenings of the present shrinking into insignificance—even absurdity—against the backcloth of eternity. The entire book is studded with similar imagery, especially the 'descent from the mountain' episode towards the close, where much of the description seems deliberately intended to lead to imagery with traditional Spanish or 'cosmic' overtones.

A further type of image frequently employed is the weather

image: the struggle between the two sides is played out not only against an alternation of sound and silence, of darkness and light, but also against the play of the seasons, which run their course unheeding. The early scenes take place in the heat of the Spanish summer: at Barcelona, 'Il faisait beau sur les corps allongés et sur le sang' (p. 25), while later, at the Madrid airfield, 'La nuit s'installe sur le champ, solennelle comme sur toutes les grandes étendues; une nuit chaude semblable à toutes les nuits d'été' (p. 65). During the siege of the Alcazar, 'Au delà des tuiles blêmes de lumière, la Castille couverte de moissons flambait avec ses fleurs roussies jusqu'à l'horizon blanc', and here the note of the eternal creeps in also, as Garcia notices the cemetery with its cypress trees: 'Garcia, possédé par toute cette réverbération, près de vomir d'éblouissement et de chaleur, découvrit le cimetière; et il se sentit humilié, comme si ces pierres et ces mausolées très blancs dans l'étendue ocre eussent rendu tout combat dérisoire' (p. 97). In these conditions death seems an illusion, an impossibility; looking at the corpses, he feels that 'ces fantômes du soleil flamboyant n'étaient des morts que par leur odeur' (p. 98). Reference to the elements at dramatic moments of the narrative continues: Marcelino, opening the bomb-trap to aim at the Alcazar, fills the cockpit with cold air and awareness at the same time: 'à l'air frais qui envahit l'avion, tous comprirent que le combat commençait. C'était le premier froid de la guerre d'Espagne' (p. 110). As winter comes on, cold and snow become the backdrop to the fighting on the Guadelajara:

> La neige cessa.
> Il y eut de nouveau un silence soudain, comme si les éléments eussent été plus forts que la guerre, comme si l'apaisement qui tombait du ciel d'hiver que les flocons ne voilaient plus se fût imposé au combat. (p. 318)

Once more the contrast is that between the contingent present of the war and the eternal flow of time. This is at times explicit: Scali, interrogating the captured airman, suddenly hears the striking of a clock, and feels the meaninglessness of his words: 'Ces pendules ... donnaient à Scali une telle impression d'indifférence et d'éternité; tout ce qu'il disait, tout ce qu'il pouvait dire lui sembla si vain qu'il n'eut plus envie que de se taire. Cet homme et lui avaient choisi' (p. 107).

Art and music form two other rich sources of imagery. Music had first been exploited in *Le Temps du mépris*, where it is one of Kassner's defences against his suffering, even allowing him to abolish the sense of time completely.[1] In *L'Espoir* its use is more complex. Loudspeaker music at times acts as a sound symbol, a poetic backcloth to the action or dialogue: 'La radio de la place cessa de jouer la Chevauchée des Walkyries; un chant flamenco monta: guttural, intense, il tenait du chant funèbre et du cri désespéré des caravaniers. Et il semblait se crisper sur la ville et l'odeur des cadavres, comme les mains des tués se crispent dans la terre' (p. 93). Here, the image helps to 'fix' the moment, to relate it to human experience in general; this technique is akin to the 'significant detail' in descriptions by Flaubert or Tolstoy which remains long in the memory of the reader. Music also, as we have seen, acts as a comforter: with its aid old Alvear can look at his blind son: 'si je fais jouer le phono, si la musique entre ici, je peux parfois le regarder, même s'il n'a pas ses lunettes . . .' (p. 234).

Later, music is given an important role at the end of the novel, where it is again seen as destroying the power of the present, and above all the will to action. Manuel plays a *kyrie* by Palestrina on the organ of a church spared from destruction: 'la voix de l'autre monde reprenait possession de l'église. Manuel était troublé, non par le chant, mais par son passé.' He goes on to say: 'J'en ai fini avec la musique. . . . Je crois qu'une autre guerre a commencé pour moi avec le combat; aussi absolue que celle qui a commencé quand j'ai pour la première fois couché avec une femme. . . . La guerre rend chaste . . .' (p. 352). But this is not the last word: the novel ends with Manuel playing Beethoven on the gramophone, and reaching at last full awareness of himself and his life in the war: 'Comme la musique supprimait en lui la volonté, elle donnait toute sa force au passé' (p. 359); 'Comme le somnambule qui soudain s'éveille au bord du toit, ces notes descendantes et graves lui jetaient dans l'esprit la conscience de son terrible équilibre — de

---

[1] Cf. Daniels, op. cit., p. 77; and also R. P. Leavitt, 'Music in the Aesthetics of André Malraux', *French Review*, xxx, pp. 25–30.

l'équilibre d'où on ne tombe que dans le sang' (pp. 359–60). Here Malraux is making action incompatible with introspection and self-awareness: the final rejection of the position of Kyo and Hernandez. The last two paragraphs of the book bring together several images in the notion of destiny, while Manuel represents the whole of Republican Spain in a last burst of lyricism:

> Autrefois, Manuel se connaissait en réfléchissant sur lui-même; aujourd'hui quand un hasard l'arrachait à l'action pour lui jeter son passé à la face. Et, comme lui et comme chacun de ces hommes, l'Espagne exsangue prenait enfin conscience d'elle-même, — semblable à celui qui s'interroge à l'heure de mourir. On ne découvre qu'une fois la guerre, mais on découvre plusieurs fois la vie.
>
> Ces mouvements musicaux qui se succédaient, roulés dans son passé parlaient comme eût pu parler cette ville qui jadis avait arrêté les Maures, et ce ciel et ces champs éternels; Manuel entendait pour la première fois la voix de ce qui est plus grave que le sang des hommes, plus inquiétant que leur présence sur la terre: — la possibilité infinie de leur destin; et il sentait en lui cette présence mêlée au pas des prisonniers, permanente et profonde comme le battement de son cœur. (p. 360)

Passages such as this can only be called poetic, and mark with great poignancy Malraux's creative imagination as well as his command over language: they are *trouvailles* comparable with any in Proust. In them imagery rises to a point at which it does not merely ornament the structure of the novel: it *is* the structure of the novel, which is constructed round key scenes just as much as round important dialogue.

There are many images too which are powerful in themselves, without any 'cosmic' or metaphysical implications: the dead man lying over the battering-ram (p. 35); the crucifixion riddled with Fascist bullets (p. 147); or the bomber flying in a halo of phosphorescence (p. 160). These do not depend on language for their effect, but on imagination alone. At other times Malraux seems to be forcing his vision somewhat, as when he describes the uneven line of revolutionaries advancing against the Fascist fire as like 'une courbe de câble dans l'eau' (p. 54); or again, at the Madrid airfield: 'Le ciel de l'après-midi d'été espagnol écrasait le champ comme l'avion à demi effondré de Darras écrasait là-bas ses pneus vides, déchirés par les balles' (p. 108). But these are rare exceptions. One new source of imagery is the cinema, to which there are numerous references, no doubt reflecting one of Malraux's developing interests at this time. 'Fusil au bras, des types apportaient des nouvelles, comme, à la buvette des studios, les acteurs viennent boire en costume, entre deux prises de vues' (p. 35). The captured Civil Guard officer has 'une tête de film mexicain' (p. 67); Scali '[un] air de comique américain dans un film d'aviation' (p. 206). But even these film images are not purely gratuitous, as another passage makes clear, stressing the apparent unreality of the war: 'Dans la pleine lumière des lampes électriques, Madrid, costumée de tous les déguisements de la révolution était un immense studio nocturne' (p. 38). All the characters are basically acting a role, even if, as for Manuel, it becomes spontaneous. The war is merely an episode in life, and is thus set in relief: 'Un jour il y aurait la paix. Et Manuel deviendrait un autre homme, inconnu de lui-même, comme le combattant d'aujourd'hui avait été inconnu de celui qui avait acheté une petite bagnole pour faire du ski dans la Sierra' (p. 360).

Another technique used by Malraux, analogously, is the introduction of anecdotes, sometimes with comic overtones. These also help to lower the tension, and to show the war as merely one episode in eternity. Thus we have Séruzier arrested as an Italian spy, after proposing to a prostitute 'l'amour à l'italienne' (p. 102); the sculptor Lopez demanding that the Duchess of Alba should pose like a hippopotamus (p. 38), or stealing stone from cemeteries when he was too poor to purchase any (p. 42). Indeed, both Lopez and Shade, the American journalist, both deliberately picturesque, have little more to do in the novel than act as a vehicle for anecdotes of this type, and for other ideas, such as Lopez's opinion, watching the enthusiasm of the Republicans in Madrid, that 'Il n'est pas possible que, de gens qui ont besoin de parler et de gens qui ont besoin d'entendre, ne naisse pas un style' (p. 40). This is an idea that will be further developed in Malraux's art philosophy. The initial conversation between the two men ends with the vision of the poor reclaiming their possessions from the pawnshops, which even to the hard-boiled and lucid Shade, only interested in 'la vie fondamentale: douleur, amour, humiliation, innocence' (p. 43), brought home the meaning of the word 'révolution'.

A neat turn of phrase and feeling for epigram is frequently shown in the novel; and this ability to set ideas in crisp formulae is developed still further in the later works. For Puig, on the first day of the war, 'Barcelone était enceinte de tous les rêves de sa vie' (p. 26); or, in Madrid, 'la nuit n'était que fraternité' (p. 16). Attignies, himself the son of a Fascist, talks about friendship: 'L'amitié, ce n'est pas d'être avec ses amis quand ils ont raison, c'est d'être avec eux même quand ils ont tort . . . ' (p. 119); le Négus speaks of death: '[Il] leva la main droite avec le geste du Christ enseignant: — celui qui a peur de mourir n'a pas la conscience tranquille' (p. 148); Ximénès tells Puig: 'Vos hommes savent se battre, mais ils ne savent pas combattre' (p. 29). Ellipsis is, of course, the essence of epigram; Malraux rarely pauses to make his thoughts absolutely clear, and moreover the psychological generalization has always been traditional in the French novel, from Mme de La Fayette onwards. Scali, interrogating the captured Fascist airman, 'éprouvait avec violence la supériorité que donne sur celui qui ment la connaissance de son mensonge' (p. 105). Yet Malraux is not afraid of indulging in lyrical passages, or even rhetoric: Scali, during the descent from the mountain, muses on his life:

> Descendant vers le torrent, il pensait aux quatre loges saumon et or qu'il n'avait jamais vues. Une maison à ramages, avec des bustes de plâtre entre les feuilles sombres des orangers. . . . Son brancard passa le torrent, tourna. En face, reparurent les taureaux. Espagne de son adolescence, amour et décor, misère! L'Espagne, c'était cette mitrailleuse tordue sur un cercueil d'Arabe, et ces oiseaux transis qui criaient dans les gorges. (p. 341)

This lyrical note of tragic beauty might be said to be the keynote of the novel: in another fine passage Magnin looks at the body of Marcelino, killed in action:

> Magnin avait vu assez mourir pour connaître l'apaisement qu'apporte la mort sur beaucoup de faces. Plis et petites rides étaient partis avec l'inquiétude et la pensée; et devant ce visage lavé de la vie, mais où les yeux ouverts et le serre-tête de cuir maintenaient la volonté, Magnin

pensait à la phrase qu'il venait d'entendre, qu'il avait entendue sous tant
de formes en Espagne; c'est seulement une heure après leur mort, que,
du masque des hommes, commence à sourdre leur vrai visage. (p. 120)

L'Espoir is an outstandingly difficult novel to attempt to judge
with any degree of finality or even confidence. For some critics,
such as Dr. Jenkins, it is 'one of the important novels of our time',
Malraux's highest achievement; for others, for example Frohock,
'it will survive more by its value as a document than as a piece
of literature'.[1] Indeed, the book stands almost as a proof of the
ultimate relativity of critical judgements. It is not difficult to see
why critics should not be unanimous in their opinion. First of all
Malraux makes a definite political stand. Although he is ready to
explore the moral implications of various aspects of the war—and
civil war is the most unpleasant form of war—there is never any
doubt to him that the Republican side is firmly in the right. This
makes the struggle between Right and Left one between black and
white, or, to use Malraux's own word, Manichean. Garcia, as
often, formulates the idea explicitly: 'Le grand intellectuel est
l'homme de la nuance, du degré, de la qualité, de la vérité en soi,
de la complexité. Il est par définition, par essence, antimanichéen.
Or, les moyens de l'action sont manichéens parce que *toute action
est manichéenne*' (p. 279). This being so, no one whose sympathies
in the Civil War, either at the time or in restrospect, have been
with Franco and the Right can really be expected to approve of the
novel, however much they may have welcomed Malraux's post-
war political activities. And this 'Manichean' aspect may be taken
further. Even among Republican sympathizers by no means all
readers will automatically accept Malraux's other *prise de position*,
that *être* must be subordinated to *faire*, that the end is more important than the means, Manuel more effective than Hernandez in the
contemporary world of *engagement*. Thus even on the Left many
readers may deplore the propaganda aspects of the novel, and
wish, now that the struggle is decided and firmly embedded in
history, that Malraux had suppressed the partisan in himself when
composing his book.

[1] C. Jenkins, in J. Cruickshank (ed.), *The Novelist as Philosopher*, p. 68; Frohock,
op. cit., p. 125.

In my own view it is precisely this note of *engagement* combined with metaphysics which gives the novel its lasting attraction. Certain facets of the novel, it is true, have tended to date. Malraux devotes a good deal of attention to the indiscriminate bombing of Madrid; after the Second World War, in which both sides had vied with each other in terror bombing, no longer a frightening novelty but one of the dreadful commonplaces of the era, he might well have treated it much more cursorily. The final outcome of the war somewhat overshadows some of the episodes in which Malraux perhaps indulges his enthusiasm a little too much: the defeat of the Italians on the Guadalajara is much less effectively described than, say, the fall of Toledo; it is both less direct and less immediate, and tinged more with partisan propaganda. Yet the novel remains—in my judgement—not only the finest *roman engagé* of the century, but indeed the only one which is fully satisfactory on both the emotional and intellectual planes. It is ironical that Sartre, to whom Malraux has become anathema after his commitment to Gaullism, should have spent so much time promoting the concept of *littérature engagée* beyond which the older writer had already evolved. Be that as it may, *L'Espoir* fulfils Sartre's design better than any other work, certainly better than Sartre's own *Chemins de la liberté*; above all, precisely because it is involved with the events of the moment, not merely reviewing the past in retrospect, and because it can therefore influence the future outcome of those present events.

The other main bone of contention between critics is more aesthetic. Formally *L'Espoir* is untidy: there is no question here of the *roman bien fait*. Yet once again this is ultimately a subjective criterion; sprawling novels are not to everyone's taste, but it is difficult to see how Malraux could have achieved the effects he does without a very loose form. He could, certainly, have given the novel a firm shape with a clear-cut ending if he had concentrated on Hernandez alone, taking him from initial enthusiasm for the revolution to later disillusionment and death, or if he had awaited the end of the war and used the rhythm of events, the parabola of hope, followed by defeat; but if he had done so he would have written a different novel, one very similar to *La*

Condition humaine, with pessimism the dominant note. This takes us immediately back to the question of *engagement* in the events of the moment, which is perhaps the greatest difference between these two novels. Malraux is now attempting something entirely different: whereas the Shanghai uprisings directly affected at most a comparatively small proportion of the population, it was impossible for anyone to opt out of the Spanish Civil War (except by permanent exile, which Moreno considers, only to reject). Individual choice and will were consequently much more circumscribed: we have only to remember that by the end of the war the vast majority of the troops on both sides were no longer volunteers, but conscripts, mobilized by the side where chance had physically found them. Again, although the novel does not have a clean ending in terms of events, attaining instead a high pitch of emotional enthusiasm, this was inevitable if Malraux were to complete it in mid war. But the idea of a sharp ending is merely a convention of the novel; substitution of *points de suspension* simply implies substitution of another convention, the 'open' ending—which has in effect become very popular, above all in drama, in the post-war period.

Above all, the looser form of the novel means greater freedom of scope for the author. Although the general pitch of intensity is lower than the almost claustrophobic level of *La Condition humaine*, there are episodes which equal anything in the earlier book. The fight with the flame-thrower in the tunnel beneath the Toledo Alcazar, presented with metaphysical and ethical overtones (pp. 99–100), the neat exposition in snatches of dialogue on the railway telephone, the crash outside Malaga, not to mention the famous episode of the 'descent from the mountain', are as dramatically poignant as the initial murder by Tchen; while at the same time Malraux seems to have more sense of aesthetic distance, to be less obsessed by his material. His style is not so forced; he switches freely in point of view and in tense, from the ordinary narrative past definite to the pluperfect, then forward to the present for immediacy of effect; lyricism alternates with matter-of-fact brevity, ellipsis with detailed description, imagery with lucid insight. The free form of loose episodes, widely ranging in setting, with some events treated at length and others presented as brief vignettes, permits the most profitable development of Malraux's basic structure of alternate action and intellectual discussion, both against a backcloth of description and imagery. Formally Malraux uses the episodic method of narration of First World War novelists such as Barbusse and Dorgelès, but adds an intellectual dimension to their emotional appeal; and as a result his novel far transcends theirs. Later war writers, such as Lartéguy, have tended to imitate *L'Espoir*, but have again fallen far short, replacing mature intellectual reflections by the clichés of journalism.

To myself at least, then, *L'Espoir* is a considerable achievement, ranking next to *La Condition humaine* as Malraux's best work. In it Malraux achieves an equilibrium between various facets of interest, at the same time virtually suppressing aspects, such as eroticism, which had seemed in the earlier novels to sit uneasily with belief in human equality and fraternity. The older themes are still present: death, dignity, and humiliation, the psychology of revolution. But violence no longer seems to hold such a fascination for Malraux: Spain was his first experience of war on a large scale, in which genuine experience of violence replaced the vicarious. The terrorist such as Hong or Tchen, to some extent glamorized, is missing from the Republican side: Manuel, watching a peasant writing 'Death to Fascism' with the blood of the executed Civil Guards, thinks, 'la gorge serrée', that 'Il faut faire la nouvelle Espagne contre l'un et contre l'autre. . . . Et l'un ne sera pas plus facile que l'autre' (p. 67). The expression of human brotherhood, the enthusiasm of fraternity, reaches its highest expression in *L'Espoir*, developing from a more or less abstract intellectual concept to a concrete physiological one, felt 'dans leur corps' (p. 46) by comrades who daily risk their lives in the service of a common ideal.

The idea of destiny is also expressed here more forcefully than in any of Malraux's earlier work. The word appears several times in the course of the novel. Principally it is used poetically, charged with emotive power as it is, transforming the political and military struggle into a metaphysical one: 'Les journaux paraissant seulement une fois par jour, le destin de l'Espagne ne s'exprimait plus que par la T.S.F.' (p. 34). There is a strong element of chance in *destin*: when Magnin's squadron, to avoid the enemy fighters, begin to fly only at night, we are told that 'Le destin avait pris la place du combat' (p. 158). But, even more than the simple arbitrary future, the word often implies death: before the bombing of the hidden airfield, 'Dans le froid des départs de nuit, chacun sait qu'il va à son destin' (p. 324). Most powerfully of all, Hernandez, taking up Moreno's idea, explains the immutable nature of destiny to his Fascist interrogator:

Un des nôtres ... évadé d'une de vos prisons, condamné à mort depuis plus d'un mois, m'expliquait que tout, dans la vie, peut être compensé. ... Mais, que la ... tragédie de la mort est en ceci qu'elle transforme la vie en destin, qu'à partir d'elle rien ne peut plus être compensé. Et que— même pour un athée — là est l'extrême gravité de l'instant de la mort. (p. 182)

Hernandez's words make destiny the instrument of tragedy: the utter finality of death, with no belief in immortality to redress the balance, forms a powerful contemporary expression of tragedy. Against destiny man has one single weapon—his will, his ability to choose. This, in Hernandez's case, is not strong enough to conquer his environment, but at least he can choose death itself, and thus encompass his own destiny despite all the contingent forces against him. Both Hernandez and Manuel are exemplary figures, in different ways: Hernandez, more nobly, of the individual values which ought to exist; Manuel, of the collective ones which in the grim reality of war do in fact reign. In the absolute, Hernandez is morally preferable; in the immediate exigencies of struggle, Manuel's attitude is the only positive one. Garcia, again, makes the point explicit, in the conversation with Scali, shortly after his famous definition of man's finest achievement: 'Transformer en conscience une expérience aussi large que possible.' Garcia is speaking expressly of Hernandez:

Pour un homme qui pense, la révolution est tragique. Mais pour un tel homme, la vie aussi est tragique. Et si c'est pour supprimer sa tragédie qu'il compte sur la révolution, il pense de travers, c'est tout. J'ai entendu poser presque toutes vos questions par un homme que vous avez peut-être connu, le capitaine Hernandez. Il en est mort, d'ailleurs. Il n'y a pas

cinquante manières de combat, il n'y en a qu'une, c'est d'être vain-
queur. Ni la révolution, ni la guerre ne consistent à se plaire à soi-même!

Je ne sais pas quel écrivain disait: 'Je suis peuplé de cadavres comme
un vieux cimetière. . . . ' Depuis quatre mois, nous sommes tous peuplés
de cadavres, Scali; tous, le long du chemin qui va de l'éthique à la
politique. (p. 283)

There is in *L'Espoir*, despite its topical theme, a much higher
concentration of ideas than in any of the previous novels: this
greater intellectual density means that the novel repays careful
reading and re-reading. Its value depends ultimately on qualities of
tension and balance: between historical events and imaginative
insight, action and reflection, purity and efficiency, moral nobility
and compromise, the partisan and the objective, the contemporary
and the eternal. Although Malraux takes sides in these problems—
and very possibly not the same side as he might have taken a few
years later—he presents the other alternative dramatically and
forcefully. The propaganda aim, always present, nowhere distorts
beyond measure. *L'Espoir* fulfils one of the most important roles
of the novel: it formulates the problems. To discover definitive
answers is the task, not of the writer, but of the reader—if he can.

7

LES NOYERS DE L'ALTENBURG

MALRAUX'S last novel, unless later manuscripts await publication, was published in Switzerland in 1943 as the first volume of a series to be entitled *La Lutte avec l'ange*. The text itself bears the date 1941; but the exact circumstances of its genesis and publication are shrouded in obscurity, like, indeed, much of Malraux's life in the first years of the war. Once again, only a detailed biography can clear up the exact sequence of events concerning Malraux in those years. At any rate certain points seem fairly clear: from 1938 his activities on behalf of the Republican Government in Spain appear to have lessened—after the shooting of the film of *L'Espoir*—with a corresponding increase in his literary activities in France. At the outbreak of general war in 1939 Malraux joined the army, in a tank regiment. From a remark in Simone de Beauvoir's autobiography it seems that Malraux had some difficulty in being accepted for military service, because of his well-known nervous tics; but his age (38) can in any case scarcely have been regarded as ideal for skilled combat service.[1] Taken prisoner in the débâcle of 1940, he succeeded in escaping and making his way to the unoccupied section of France. His activities in the Resistance movement were to be distinguished —unlike many Maquis 'colonels' he was incorporated into the French army with that rank in 1944—but it is unclear precisely what he was doing before 1943. To write a novel of moderate length such as *Les Noyers* he must, in 1941, have enjoyed a certain

---

[1] Simone de Beauvoir, *La Force de l'âge*, p. 417. One of the minor biographical problems of Malraux's life, his missing military service in the early 1920s, has now been elucidated: according to Clara Malraux he was briefly incorporated into a hussar regiment at Strasbourg, but was invalided out owing to a fortunate conjunction of a history of rheumatism in childhood, a sympathetic medical officer, and 'une absorption massive de granules de caféine' (*Nos vingt ans*, pp. 104–8).

amount of leisure, and the generally reflective mood of the book, for what it is worth as an indication, gives the same impression of contemplation rather than action. This is, indeed, one of the most obvious differences between *Les Noyers* and Malraux's earlier novels.

In conception, *Les Noyers* was apparently to be only the first part of a much longer work; and in his prefatory note to the 1948 edition Malraux states that 'La suite de *La Lutte avec l'ange* a été détruite par la Gestapo'. How far composition had proceeded is not clear; and, indeed, the manuscript may even have survived, since it was the Gestapo's custom to file documents, rather than to destroy them, and it seems difficult to know how Malraux—at the time, if his home had been raided, presumably on the run—could have discovered the precise fate of his work. At any rate it is evident that in 1948 Malraux still hoped to complete his novel: 'On ne récrit guère un roman. Lorsque celui-ci paraîtra sous sa forme définitive, la forme des *Noyers de l'Altenburg* sera sans doute fondamentalement modifiée.' The note runs on, indicating probably that at that time Malraux was not yet working on the book: 'La présente édition ne s'adresse donc qu'à la curiosité des bibliophiles.' So far no later work has appeared, and the firm statement in the *justification de tirage*, 'CET OUVRAGE QUI NE SERA PAS RÉIMPRIMÉ', has also not been borne out, since both French editions and translations have in fact been subsequently published.

Les Noyers must therefore be taken on its own; and, indeed, it is arguable, as Frohock points out, that 'There is abundant interior evidence that [it] is complete within itself'.[1] Its form is deliberately symmetrical: the narrator, a prisoner in a makeshift German camp at Chartres in 1940, first reflects on his situation there, and is led by his own experiences to reflect on those of his father. The middle three sections of the book treat episodes in the life of the latter, Vincent Berger, first in Turkey and the Near East, and then back in his home province of Alsace, then on the Vistula in the First World War. The final section of the book, printed like the first in italics, takes us back to the nominal narrator, serving in a tank regiment during the brief campaign before he is captured. Thus

---

[1] Op. cit., p. 126. Frohock again gives a thorough formal analysis of the novel.

the unity of the book is assured by its construction: the present, followed by a series of flashbacks, returning ultimately to the present once more. It is, in fact, not easy to see how Malraux could have continued without damaging the existing unity: since the crucial episodes in Vincent's life had been dealt with, and his experiences on the Eastern front apparently end in his death, it would be difficult to make much more of them. On the other hand, *Les Noyers*, written in 1941, can only cover the events up to the downfall of the Third Republic; clearly later events in the Second World War would have provided ample material, but in 1941 Malraux could not know what they were to be. So although he may have wished to use them he could have had little definite plan. However, he could have presented episodes from the life of the narrator, now barely even a sketch, characterized by little more than his relationship to Vincent and his artistic culture. Perhaps a remark Malraux apparently made to Claude Roy in 1945 should be considered here: 'Dans l'ordre humain aussi, cette guerre m'a enseigné pas mal de choses que ne m'avaient enseignées ni l'Asie, ni l'Espagne. . . . Ce sera pour la suite de *la Lutte avec l'ange*.'[1] It may be that Malraux was implying personal bereavements in his use of the term 'l'ordre humain'; certainly it shows an interest in aspects of life which are rather summarily treated in *Les Noyers* as we have it.

The most evident feature of *Les Noyers* is that it is not, as it stands, a novel of the Second World War at all, much less one of the Resistance. There is no mention in it of General de Gaulle's flight to London—or for that matter of any of the political figures of Europe in 1939–40 at all. Although written in 1941, the book has its temporal centre of gravity in the First World War and the half dozen years before. There could be no clearer contrast with *L'Espoir*, written equally in mid war, and intimately bound up with that war; now it is as if Malraux had deliberately turned his back on current events—and on his own previous *engagement*—in order to concentrate on the ultimate, non-topical significance of his material. There is, for instance, no explicit anti-Fascism in the novel, which can only be intentional.

[1] C. Roy, *Descriptions critiques*, vol. 1, p. 223.

The general narrative mode is, therefore, reflective: this is Malraux's only novel to cover any considerable time-span. The narrative viewpoint in the three central sections of the novel forces most events to be stated indirectly in the past rather than presented dramatically in the present,[1] and in thus abandoning the violent immediacy of his earlier novels Malraux is deliberately intellectualizing his themes. In *Les Noyers* action is generally subordinate to thought; indeed, the whole novel may be read as a parable on the theme of the Altenburg colloquy: 'Existe-t-il une donnée sur quoi puisse se fonder la notion d'homme?' (p. 150).[2] Every episode is closely linked to this problem, to the extent that the novel is mainly composed of scenes which provide evidence for or against. Malraux's technique is again one of contrast and juxtaposition, but of a different kind: the purely intellectual considerations introduced all tend to give a negative answer to the fundamental question, while others lead intuitively and emotionally towards a powerful affirmation. The novel is thus focused on the antithesis of intellect and experience; in Malraux's earlier novels this dichotomy had been a unity, with the two elements cemented by a socialistic faith. Now Malraux has returned to the moral problem of his youth and *La Voie royale*: what are the ethical implications of pure individualism without a transcendental religious belief? More mature, both intellectually and emotionally, he attempts to give a more adequate answer.

The crucial development in Malraux between 1938 and 1941 is obviously his rejection of communism. Although it is easy now to discern numerous elements in his earlier novels which do not sit well with a Marxist philosophy, there is little doubt that Malraux was as close to communism in the 1930s as, say, Sartre in the 1950s. Although critics on both sides have since tried to minimize this— Marxists claiming that he was never a real Communist at all, and men of the Right equally understating his former commitment to their political enemies—it remains a fact. And his change of atti-

---

[1] It is noteworthy that both Thomas Mann in *Doctor Faustus* and Roger Martin du Gard in his unfinished *Colonel Maumort* wished similarly to juxtapose direct experience of the Second World War and reflection on the First.

[2] Quotations are taken from the 1948 (Gallimard) edition of *Les Noyers*.

tude after *L'Espoir*, if very understandable, nevertheless represents a sharp break with all his political acts of the previous fifteen years or so. We can surmise what the causes were: after Gide's return from the U.S.S.R. and repudiation of communism (Gide and Malraux were close friends in the 1930s), the failure of the Popular Front in France itself, increasing scepticism about the role of the Communists in Spain—which may well have coincided with Malraux's disengagement from the Spanish Civil War—and above all, of course, the Nazi–Soviet Pact preceding the invasion of Poland and outbreak of the Second World War. The indications are that during the years of the Occupation Malraux was thinking out his political position anew and that he had no close ties with any political party until his meeting with de Gaulle in late 1944, which led to his firm adhesion to the Gaullist cause.

It is no doubt this transitional stage in Malraux's political attitudes which underlies the prevailing tone of *Les Noyers*.[1] He goes out of his way to remove any suggestion of political partisanship, so that an all-embracing compassion for common humanity pervades the novel, just as in the First World War books of Duhamel or Barbusse, or, on the other side, Carossa. Alsace is deliberately chosen as the home of the Berger family: German territory in 1914, French in 1939.[2] Vincent is therefore German, his son French, and natural patriotic loyalties are effaced by pure contingency. Human experience is presented as basically the same for all soldiers, whether French or German: the power of rumour among the prisoners at Chartres is echoed, at some length and therefore deliberately, among the Germans awaiting the signal to attack in Poland. The Altenburg itself forms a microcosm of intellectual Europe, and is as consciously chosen for this symbolic value as the Davos sanatorium in *The Magic Mountain*. There is only one apparent exception to this exclusion of politics: Vincent's fascination with Enver and Turkish politics. But here again Vincent

[1] R. D. Reck in her helpful study uses this term to characterize the novel: 'Malraux's Transitional Novel: "Les Noyers de l'Altenburg"', *French Review*, xxxiv, pp. 537–44. The book is transitional in two ways: both in form, as the intermediate work between the earlier novels and the art philosophy, and in content.

[2] It is ironical that Malraux himself should have been fighting there in the winter of 1944–5.

plunges into political activity only to reject it absolutely later on, when he realizes that Enver's dream of the Turan, the Pan-Turkish state, is, precisely, a dream, untranslatable into reality. Back in Europe, Vincent turns from politics to humanity, and his life in the East may possibly be viewed as a parable of Malraux's own political involvement with communism, ending equally in cruel disillusionment.

Parable is perhaps the crux of the affair: *Les Noyers* is, fundamentally, a parable of humanity. Practically every scene, every dialogue, is primarily symbolical; each character is representative. Despite attempts to individualize them by personal traits, the speakers in the colloquy are really no more than what they say. Only the character of Vincent is developed beyond a simple vignette; and even Vincent we only know from the single aspect of the community of mankind.

It follows therefore that there is a close, indeed almost exact, correlation between the scenes Malraux chooses to present and the ideas he wishes to develop; he is not bound, more or less, by a series of events as in *L'Espoir*. Some of the episodes do probably have their origin, it is true, in Malraux's own experiences: he was a prisoner at Sens, after serving in the tanks; while Vincent's feelings on returning to Marseille after a long absence may be based on Malraux's own, after his journeys to the East. But their value does not depend on their accuracy as autobiography. Again, certain of the characters may be based on real persons, just as the Altenburg colloquies were certainly based on Paul Desjardins's *Décades de Pontigny*, about which writers such as Gide, Martin du Gard, and Maurois have written eloquently. But it is ultimately irrelevant whether Ravaud, say, was based on Charles Du Bos,[1] or Möllberg on Frobenius. Malraux's primary interest is in ideas, not transcription of *réalité vécue*, and the original source of his ideas matters less than the use he makes of them.

The introductory section sets the tone for the whole novel in being based, not on event, but on experience. The core of that experience is that captivity is not a unique event, happening to unique individuals in the mid-twentieth century, but merely an

[1] Cf. A. Maurois, *De Proust à Camus*, p. 308.

aspect of the eternal endurance of mankind. Malraux sets the scene in Chartres cathedral, rather than at Sens, clearly because of the historical and artistic associations of Chartres, which lend great force to his underlying idea; just as the narrator finds himself, at the outbreak of war, at Beaulieu-sur-Dordogne with its Romanesque carvings. The most powerful expression of history, for Malraux, is in art. Throughout the episode his vocabulary illustrates his historical and 'cosmic' preoccupations; he is developing an aspect of *L'Espoir* (one running counter to the political *engagement* of that novel), which now becomes the central theme. The crucial image is that of the faces of the prisoners, unshaven, who become physically just like medieval peasants:

Ceux qui m'entourent, eux, vivent au jour le jour depuis des millénaires.

Dès les premiers temps de la guerre, dès que l'uniforme eut effacé le métier, j'ai commencé d'entrevoir ces faces gothiques. Et ce qui sourd aujourd'hui de la foule hagarde qui ne peut plus se raser n'est pas le bagne, c'est le moyen-âge. Même chez ceux des Méditerranéens dont j'attendais des visages de pêcheurs helléniques, de maçons romains: peut-être parce que le moyen-âge s'est chargé de représenter les hommes, et que nous ne sommes pas dans un endroit d'où sortent les dieux. Mais le moyen-âge n'est que le masque de leur passé, si long qu'il fait rêver d'éternité. Leur amour, c'est un secret, même pour eux; leur amitié, la chaleur humaine d'une présence auprès de quoi l'on se repose sans parler, — un échange de silences. Leur joie, toute en bourrades et en éclats, elle n'a pas changé depuis Breughel, depuis les fabliaux; ces claques et ces rires, comme leur son monte d'une fosse plus insondable, plus fascinante que tout ce que nous connaissons de notre race, fascinante comme leur patience! Ici, un prêtre ami m'a dit: 'Au fond, croyants ou incroyants, tous les hommes meurent dans un mélange bien enchevêtré de crainte et d'espoir. . . .' (p. 28)

This is the essence of the narrator's emotional experience of humanity: that, *sub specie aeternitatis*, mankind is a unity; despite apparent differences, a fundamental experience such as defeat in battle will bring out the common denominator. This feeling is related to the narrator himself, who is evidently a writer (although this is not further explained):

Que m'obsède ce lourd et mystérieux demi-sommeil sur quoi le présent, le christianisme même tournoient comme la poussière sur tous nos corps couchés, comme nos rêves! Écrivain, par quoi suis-je obsédé depuis dix ans, sinon par l'homme? Me voici devant la matière originelle. Et je pense une fois de plus à une phrase de mon père que la constance de la mort a imposée à ma mémoire, que la captivité me ressasse inexorablement:

'Ce n'est pas à gratter sans fin l'individu qu'on finit par rencontrer l'homme.' (pp. 28–9)

The permanence of man, the central intuition in the whole novel, is not entirely original. There is something of the same feeling in Pierre Bezukhov's experiences as a prisoner in Moscow in *War and Peace*; while Duhamel uses a very similar image in *La Vie des martyrs*, describing two wounded soldiers arriving in hospital: 'Ils paraissaient sans âge; ou plutôt, n'avaient-ils pas tous deux mille ans et plus, l'âge même des momies ficelées dans le fond des sarcophages?'[1] However, Malraux makes much more systematic use of the intuition—indeed, the personal experience—that in war, despite destruction and bloodshed, there is a compensating factor in the stripping away from man of his veneer and the revelation of the common essence of humanity beneath. Surrounded by barbed wire in the makeshift camp, each soldier begins to construct for himself a 'domaine', with bricks, cans, pieces of wood, or whatever other materials are to hand, thus re-enacting primitive man's sense of property (a vision which may possibly symbolize Malraux's rejection of Marxist beliefs): 'Des types qui n'ont trouvé que quelques briques ont délimité un terrain personnel et rêvent, les genoux entre les mains, au centre de leur domaine imaginaire . . . ' (p. 19). At times the imagery verges on the strained, but the meaning is clear: 'Dans la masure babylonienne, faite de piliers trapus, de drains et de branches, ils sont maintenant trois qui écrivent sur leurs genoux, recroquevillés comme les momies du Pérou' (p. 25). Handing in their letters to their families, the prisoners resemble 'des mendiants de naguère' (p. 17); snippets of conversation from the German guards reveal that they are talking of Bamberg cathedral: 'Bamberg, la Chartres allemande . . . ', thinks the narrator (p. 15). The only reality is human solidarity,

[1] G. Duhamel, *La Vie des martyrs*, new edn., Paris, 1950, p. 9.

besides which even time pales into insignificance: prisoners and guards alike are waiting until 'le destin s'use'. And the only positive act which can be attempted is to write, even though what is written may never survive, like the undelivered letters which flutter back over the camp. 'Ici, écrire est le seul moyen de continuer à vivre' (p. 30): this statement, which ends the first section, may be taken symbolically as Malraux's belief that art is man's principal way of challenging his destiny.

The second section of the novel is the first to be headed *Les Noyers de l'Altenburg*, and immediately introduces the narrator's father, Vincent Berger. Vincent, not the original narrator, is the central character of the novel; although both share the same preoccupations and, in the end, the same insights. Obviously there is much of Malraux himself in Vincent, with perhaps a touch of wish-fulfilment. His own experiences in searching for Graeco-Buddhist art in Afghanistan are a point in common with Vincent, and at times the latter even seems a physical self-portrait: 'Cet homme . . . qui lui semblait trop jeune pour le rôle qu'il avait joué (encore que l'autorité ne manquât pas à celui qu'il jouait présentement), cet homme dont le débit saccadé s'accordait au visage finement osseux et aux mains fébriles . . . ' (p. 63). Vincent's motives are 'son besoin de s'écarter de l'Europe, l'appel de l'histoire, le désir fanatique de laisser sur la terre une cicatrice, la fascination d'un dessein qu'il n'avait pas peu contribué à préciser, la camaraderie de combat, l'amitié . . . ' (p. 64). A remark about Vincent later in the novel shows that Malraux is fully conscious of the gap between life and legend: 'Il rencontrait devant lui sa légende — décor romanesque, action secrète, indifférence au profit et peut-être au pouvoir — comme s'il eût couru derrière elle' (p. 102). The parallel with Lawrence is equally evident, while Vincent also closely resembles Garine, the most Lawrentian of Malraux's other fictional heroes, and shares, at this stage, Perken's ideals. At any rate Vincent is in the tradition of the outstanding individual, the lucid adventurer, the intellectual man of action fascinated—like Garine—with power intrigues and the manipulation of public opinion through propaganda techniques. Malraux's choice of Turkey as the field of Vincent's action is interesting, especially the pre-1914 Turkey already tending to disintegrate under the pressure of nationalism. Vincent's action is thereby made to anticipate Lawrence's—of which it is to some degree the counterpart, with Turanism taking the place of Arab nationalism. In describing Vincent's relationship with Enver and the Young Turks, Malraux is using, as in his China novels, a little-known episode in quite recent history, in which the fictional Vincent can be grafted on to the stem of authentic events, such as the 1908 revolt in Macedonia which brought the Young Turks to the fore, and the pro-Turkish revolt of the Senussi tribes in Cyrenaica in the Italo-Turkish War of 1910, used to make Vincent appear an initiator of guerilla warfare. In addition Turkey forms part of the East, and Malraux's use of it is exotic as well as political, with anecdotes about Sultan Abdul Hamid's capricious despotism.[1] But the whole Turkish episode in Vincent's life is important only in its conclusion: his utter failure. Youthful admiration for Enver and his dream of a Young Turk Empire, its capital at Samarkand, bringing together all the Turkoman races, turn to bitter realization that this is an empty illusion—indeed, absurd—since the apparent feeling for Turkey in certain tribes in Central Asia depends on community of religion, not of race, and Enver's hopes are even less realistic than the Pan-Mohammedanism of Abdul Hamid. The moment of lucidity, following an attack by a lunatic, is the end of Vincent's *engagement* in the East; and the experience providing this insight is, once more, that of humiliation. And behind humiliation, there lies the absurd —'cette Asie Centrale menteuse, idiote et qui se refusait à son propre destin' (p. 74)—the disproportion between effort and result, which disillusions Vincent for good and sends him, sick, back to Europe.

Return to Europe furnishes Vincent's second major insight: an immense feeling of freedom from the past, and wonderment at the simple details of European life, of which he no longer feels himself a part. This insight is not analysed intellectually, but is described in

[1] As so often, Malraux seems unduly fascinated by colourful and violent anecdotes; in the present case it is not unfair to say that sometimes this section recalls John Buchan's *Greenmantle*, the other best-known novel of secret political intrigues in Turkey.

poetical terms, often very close to the rhetoric of *La Tentation de l'Occident*:

Jeté à quelque rive de néant ou d'éternité, il en contemplait la confuse coulée — aussi séparé d'elle que de ceux qui avaient passé, avec leurs angoisses oubliées et leurs contes perdus, dans les rues des premières dynasties de Bactres ou de Babylone, dans les oasis dominés par les Tours du silence. A travers la musique et l'odeur de pain chaud, des ménagères se hâtaient, un filet sous le bras; un marchand de couleurs posait ses volets arlequins où s'attardait un dernier rayon; la sirène d'un paquebot appelait; un commis en calotte rapportait un mannequin sur son dos, à l'intérieur d'un étroit magasin plein d'ombres, — sur la terre, vers la fin du second millénaire de l'ère chrétienne. . . . (pp. 78–9)

This 'cosmic' feeling of detachment, or alienation, to use the Existentialist term, is accompanied by a new awareness of the individuality of European life: 'L'absence du voile musulman, l'apparition des visages' (p. 77); it marks an essential stage in Vincent's maturity—transcendence of pure action, and an appreciation of the humble details which make up the real texture of human existence. He is now ready for further insights.

Malraux's narrative viewpoint, Vincent's son writing about his father in the third person, gives the central sections of *Les Noyers* a unique tone in Malraux's works. Obviously a certain detachment is the aim: the narrator can select those of Vincent's experiences he wishes, and contrast them with his own. We are told that he has had access to his father's notes and papers; though in fact this cadre is a little strained—Vincent's conversation with the German ambassador in Turkey, for instance, seems to show that the narrator is not only privileged but in fact omniscient. But the occasional implausibilities of the narrative method are less important than its consequences: everything has to be *stated*, in the past, rather than *presented* dramatically. The narrative is therefore much more indirect and less immediately forceful than in the earlier novels. Narration of action does not, in this section, go further than pure anecdote, often very slim; while characters are themselves no more than brief sketches. Vincent's family at Reichbach in Alsace, his father Dietrich and uncle Walter, appear to have

more individuality, but this is only lent to them by the introduction of other curious anecdotes such as Dietrich's visit to Rome to
see the Pope, or his welcoming a travelling circus in his house. The
characters, indeed, lack body, the physical and perhaps above all
the emotional dimension. This may well be deliberate: man,
Malraux insists, is more than his secrets, and the whole episode of
Dietrich's suicide, which closes the section, a week after Vincent's
return, is intended to focus attention on the ultimate mystery in
human life. The motive of this suicide is intentionally inexplicable,
undiscoverable. But, from the reader's side, it is unclear, and there
is perhaps an element of mystification in Malraux's use of it, and in
the words he makes Dietrich use, in full consciousness, immediately
before his suicide: 'Eh bien, ma foi, quoiqu'il [sic] arrive, si je
devais revivre une autre vie je n'en voudrais pas une autre que
celle de Dietrich Berger . . . ' (p. 87).[1]

For the most part the historical and 'cosmic' imagery, brought
in as an almost automatic technique in the introductory section of
the novel, is absent in this one. There is the occasional burst of
rhetoric, as when Vincent, wandering, feverish, through the
Hindu Kush, dreams of the West, 'O Europe verte! sifflets des loco-
motives dans la nuit, grelots et sabots des fiacres attardés . . . '
(p. 70), but there is no gratuitousness, since the passage represents
Vincent's semi-delirium. But in the main Malraux's use of
imagery and historical parallels is more sketchy, and he relies much
more on pure description, treating Afghanistan, or anecdotic
narrative, dealing with Turkey, where his personal experience was
more lacking. Neat formulations of ideas, or antitheses, are again
frequently used: there are many effective examples: 'un homme
est plus *signifié* par sa valeur que par ses secrets' (p. 50); 'Il est peu
d'actions que les rêves nourrissent au lieu de les pourrir' (p. 64);
'l'arme la plus efficace d'un homme, c'est d'avoir réduit au minimum sa part de comédie' (pp. 49–50).

Vincent's experiences in the East are, ultimately, no more than a

_____

[1] Suicide, indeed, has exercised a peculiar fascination on many modern French
novelists, especially in its metaphysical aspect as an act of will *in extremis*, man's
last defence against the contingent or the absurd: Martin du Gard, Camus, and
Sartre share Malraux's preoccupation here.

prologue to the section of the novel which contains the bulk of the intellectual content: the central episode of the colloquy at the Altenburg. At the same time it seems to be forcing the significance of the novel to assume, with Frohock, that because Malraux introduces the idea of the 'shaman' he intended this, with its pattern of withdrawal, enlightenment, and return, to be of fundamental importance. Indeed, Malraux's reference to the shaman is very brief and his reasons far from explicit; he scarcely passes beyond lists of men who were shamans (Trotsky, Dostoevsky, Mirabeau, Hölderlin, Poe), or who were not (Lenin, Pushkin, Robespierre, Goethe), merely suggesting that Vincent's strength and weakness derived from the shaman in him (p. 49). The remarks are even somewhat artificially introduced by a sudden return to a later period, long after Vincent's death; the episode remains unclear, and seems to be little more than an idea Malraux toyed with, without extracting from it all the possible implications; indeed, his knowledge of shamanism may not have been very extensive, since he makes no mention of one of its most vital elements, ecstasy, and seems to equate the shaman with any mystic with epileptic or neurotic traits, uprooting him from his religious context.[1] On the other hand, the theme of initiation recurs in many of Malraux's novels.

The dominant note in the treatment of the Altenburg colloquy is one of irony, almost of debunking. Before we see the participants actually at grips with each other, Malraux uses the character of Hermann Müller to set the desired tone. A decaying rake—'gigolo vieilli à cravate frivolette' (p. 101)—Müller, as Walter Berger's cousin and assistant, is in a privileged position in knowing more about the men present than Vincent. Walter, in fact, is shown up almost as a fraud, with his inordinate vanity, altering Vincent's telegram 'SERAI ALTENBURG 2 JUIN' to read 'TRÈS SENSIBLE HONNEUR COLLABORER A VOS RECHERCHES. AFFECTIONS RESPECTUEUSES', or preserving letters from Nietzsche, the pride of his library, yet which are, Müller assures Vincent, nearly all 'des engueulades'. The irony is not only at Walter's expense, but

[1] Cf. M. Éliade, *Le Chamanisme et les techniques archaïques de l'extase* (English translation: *Shamanism*, London, 1964).

against intellectuals generally: they are like women, claims Müller, fascinated by uniforms, and their reasons for attending the colloquies are partly to indulge their natural tendency to be 'bavards', partly perhaps also to eat choice trout, washed down by Rhine wine, at nearby inns. The effect of this irony is to discount, in advance, the conclusions of the discussions: however impeccable intellectually, there remains a hollowness about them, just as it is difficult to take entirely seriously a man like Thirard, who has given up his university post in order to teach in a school in an area where the *vin du pays* is outstanding. A certain disillusionment with the 'intellectual' as hero, already noticeable in *L'Espoir*, now becomes prominent.

The intellectual content of the colloquy is, however, considerable: this central section in the novel is bursting with ideas. These ideas are very much the ones with which Malraux himself was concerned: although he introduces many famous names—'Des textes de Max Weber, de Stefan George, de Sorel, de Durkheim, de Freud étaient nés de ces colloques' (p. 44)—not many of the ideas have much to do with these figures (and since George was a poet rather than a thinker he seems a little out of place in this list). The fundamental question discussed—'Existe-t-il une donnée sur quoi puisse se fonder la notion d'homme?'—is in fact merely one aspect of the ultimate philosophical problem: is there a meaning in life at all? All the participants accept Nietzsche's dictum, that God is dead, and are, basically, discussing the possibility of making any kind of a transcendental reality out of man himself. Intellectually Möllberg's conclusion is unchallengeable: there is no unity of man, only successive, and different, men: 'Les états psychiques successifs de l'humanité sont irréductiblement différents' (p. 148). This intellectual conclusion, after a life's work in the field of ethnology, coincides with Vincent's own experience in Asia; yet Möllberg has hardly enunciated it before Vincent has the even more powerful intuition that, despite everything, a human continuity remains, expressed in the symbol of the trees surrounding the Altenburg, the apple-trees, the pines, and above all the gnarled 'noyers', centuries old, which give the novel its title. Beyond the reach of intellectual inquiry there remain intuitions that are almost involuntary affirmations of value, and these are the fundamental experiences of man.

Close examination of this section reveals that Malraux has been working towards this conclusion throughout. First there is the irony already discussed; and even a certain insincerity in Walter: talking with Vincent about his father's suicide, Walter claims that increasing age has freed him from fear of death, but Vincent 'était certain que Walter mentait; il sentait affleurer l'angoisse' (p. 88). Already at this point, before the opening of the discussions, Dietrich's suicide leads to similar affirmations, intuitions, rather than intellectual conclusions. Against Walter's almost condescending statement (and the gesture with which Malraux makes him accompany it is significant) Vincent affirms the power of will:

— Pour l'essentiel, l'homme est ce qu'il cache. . . .
Walter haussa les épaules et rapprocha ses vieilles mains, comme les enfants pour faire un pâté de sable:
— Un misérable petit tas de secrets. . . .
— L'homme est ce qu'il fait!' répondit mon père presque avec brutalité. Par tempérament, ce qu'il appelait la psychologie-au-secret, comme il eût dit le vol-à-la-tire, l'irritait.
A supposer que le suicide de mon grand-père eût une 'cause', cette cause, fût-elle le plus banal ou le plus triste secret, était moins significative que la strychnine et le revolver, — que la résolution par quoi il avait *choisi* la mort, une mort qui ressemblait à sa vie. (pp. 89–90)

This antithesis has been widely taken, almost certainly with justice, as a central feature in Malraux's own *Weltanschauung*, with Vincent's views representing his own. Yet it is fundamentally a poetical, rhetorical, formulation rather than a satisfactory philosophical analysis: for may not a man's deeds in fact be his secrets? The acts of an individual are not known, except in so far as he or someone else makes them known; this is to make acts, Malraux's essential values, dependent on communication, even on words, and on recognition by others. The essence of personality is thus thrown back on what is, or appears to be, publicly known about an individual: legend. This affirmation, however revealing it might be about Malraux's own life and his attitude to it, nevertheless remains no more than a neat formulation, which, analysed, leads to more problems and difficulties than it solves.

At the same time, although Vincent's position is privileged, he is not the only character to express ideas which are obviously Malraux's own. Only a few pages after the exchange quoted above, it is Walter, despite the ironic treatment of him—'Michel-Ange à la fin d'une longue carrière universitaire' (p. 84)—who formulates the idea of the *anti-destin*. Describing, in a well-known passage, how he had brought Nietzsche, insane, back from Italy, through the St. Gotthard tunnel,[1] and how in the complete darkness the philosopher had begun to sing his poem, *Venice*, Walter realizes that this is a symbol of man's power to conquer his destiny. Nietzsche's song was as powerful as the whole of the universe: 'Et dans ce wagon, voyez-vous, et quelquefois ensuite — je dis seulement: quelquefois . . . — les millénaires du ciel étoilé m'ont semblé aussi effacés par l'homme, que nos pauvres destins sont effacés par le ciel étoilé . . .' (p. 97). This, one of the key ideas in Malraux's work, already hinted at in the earlier novels, will provide the essence of *Les Voix du silence*; again it consists of an affirmation, not a reasoned argument: the affirmation of the supremacy of will, that man can give life the meaning he wishes it to have. This is man's greatest gift; as Walter goes on: 'Le plus grand mystère n'est pas que nous soyons jetés au hasard entre la profusion de la matière et celle des astres; c'est que, dans cette prison, nous tirions de nous-mêmes des images assez puissantes pour nier notre néant' (pp. 98-9). In this expression of will, man's freedom to choose, we recognize the Existentialist denial of determinism and faith in action. In this case, then, it is Walter who is given Malraux's ideas, and even some of his traits, such as his way of speaking in 'ces ellipses, ces images bousculées et instinctives' (p. 97); and this insight is not fatally weakened by Müller's later attempt to debunk Walter's role in Nietzsche's life—that of a 'raseur sérieux', who, in bringing the philosopher back to Basle, only did what any *concierge* might have done. The whole episode is, of course, an invention on Malraux's part, but a plausible one,

---

[1] An act in fact carried out by Nietzsche's friend and former colleague at Basle, Franz Overbeck.

a successful poetical equivalent of an intellectual idea; and we may well take Vincent's reasons for liking Nietzsche as Malraux's own: 'Mon père aimait Nietzsche plus que tout autre écrivain. Non pour sa prédication, mais pour l'incomparable générosité de l'intelligence qu'il trouvait en lui' (pp. 94–5).

What Malraux is in fact doing, then, throughout the colloquy, is turning his own ideas into dialogue. All the participants, Walter, Stieglitz, and Rabaud, just as much as Möllberg and Vincent, are obsessed with the same set of problems and concepts, and use similar terms and elliptical formulations: 'destin', 'fatalité', 'métamorphose', 'volonté', and the rest of them. These are, of course, the same key terms as in the earlier novels; the chief new intellectual component is the extensive use of ethnology and anthropology: reference to the *potlatch*, work done in Melanesia, or even the contents of a certain showcase in the Cairo Museum. This gives what is perhaps only a superficial brilliance to the intellectual dialogue, although few of the references and ideas are developed in any detail. To do this Malraux will later abandon the novel altogether. For the moment the dialogue is primarily intended to deepen and further Vincent's first intuition that man is not a unity, that Moslems lead a life so different from Europeans that they might as well be a different species. Self-consciousness is unknown to them; as he tells his uncle, 'La vie des Musulmans est un hasard dans le destin universel: ils ne se suicident jamais' (p. 88). His conversation with Müller reflects this again. Even Western man does not provide a continuity, Müller claims: 'les grands voyages sont devenus communs, et l'ethnologie est venue troubler nos historiens, qui commencent à se demander si un Romain n'était pas aussi différent d'eux qu'un Chinois, par exemple' (p. 106). Action and ambition, Vincent has stated, are the most constant elements in human personality; but even this is seen as doubtful.

The colloquy itself continues the same lines of argument, and the various ideas, some contradictory, some complementary, are expressed by the participants in turn. Rabaud sees the idea of art as the basis of man, and as the key to the eternal:

le grand artiste . . . établit l'identité éternelle de l'homme avec lui-même. Par la façon dont il nous montre tel acte d'Oreste ou d'Œdipe, du prince Hamlet ou des frères Karamazoff, il nous rend proches ces destins si éloignés de nous dans l'espace et dans le temps; il nous les rend fraternels et révélateurs. Ainsi certains hommes ont-ils ce grand privilège, cette part divine, de trouver au fond d'eux-mêmes, pour nous en faire présent, ce qui nous délivre de l'espace, du temps et de la mort. (pp. 112–13)

This idea is close to that of art as an *anti-destin*, though Rabaud is not given Malraux's own terminology; but Rabaud only speaks so that Thirard can then proceed to ask what is meant by knowing man. There is more to man, Thirard claims, than art: 'la culture ne nous enseigne pas l'homme, elle nous enseigne tout modestement l'homme cultivé, dans la mesure où il est cultivé' (p. 115). There is a Mandarin quality about art which separates it from the reality of life: '[l'objet de la culture] a toujours été de fonder la vie en qualité, si j'ose dire, mais c'est tout autre chose que de la fonder en vérité' (p. 116). Nor is psychology an effective way of knowing man; introspection tells us nothing about man in general, merely something about introspective man. Thirard goes on to distinguish between the two forms of knowledge of man: formal knowledge, the attempt to reduce man to a system of psychological laws, and the intuitive knowledge shown by novelists—he cites Stendhal, Tolstoy, Meredith, Dostoevsky—and Montaigne, who is making the same kind of inquiry. Their knowledge of man is in a way negative: it is simply 'Ne plus pouvoir être surpris par lui' (p. 117). It is precisely in this, reflects Vincent, that he did not really know even his own father, whose suicide remains completely inexplicable to him.

The initiative at this point passes to Stieglitz, a pugnacious German professor, who calls the knowledge of novelists artificial and contrived—'un véritable tour de passe-passe'. A friend of his who had spent some time in prison claimed that only three books could adequately resist the atmosphere of prison: *Robinson Crusoe*, *Don Quixote*, and *The Idiot*. In each case, the initial *donnée* is a man separated from his fellows, by shipwreck, madness, or innocence, a man who fights to destroy his solitude and rejoin humanity, by work, dreams, or *sainteté*. Although none of the authors had undergone the experiences about which they wrote, all had suffered from the most common experience of isolation from one's fellow men, humiliation and shame: Cervantes had been a slave, Dostoevsky a convict, Defoe in the pillory. Ultimately their work is still based not on real knowledge of man but on introspection; for Stieglitz, 'L'homme commence à l'autre' (p. 122). Here, too, Stieglitz is putting forward ideas of Malraux's own, developed later more extensively in the marginal comments to Picon's *Malraux par lui-même*. Stieglitz, in fact, makes a fundamental challenge to psychology, the very basis of Western thought, as an element of human experience which is contingent and might equally well be absent. Here Vincent can bring forward his own experience: Moslem art, and perhaps that of the whole of Asia, excludes all psychology. Its plastic art is abstract, and its literature fantastic.

Il n'y a *besoin* de psychologie qu'en Occident. Parce que l'Occident s'oppose au cosmos, à la fatalité, au lieu de s'accorder à eux. Et que toute psychologie est la recherche d'une fatalité intérieure. Le coup d'état du christianisme, c'est d'avoir installé la fatalité *dans* l'homme. De l'avoir fondée sur notre nature. Un Grec était concerné par ses héros historiquement — quand il l'était. Il extériorisait ses démons en mythes, et le chrétien intériorise ses mythes en démons. Le péché originel concerne chacun. La crucifixion concerne chacun. (p. 125)

In fact all that modern psychoanalysis has done, Stieglitz interrupts, is to take up again the idea of original sin; the unconscious is always *a priori* seen as evil. And Vincent rounds off this stage of the argument: only the West confuses knowledge of man with that of his secrets. Psychological analysis alone is insufficient basis for art; for this analysis to become true art, 'il faut qu'elle entre en lutte avec la conscience que nous avons de notre destin' (p. 127). Here Vincent gives a definition of *destin*, the closest indication of the meaning of this concept to be found in Malraux's works, and an excellent formulation of the basic Existentialist predicament.

— Nous savons que nous n'avons pas choisi de naître, que nous ne choisirons pas de mourir. Que nous n'avons pas choisi nos parents. Que nous ne pouvons rien contre le temps. Qu'il y a entre chacun de nous et la vie universelle, une sorte de . . . crevasse. Quand je dis que chaque homme ressent avec force la présence du destin, j'entends qu'il ressent

— et presque toujours tragiquement, du moins à certains instants —
l'indépendance du monde à son egard. (p. 127)

This is immediately followed up by the central thought of Malraux's art philosophy: that art is man's supreme way of escaping
his *destin*, and even dominating it:

L'homme sait que le monde n'est pas à l'échelle humaine; et il
voudrait qu'il le fût. . . .
Notre art me paraît une rectification du monde, un moyen d'échapper
à la condition d'homme. La confusion capitale me paraît venir de ce
qu'on a cru — dans l'idée que nous nous faisons de la tragédie grecque
c'est éclatant! — que représenter une fatalité était la subir. Mais non!
c'est presque la posséder. Le seul fait de pouvoir la représenter, de la concevoir, la fait échapper au vrai destin, à l'implacable échelle divine: la
réduit à l'échelle humaine. Dans ce qu'il a d'essentiel, notre art est une
humanisation du monde. (p. 128)

At this point in the colloquy there is a temporary break, and
Vincent's definition of art is not immediately taken up. Instead the
pièce de résistance of the talks, Möllberg's address, is prepared.
Möllberg is perhaps the most interesting participant in the
colloquy; he has already appeared on the previous day, interrupt-
ing Vincent's conversation with Müller. An ethnologist with an
international reputation, he shares with Vincent (and Malraux)
the quality of being a man of action as well as a thinker (all the
participants show great deference to both of them, perhaps because of this). He is described in some detail, both physically and
biographically, and it appears that Malraux had a model in mind:
Léopold Chauveau for the physical portrait, and Leo Frobenius for
the biographical study.[1] In particular Möllberg's monsters, small
bronze or clay objects, half human, half fantastic like Goya etch-
ings, which somehow symbolize his detachment from normal
humanity, had their origin in similar creations of Chauveau's. At

---

[1] Cf. the interesting article by Armand Hoog, 'Malraux, Möllberg and
Frobenius', *Yale French Studies*, 18 (Winter 1957), pp. 87–96. At the same time I
find it difficult to agree with Hoog's contention that Frobenius marked Malraux's
thinking between 1918 and 1923, since he was hardly known in France at that time.
(Nor was Frobenius's Institute founded, as Hoog states, in Frankfurt at the end of
the First World War; it was in Munich until 1925, and moved to Frankfurt then.)

the same time the resemblance between Möllberg and Frobenius is perhaps more limited. Leo Frobenius (1873–1938) was one of the great names of ethnology; he wrote many books, articles, and pamphlets, and investigated prehistoric art in the Alps, Norway, Spain, the Libyan and Sahara deserts, Jordan, Rhodesia, and the Bushman caves of South Africa. Between 1904 and 1935 he made no less than twelve expeditions to Africa. He was, however, more an archaeologist in temperament than an anthropologist: he combined deep respect for the African past—and was one of the principal discoverers of the former existence of an indigenous African civilization—with a biting contempt for living Africans, and for what he considered the excessively soft treatment of them by humanitarian missionaries, especially British ones.[1] This low opinion of negro capacities he took almost to the point of developing a racialist anthropology, while in 1910 he claimed to have conclusive proof that the lost continent of Atlantis existed in West Africa. There was, certainly, a good deal of the Romantic in him, and he recalls Schliemann in his direct methods of obtaining objects for his museum; even dubious methods, such as bribery and theft, were used (and the parallel with Claude Vannec—and the young Malraux himself—is interesting, although it is not sure how much Malraux knew of Frobenius at that point of his career).

This colourful, if erratic and emotional, figure was not merely an ethnologist, but also a *Kulturphilosoph*. A pupil of Ratzel's, he developed the latter's concept of 'cultural complexes' into that of 'cultural circles', and started his own 'Research Institute for the Morphology of Civilization'. The comparison with Spengler is evident; but Frobenius in fact anticipated Spengler (nor was he the only one to do so) in evolving a theory of cultural cycles. Perhaps his most important work was *The Cultural History of Africa*, which appeared in 1932 and was translated into French in 1936. Some of Malraux's knowledge of Frobenius is evidently mainly due to his reading of this work, and of *The Destiny of Civilizations* (French translation, 1940), though he had no doubt a certain amount of second-hand knowledge from, among other sources, conversations

[1] H. R. Hays devotes a chapter to Frobenius in his most readable informal history of anthropology, *From Ape to Angel*.

with Groethuysen and his attendance at the Pontigny *décades*;
most of Frobenius's other work was not translated into
French. Certainly Malraux draws on these books for Möllberg's
description of the ritual life and death of the 'moon' king
(pp. 130–3).[1] Professor Hoog has also shown that certain ideas ad-
vanced by Möllberg—the knowledge of the meaning of death, of
eternity, of identity with other tribes and other races, all of which
are not common to all men—can be found in *Aus dem Flegeljahren
der Menschheit*, an early book by Frobenius, published in 1901. But
Frobenius, if a flamboyant 'intellectual adventurer' of the type one
might expect Malraux to admire, was also one of the founders of
the diffusionist school in anthropology, whose main teaching was
precisely that cultural developments were not invented indepen-
dently in different societies, as the evolutionists had held, but passed
on from one to another. The ritual killing of the king, for instance,
which Frobenius actually found in Southern Africa, he tried to
prove to be the mark of a 'culture-complex', with its primary
origin in India. Möllberg, on the other hand, uses this ritual as his
main proof that mental structures of different societies are mutually
exclusive. Here the influence is more that of Spengler, although
Malraux uses Frobenius's material.[2] In Möllberg's arguments there
is nothing of this; nor for that matter are there any ideas that were
not common coin among anthropologists long before 1940.[3] In
fact we might conclude that Malraux used Frobenius's writings, or
those of which he knew, chiefly because they were the anthropological works with which he was most familiar. And the importance of those ideas which Möllberg develops—not all of them, or
even the apparent facts, are accepted among anthropologists as
more than hypothetical—lies less in the ideas themselves than in

[1] Cf. J. Huizinga, *Homo Ludens*, English translation, pp. 15–16: 'As Leo Frobenius puts it, archaic man plays the order of nature as imprinted on his consciousness.' Huizinga draws extensively on *Kulturgeschichte Afrikas* in developing this
idea. Cf. also Hoffmann, op. cit., pp. 263–5.

[2] It is largely because diffusionism is now, in the main, superseded, together
with Frobenius's unorthodox and imperialistic approach to his subject, and perhaps a streak of paranoia and charlatanism in his character, that his name rarely
appears in current Anglo-Saxon anthropological textbooks.

[3] Cf. any standard introduction to the subject, such as Ruth Benedict's
Patterns of Culture, first published in 1934.

Malraux's use of them to dramatize his novel. And, as so often, he translates them into his own terminology, giving them striking form; the idea that men are fundamentally shaped by their intellectual and cultural environment, just as much as by their physical and material one, is treated in terms of *fatalité*: 'les hommes sont le plus profondément définis, et séparés, par la forme de leur fatalité' (p. 139). In the twentieth century this implies nationalism, consciousness of race or social class; but—and it is Walter, not Möllberg, who makes this point—behind all these is modern man's sense of history. This, Möllberg himself can then go on, itself depends on a sense of time. Here he rejoins Vincent's own experience once again: just as, according to the German, the Middle Ages had no sense of time, Vincent returning to Marseille from Central Asia had felt that he was returning not so much to Europe, as to 'le temps'. Möllberg sees history as the key to the meaning or meaninglessness of life; here his ideas are Malraux's own, rather than Frobenius's, and the passage is charged with the same peculiar intensity and vocabulary with which Malraux has always clothed his thought:

— C'est l'histoire qui est chargée de donner un sens à l'aventure humaine — comme les dieux. De relier l'homme à l'infini. . . .

Nous ne sommes hommes que par la pensée; nous ne pensons que ce que l'histoire nous laisse penser, et sans doute n'a-t-elle pas de sens. Si le monde a un sens, la mort doit y trouver sa place, comme dans le monde chrétien; si le destin de l'humanité est une Histoire, la mort fait partie de la vie; mais sinon, la vie fait partie de la mort. Qu'on l'appelle histoire ou autrement, il nous faut un monde intelligible. Que nous le sachions ou non, lui, lui seul, assouvit notre rage de survie. Si les structures mentales disparaissent sans retour comme le plésiosaure, si les civilisations ne sont bonnes à se succéder que pour jeter l'homme au tonneau sans fond du néant, si l'aventure humaine ne se maintient qu'au prix d'une implacable métamorphose, peu importe que les hommes se transmettent pour quelques siècles leurs concepts et leurs techniques: car l'homme est un hasard, et, pour l'essentiel, le monde est fait d'oubli. (pp. 141–2)

Here Möllberg leans to metaphysical pessimism, and his interrogation and response are, in essence, little different from, say,

Camus's concept of the absurd or Sartre's atheistic Existentialist premiss. The term 'absurd' itself is used shortly afterwards by Stieglitz, who defines Möllberg's subject as 'l'absurdité ou la non-absurdité du monde' (p. 143). Malraux's close affinity with Existentialist writers is clearly demonstrated in passages such as these (which also inspire Christian apologists with the hope that he will ultimately, presumably because of the intolerability of this pessimism, go over to the Church). But again one may doubt the originality of the thought, as opposed to the expression; the meaninglessness of a world without God and the pessimism resulting from an acceptance of this position have been familiar to European thought for well over a century.

The remainder of the discussion consists of an elaboration of Möllberg's question. First, Stieglitz argues that even between modern European and medieval man there is a huge difference in mental structure, illustrated by their attitudes to the concept of miracles, or the difference between a genuine Gothic cathedral and a modern neo-Gothic church. Thirard asks if this difference in mental structure is valid for simple peasants, as well as for members of more specialized occupations; to this, Möllberg replies that the millions of peasants through the ages may be alike, but that they are not, ultimately, significant:

L'homme n'est pas intéressant en soi, il l'est par ce qui le fait réellement homme: c'est malheureusement ce qui fait sa différence essentielle. Moins les hommes participent de leur civilisation et plus ils se rassemblent, d'accord! mais moins ils en participent et plus ils s'évanouissent. . . . On peut concevoir une permanence de l'homme, mais c'est une permanence dans le néant. (p. 145)

This statement acts as a cue for Vincent's question, 'Ou dans le fondamental?', and brings the reader back to the experience of the narrator, imprisoned at Chartres, in the introductory section of the novel. Möllberg takes the negative view: outside thought there is no basic residue of fundamental man. 'Une civilisation n'est pas un ornement, mais une structure.' 'Il n'existe pas un homme fondamental, augmenté, selon les époques, de ce qu'il pense et croit: il y a l'homme qui pense et croit, ou rien' (p. 146).

Indeed, apart from his capacity for thought, a man is no more than an animal, for what he has in common with other men, eating, drinking, sleeping, copulating, is precisely what he has in common with all living creatures: 'Qu'il y ait ou non une permanence du néant, que nous importe, si précisément ce qui fait la dignité de l'homme est à jamais condamné!' (p. 147). Rabaud maintains that at least this is man's finest achievement, his nearest approach to eternity: 'Quelque chose d'éternel demeure en l'homme — en l'homme qui pense . . . quelque chose que j'appellerai sa part divine: c'est son aptitude à remettre le monde en question . . .'; but Möllberg retorts (using Camus's symbol) 'Sisyphe aussi est éternel.' He is categorical: 'Les états psychiques successifs de l'humanité sont irréductiblement différents. . . . Sur l'essentiel, Platon et Saint-Paul ne peuvent ni s'accorder, ni se convaincre: ils ne peuvent que se convertir' (p. 148). And hence his dramatic gesture of throwing away sheet by sheet the manuscript of his *magnum opus*, the fruit of many years' work, as he crossed Africa; his last words fully express his bitterness and irony: 'rien de meilleur que de regarder les termitières pour être fixé sur l'homme . . .' (p. 149).

Here the discussion ends, and Vincent goes off through the fields, where, in a lyrical and rhetorical passage, he contrasts intellectual arguments with fundamental life, and has the intuition already mentioned:

Combien d'interrogations étrangères avaient été poussées avec la même passion, sous les voûtes mêmes de ce prieuré. Le soleil se couchait, allumant les pommes rouges des pommiers. Vaine pensée, vergers aux inépuisables renaissances, que toujours la même angoisse éclaire comme un même soleil! . . .

La plénitude des arbres séculaires émanait de leur masse, mais l'effort par quoi sortaient de leurs énormes troncs les branches tordues, l'épanouissement en feuilles sombres de ce bois, si vieux et si lourd qu'il semblait s'enfoncer dans la terre et non s'en arracher, imposaient à la fois l'idée d'une volonté et d'une métamorphose sans fin. (p. 151)

Here is the intuition of life itself, expressed not in man but in trees, and it embodies a permanence through time: this is the silent affirmation, which refutes all Möllberg's pessimistic arguments.

Experience on its deepest levels is not subject to logical analysis; and the intuition of life, the 'banal mystère' (a term which
Malraux uses twice, on pp. 115 and 151), is more powerful than
any 'dialogue avec la culture'. Indeed, the conclusion has been
several times anticipated: while Möllberg was talking, men outside had been going about their daily work as from time immem-
orial, unheeding and unaffected by the logic of Möllberg's analysis:

> [Möllberg] parlait maintenant avec passion; dehors, des hommes
> chargeaient des troncs semblables à ceux que mon père avait pendant
> quarante ans fait empiler devant la mairie de Reichbach, semblables à
> ceux qu'empilaient les bûcherons de la Sainte-Forêt dans le soleil du
> Moyen-Age, — et la fontaine de la place marmottait dans le soir. (p. 141)

Both the Altenburg and Reichbach are no doubt selected because
of their long history stretching back to medieval times and beyond,
so that the colloquy stands out as a brief moment against the
centuries (the same technique as in *L'Espoir*, where the brief
present struggle of the Civil War is contrasted with ancient cities
such as Toledo). Even the Altenburg library, in which the discussions were held, adds to this impression with its Gothic sculptures.

The use of vegetation as imagery is repeated several times: the
smell of sawn wood is one of Vincent's most pervading childhood
memories (p. 43); the sight of branches and leaves and the smell of
the forest entering the windows of the priory at night punctuate
Vincent's initial conversation with Walter. This use of vegetation
is deliberate: in the next section of the novel the full horror of the
German gas is expressed by its ability to kill off even the vegetation over which it passes, and again vegetation represents life even
more fully than do men. Walter and Vincent themselves are seen
as essentially akin to the peasants and woodcutters; their conversation about death ends with Vincent looking at Walter's hands,
'les mêmes que les siennes quoique plus fortes, les mains de
bûcherons des Berger de Reichbach, cordes et poils gris' (p. 100).
During the discussions themselves a considerable amount of
imagery is used to punctuate the argument. Much of it is slightly
ironic, depreciating the intellectual value of the propositions made,

as when Walter is interrupted by 'des cris idiots de poules' coming through the window from outside (p. 87), or when Möllberg makes an affirmation 'avec la sourde violence des incurables à qui l'on parle imprudemment de leur maladie' (p. 148). Malraux again indulges his predilection for striking sound images: Möllberg, after pausing in his argument, which provokes a round of chair-scraping and throat-clearing, takes it up again: ' — Autre domaine, reprit-il, retrouvant aussitôt le silence strié de mouches' (p. 134). Describing Dietrich's deathbed, Malraux makes extensive use of both sound and insect images, which link this individual destiny to the whole living world:

Sur le bord du cendrier, une fourmi courait. Elle avait continué en ligne droite son chemin, grimpé sur le revolver déposé là. A part une trompe d'auto lointaine et le clip-clop d'un fiacre dans la rue, mon père n'entendait que le bruit indifférent de la pendulette de voyage, pas arrêtée encore. Mécanique et vivant comme ce grattement, sur toute la terre s'étendait l'ordre des communautés d'insectes au-dessous de la mystérieuse liberté humaine. La mort était là, avec l'inquiétante lumière des ampoules électriques lorsqu'on devine le jour derrière les rideaux, et l'imperceptible trace que laissent ceux qui ont emporté les cadavres; du côté des vivants venaient le bruit constant de la trompe, le pas du cheval qui s'éloignait, des cris d'oiseaux du matin, des voix humaines, — étouffés, étrangers. A cette heure, vers Kaboul, vers Samarkande, cheminaient les caravanes d'ânes, sabots et battements perdus dans l'ennui musulman. . . .

L'aventure humaine, la terre. Et tout cela, comme le destin achevé de son père, eût pu être autre. . . . (p. 91)

This imagery thus builds up a haunting sensory equivalent of the feeling Vincent has of destiny and the mystery of life: 'un secret qui n'eût pas été moins poignant si l'homme eût été immortel' (p. 93).

The Altenburg colloquy is deliberately made to take place on the very eve of the First World War, although this is not apparent until the end of the Altenburg section, which, after Vincent's lyrical intuition of the permanence of the trees, overlying 'l'angoisse des hommes', is concluded by the single remark, 'Il y avait quarante ans que l'Europe n'avait pas connu la guerre' (p. 153).

The fourth section of the book then begins with the bald state-ment: 'Un peu moins d'un an plus tard — le 11 juin 1915 — mon père attendait dans l'anti-chambre du P.C. du général Von Spitz, sur le front de la Vistule' (p. 157). This timing is significant: the 'European' colloquy (though in fact only Frenchmen and Germans are present) is utterly swept away by events outside the control of the intellect, just as Vincent's intuition of life completely contra-dicts his intellectual convictions. The scenes on the Eastern front are as conspicuously lacking in intellectual dialogue as the Alten-burg discussions were coruscating with brilliance; there is an in-tentional contrast here between the intellectual and the ordinary man. The experience of war, in fact, is shown as reducing men to the lowest common denominator: 'Il suffit de tirer les hommes de leur milieu pour qu'ils ne sachent plus grand'chose, sinon quelques noms et des mots' (pp. 158-9). Vincent's feelings as a soldier may perhaps have been modelled on Malraux's own in 1939 and 1940: dislike of his superiors, inability to communicate with his fellows on an intellectual level, but a certain comradeship of 'bavardage', plus the virile fraternity of courage so powerfully expressed in the earlier novels.

Although most of the fourth section of *Les Noyers* is taken up with the gas attack, the initial episode, the interrogation of a sus-pected woman spy by Wurtz, a German counter-intelligence officer, deserves attention. This scene of interrogation super-ficially resembles several other such scenes in Malraux's novels, notably Garine's interrogation of the two men suspected of poisoning wells. But the episode is certainly introduced to arrive at the opposite conclusion: whereas Garine is proud of his ability to extract a confession—it is his last flash of activity before his ill-ness—and the violence involved is ignored, now Malraux uses the episode to show Vincent's disgust at Wurtz's brutality. The inci-dent constitutes a parable of the violence engendered by war, foreshadowing the gas attack which follows. For Vincent—and, we may assume, for Malraux at this period—the end does not justify the means. It is as if Malraux were intentionally rewriting his earlier novels; the deliberate humanitarianism is unmistakable.

The gas attack marks the ultimate point of Vincent's experience of man: it, even more than the Altenburg colloquy, can be called the crucial episode in the novel. After the discussions were over, his intuition of the permanence of man, if profound, was passive in nature; and again, after the interrogation of Mme Rosnowa, the suspected spy, his role was limited to the passive one of asking to be posted to a different branch of the service. Now, faced with the horror of a gas so deadly that it kills even foliage, he finds himself impelled to act, and thus to transform the passive intuition into a basis for action, even at the cost of his own life. The horror of gas warfare has perhaps been overshadowed now, in the era of atomic weapons, but at the time when Malraux wrote gas was still the most terrible and deadly weapon of war so far developed and used. No gas used seems, however, to have possessed such destructive qualities as the one described by Malraux, and there is no reason to believe that the episode is anything but entirely fictional. First of all Vincent meets Professor Hoffmann, the expert on poison gases, a deliberate caricature of the unfeeling scientist, for whom the deaths of enemy soldiers merely represent the outcome of a successful experiment, and another instance of the rejection of the 'intellectual', who dehumanizes individual man. Then, before the emission of the gas takes place, Malraux devotes a number of pages to the conversation of the German soldiers in the trenches, as they wait for the signal to begin their attack. This episode is probably in part intended to heighten suspense, but it is also significant for the disconnected scraps of dialogue, which drive home again the message of the community of man, recalling the scenes at Chartres in the opening section. There is also, perhaps, an echo of the trench scenes in *L'Espoir*; but the emphasis has changed: there the dialogue was charged with direct meaning, whereas now the individual remarks have significance only in revealing the essential humanity of the soldiers. Malraux emphasizes that in hearing these snippets of conversation Vincent for the first time begins to know ordinary men (and it is likely that the experience was Malraux's own, in 1939 and 1940; earlier he had known only dedicated militants):

Pour la première fois, à l'écoute de cette obscurité vivante, mon père entendait le peuple allemand. Le peuple tout court, peut-être: les hommes. Une voix toute proche de l'obscurité primitive, comme ces silhouettes à peine distinctes des ténèbres. Les soldats avaient toujours eu avec lui le rapport le plus faux, celui qu'ils ont avec l'officier qui ne les commande pas; depuis un an, il côtoyait un monde qu'il avait cru connaître — comme s'il suffisait d'être un homme pour connaître les hommes. . . . Il savait ce que ceux-ci avaient appris à l'école, mais non ce qu'ils avaient oublié depuis. (p. 190)

But all individuality is lost at the same time as their common humanity is affirmed:

L'obscurité était de nouveau tout habitée de voix, voix d'indifférences et de rêves séculaires, voix de métiers — comme si les métiers seuls eussent vécu, sous les hommes impersonnels et provisoires. Les timbres changeaient, mais les tons restaient les mêmes, très anciens, enrobés dans le passé comme l'ombre de cette sape — la même résignation, la même fausse autorité, la même absurde science et la même expérience, la même inusable gaîté, et ces discussions qui ne connaissaient que l'affirmation de plus en plus brutale, comme si ces voix de l'obscurité ne fussent jamais parvenues à individualiser même leur colère. (p. 199)

These men are no better and no worse than any in the various battling armies, and their topics of conversation the same: sex, civilian life and work, rumour, apprehension. Yet they are the men who will, spontaneously, refuse to continue fighting with a gas which so completely annihilates life, and instead will try to save their stricken enemies. Malraux again uses images to show that these men and their reactions are age-old, quintessentially human: a voice in the darkness is 'la voix lente et basse du peuple en face du mystère, cette voix qui fait soupçonner combien celle des sorciers de jadis était sans doute infantile' (p. 194); the gas itself is seen as a 'fléau' (p. 208). The idea of destiny is also several times evoked, as with one soldier playing with a pack of Tarot cards; here it might be argued that the image is rather forced: the description ends, 'Dans l'ombre peuplée de glissements, cette main sans corps semblait courir sur les cartes de toute éternité' (p. 200). Vincent sees the soldiers as if the sword of destiny were suspended above them, like soldiers in the Crusades, and the line of Russian trenches is seen as the place 'où peut-être commençait le destin de cette guerre' (p. 213).

Some of Malraux's images recall those in *L'Espoir*: the burning sun, seeming more real than the battle (p. 213); the horse, running wild in no-man's land, its sudden wild neighing contrasting with the prevailing silence (pp. 204–5); the migration of the birds far above the fields (p. 211). Again, incidental moral problems of command are presented: the question of volunteers, who may well be condemning themselves to death (p. 193); or the nature of courage and action, weakened by intellectual arguments (p. 179). But the dominant tone is quite different: the virile fraternity of *L'Espoir* is a struggle by men against other men for an idea which is ultimately political; now the fraternity implies a solidarity of all men against a horror which is non-human, destructive of all life. Malraux still uses the word 'fraternité', but without the virile epithet; and the term is used in connexion with a German who is staggering back towards his own lines, carrying a stricken Russian on his back, with the terse explanation: ' — Faut faire quèque chose . . . ' (p. 224). Vincent's full realization of the incredible effect of the gas is well shown by the image of the dead tree—dead for years already—which seems 'dans cet univers de pourriture, le dernier vestige de la vie' (p. 220). The silence is used to emphasize this horror: 'Le silence préhistorique' (p. 232) of a world without life, and it recalls the General, speaking the day before about the effects of the gas, above the contented chirping of crickets (p. 168), or Professor Hoffmann, its inventor, enumerating its qualities and drawbacks, punctuated by the sound of bird-calls in the evening (p. 175). The only possible human reaction to this horror, once personally experienced—Vincent cannot understand the reaction of the attacking troops until he himself has experienced the 'boule-versement panique'—, is to fight against it in the name of life itself: 'L'Esprit du Mal ici était plus fort encore que la mort, si fort, qu'il fallait trouver un Russe qui ne fût pas tué, n'importe lequel, le mettre sur ses épaules et le sauver' (p. 233). Thus the essence of the whole episode is in this reaction: 'lutter contre l'inhumain' (p. 235). Pity and compassion are now shown as fundamental human emotions, inevitable even: 'Pour avouer leur pitié, ils en parlaient comme d'une fatalité' (p. 227).

The final pages of this section of the novel remain strangely blurred; it is as if Malraux became undecided about his attitude while writing. The message of humanity and compassion seems initially clear enough (if weakened at times by indulgence in rhetoric); then Malraux seems to have had afterthoughts. The unfinished remark to Vincent by a German N.C.O.—'Si la guerre devient comme ça...' (p. 229)—was, within a few years of publication of the novel, to become a pious hope, bitterly ironical: not merely gas warfare, but wholesale slaughter in atomic holocausts, was to be accepted as justified in the very name of humanity. And Vincent thinks, as he arrives at the field ambulance, that 'le barrage de la pitié ne serait pas efficace plusieurs fois' (p. 241); already he had seen the N.C.O. drop the Russian he was carrying as soon as he realized that the poison had begun to take effect upon himself. His next thought is again cruelly ironical: 'Il n'y a qu'à mourir que l'homme ne s'habitue pas'; at this moment he is poisoned himself, as a direct result of the same compassion. What had seemed to be pity was perhaps a deeper, more metaphysical drive:

il s'agissait d'un élan bien autrement profond, où l'angoisse et la fraternité se rejoignaient inextricablement, d'un élan venu de très loin dans les temps — comme si la nappe des gaz n'eût abandonné, au lieu de ces Russes, que des cadavres amis d'hommes du quaternaire. .... (p. 243)

This experience is specifically linked to Vincent's earlier intuitions, seen as pale compared with the horror of wholesale annihilation of life, utterly incomprehensible:

Qu'était même l'aventure terrestre apparue derrière la fenêtre de Reichbach, auprès de cette Apocalypse de l'homme qui venait de se prendre à la gorge, de cet éclair qui en avait une seconde illuminé les profondeurs chargées de monstres et de dieux enfouis, le chaos semblable à la forêt où possédés et morts fraternels glissaient sous les capotes ensanglantées, gesticulantes de vent? Un mystère qui ne livrait pas son secret mais seulement sa présence, si simple et si despotique qu'elle jetait au néant toute pensée liée à elle — comme sans doute le fait la présence de la mort. (pp. 243–4)

At this point the apprehension of death is still not personal; it is only a moment later that Vincent, lighting a cigarette, realizes that he too is poisoned, and dashes towards the field ambulance in a panic, his last feeling being that happiness was the only worthwhile value in the world of 'flamboyante absurdité'. Malraux, in his preface, specifically denies that this is his, as opposed to Vincent's, last word: 'L'appel au bonheur est ici une simple réaction psychologique.' Yet before he realized he was gassed, and thus before any reaction to this knowledge was possible, Vincent's thoughts were already moving in this direction. The ultimate impact of the section is not fully clear, although it certainly seems, like much else in the book, to indicate that life is no longer seen as a struggle between the individual and the 'other', and that Vincent has become reconciled to mankind; perhaps subsequent, but unwritten, sections of the novel as originally planned might have cast more light here, but at present we cannot know.[1]

The fifth and final section of Les Noyers, entitled 'Camp de Chartres', takes the reader back to the Second World War and to the original narrator, Vincent's son. In this way a certain symmetry is achieved. However, this is largely formal; and in other ways the final section is the least satisfactory in the book, forming a distinct anti-climax after the weight of ideas in the middle section, and the emotional force of the gas episode on the Eastern front. The narrative tone is unclear: presumably everything is again seen at second-hand, as the narrator ruminates about his war experiences prior to his imprisonment: the outbreak of war, life in barracks, the disparate group of men (a pimp, a fireman, a conscientious socialist worker, and himself) who are moulded together into a tank-crew, and then an experience during the German attack when the tank falls into a trap, but manages to escape. In the latter episode, no doubt the most significant but where even the action is confused, the narrative tense moves to the dramatic present; and the novel ends with the narrator reaching something very close to the same insight as Vincent when he was gassed. Vincent's own ultimate fate remains mysterious: we are led to believe that his gas-poisoning brought about his death (like Antoine Thibault), but if so when did he marry and have the son who is the present narrator? The narrator, moreover, appears to be no

[1] It may possibly be relevant that Malraux seems to have been interested in Marcus Aurelius about this time. Cf. Gide, *Journal 1939–1949*, p. 94.

longer a youth, but a man of at least 30; yet there is no mention of Vincent's marriage or wife, if he is supposed to have been married throughout the period of his Eastern adventures.

To the slightly hesitant line of narrative we may add the vague and repetitious nature of the narrator's insights. First, like old Alvear, he seeks comfort in *anti-destins*, linking them to attitudes already presented:

De même que l'ami de Stieglitz, dans sa prison, ne pouvait penser qu'aux trois livres qui 'tenaient' contre la honte et la solitude, je ne pense qu'à ce qui tient contre la fascination du néant. Et, de jour perdu en jour perdu, m'obsède davantage le mystère qui n'oppose pas, comme l'affirmait Walter, mais relie par un chemin effacé la part informe de mes compagnons aux chants qui tiennent devant l'éternité du ciel nocturne, à la noblesse que les hommes ignorent en eux — à la part victorieuse du seul animal qui sache qu'il doit mourir. (p. 250)

This passage, as it stands, seems more like Malraux's own thoughts about the subject of his novel; and it is in precisely the rhetorical tone (the long period, contrived inversion, constant use of abstract nouns) of the later art philosophy. But solitary reverie is not a dramatic mode, and this type of insight had been perfectly adequately expressed in Vincent's reactions to his experiences. Again, as the tanks rumble off to fight, the sentiment is a repetition of that of the aviators in *L'Espoir*: 'La vie de chacun de mes compagnons devient un destin: c'est peut-être cette nuit qu'ils vont mourir' (p. 252). Much of this final section adds little to what Malraux had already said better elsewhere; and the entire tank episode recalls too closely the scenes with armoured trains which Malraux had used in two earlier novels.

There are, indeed, structural weaknesses in the very event Malraux wishes to treat: tension is heightened, on the expectation that the tank, caught in the ditch, will be shelled, and when nothing at all happens, anti-climax is inevitable. So is contrast with the previous section, where Vincent's reactions are successfully portrayed; but now the first-person narration tends to weaken the general impact—'Je hurle aussi. La reprise du moteur couvre toute voix' (p. 274)—and even to lend an excessively self-conscious, slightly hysterical note to the episode, somewhat reminiscent of

La Voie royale. There is, moreover, something of an evasion of the issues of war. The enemy are not so much ordinary men of flesh and blood (which might damage Malraux's general claim of human solidarity), but are represented by a mechanical device: an anti-tank ditch with, presumably, a gun trained on it. The struggle of the crew is not with their enemies at all, but with the slippery sides of the ditch. The narrator does say to himself, it is true, 'Ah! que la victoire demeure avec ceux qui auront fait la guerre sans l'aimer' (p. 271), but this hope is not much more than a slogan. It is this rupture between war and ordinary life that Malraux stresses: 'Du vieil accord de l'homme et de la terre, il ne reste rien: ces blés où nous tanguons dans l'obscurité ne sont pas des blés, mais des camouflages' (p. 269); while avoidance of the moral issues of war is at its strongest in the narrator's reaction to his escape, when the tank reaches a village evacuated by the Germans. The crew look around them at the natural sights of village life—pecking chickens, water troughs, spiders' webs, a brook—with entirely new eyes, like Vincent returning to Marseille. These things are seen as the essence of life, indelibly marked with centuries of human use and custom; Malraux again uses time imagery: 'J'entends bruire sous cette profusion pittoresque tout un bourdon de siècles' (p. 287); the barns are 'les granges des temps gothiques'; the tanks themselves, 'monstres agenouillés devant les puits de la Bible' (p. 288). All this represents the insoluble mystery of life, and is summed up in a typically rhetorical ending:

Portes entr'ouvertes, linge, granges, marques des hommes, aube biblique où se bousculent les siècles, comme tout l'éblouissant mystère du matin s'approfondit en celui qui affleure sur ces lèvres usées! Qu'avec un sourire obscur reparaisse le mystère de l'homme, et la résurrection de la terre n'est plus que décor frémissant.

Je sais maintenant ce que signifient les mythes antiques des êtres arrachés aux morts. A peine si je me souviens de la terreur; ce que je porte en moi, c'est la découverte d'un secret simple et sacré.

Ainsi, peut-être, Dieu regarda le premier homme. . . . (pp. 291-2)

This makes a fine ending, but should it not perhaps be regarded as a purely psychological reaction, like Vincent's thirst for happiness on realizing he is gassed? Surely the narrator's reactions would have been very different if, on reaching the evacuated village, he had found the two old peasants not sunning themselves on a bench, but mutilated corpses rotting in the heat? It is arguable that this is more the essential experience of war than that passed through by the narrator on this occasion, more an image of the human condition to which (in connexion with Pascal) Malraux has just referred.

In dealing with *Les Noyers* critics have often seemed split within themselves between two basic attitudes. The first, in keeping with the modern tendency to equate literary value with intellectual content, is that the novel, whatever its formal drawbacks, must have a deep significance. The other is the uneasy feeling that these same formal drawbacks cannot be ignored, that the structure of the novel and the line of the narrative are altogether too fragmentary. Certainly the novel appears to me to be in some ways an unsatisfactory work. There is in it much less of the texture of the traditional novel than in Malraux's earlier work, and there is a tendency towards mannerism, especially in the use of 'cosmic' imagery.[1] Too much use, for instance, is made of the image of *destin*, so that it tends to lose its power and become mere rhetoric. There is also a temptation to parade knowledge, somewhat akin to that in Thomas Mann; despite the weight of ideas, there is at times a false, almost pseudo-intellectual note present. Indeed, in one way *Les Noyers* is profoundly anti-intellectual: the Altenburg colloquy is just idle talk, immediately refuted by Vincent's own experience, and smashed completely by the reality of human existence—the First World War.

As the book stands, the conclusion seems inescapable that Malraux has not adequately objectified his experiences into the novel form. The double level of the two protagonists, in two wars, is not entirely successful; we do not know enough about either the narrator or Vincent (how did Vincent die, and how does he transmit his experiences and insights to his son?). There is an unevenness, a jerkiness even, in the space allocated to the different

[1] Simone de Beauvoir quotes, evidently with approval, Bernard Groethuysen's comment, 'Malraux est en pleine possession de ses défauts', *La Force des choses*, p. 22. Cf. also Gide's interesting comments, in *Journal 1939–1949*, p. 272.

episodes, while at other times incidents which seem as if they might be developed further are treated quite casually and perfunctorily. Dietrich's suicide, for example, if useful to introduce the idea of the impossibility of one human being ever really knowing another, is in other ways irrelevant and coincidental at that juncture: in fact Dietrich's only function in the novel is to commit an inexplicable suicide at that point. Above all, the ideas are not the total content of the novel—or of any novel; indeed, there is a certain confusion in them. In the opening and final sections, is the narrator himself one of the 'eternal peasants' whom he perceived in his fellow men, or does he separate himself from them by his very lucidity, like Vincent in the trench before the gas attack? This confusion and unevenness becomes more evident on rereading: *Les Noyers* does not, for me, at least, stand up very well to this test, for what it is worth.

The real reason why Malraux has never rewritten or continued *Les Noyers* is perhaps to be seen in his further change in basic attitudes, probably as a result of events in the war after 1941. In *Les Noyers* he comes as near to humanism in the more popular twentieth-century sense of 'humanitarianism' as he ever does; the tone of much of the novel is in fact very close to that of Camus in *La Peste*: Vincent's attitude, his intuition of humanity as a universal fraternity of all men, rather than a partisan political one as in *L'Espoir*, is close to that of Dr Rieux, with his emphasis on 'honnêteté' rather than heroism. But this note is only present in the one novel; after the war Malraux's ideas have evidently moved back towards belief in will.

Writing later, although he might well have kept the First World War episodes, he could scarcely have limited himself in the Second World War to the 1940 campaign alone; the latest events in the novel can now be seen as a beginning, not an ending, of the real Second World War. Malraux's use of the idea of the common humanity of the French and German soldiers, on the basis of their being 'eternal peasants', would not apply equally well to American, Japanese, or Russian troops. And the entire gas episode, with its moral implications, pales beside the idea of atomic war, even if the moral arguments for and against remain substantially the same. In addition, very early on in the post-war period he began to conceive the international political situation in terms of a Third World War, and even to welcome the Cold War. The rejection of violence implicit in *Les Noyers* seems to have been only temporary. This alone would be adequate to explain why the book has been left untouched. But there may be other reasons. After 1945 his interests—like those of Aldous Huxley slightly earlier—seem to have moved to general ideas. He now evidently began to see himself less as novelist than as philosopher; and he may have found imaginative work less attractive, or perhaps thought that he was unlikely to achieve again such a widely acclaimed success as *La Condition humaine*. In 1948, as we have seen, he appears to have intended continuation of *La Lutte avec l'ange*; but the success of his *Psychologie de l'art* may well have encouraged him to pursue this new line of development and drop *La Lutte*. At any rate, he has now, as a novelist, been silent for well over twenty years.

8

ART PHILOSOPHY

No part of Malraux's work has aroused such keen discussion and controversy as his writings on art, which occupied most of his creative life from 1945—and some of it before—until his return to ministerial office in 1958. These books began with a three-volume series, *La Psychologie de l'art*, published in Geneva in 1947-9, reissued in Paris with revisions and fewer illustrations as *Les Voix du silence* in 1951. Since this latter volume has been the most widely diffused and discussed, I shall concentrate on it. Part of the argument of *Les Voix du silence* has been further developed in *La Métamorphose des dieux*, of which the first volume appeared in 1957, still to be followed by a second. Other works include *Saturne* (1950), an extensive essay on Goya; *Le Musée imaginaire de la sculpture mondiale*, in three volumes (1952-4); and two volumes in Gallimard's *Galerie de la Pléiade*, of which Malraux was the general director, *Tout Vermeer de Delft* and *Tout l'œuvre peint de Léonard de Vinci*.[1]

Reactions to Malraux's art philosophy have differed widely, with certain critics—especially literary ones such as André Rousseaux, Gaëtan Picon, and Edmund Wilson—wildly enthusiastic, yet others dismissing it out of hand as inflated nonsense. Professional art historians, as might perhaps be expected, have taken a suspicious view of an amateur, however gifted, invading their territory with a supreme unconcern about academic method and scholarly apparatus, and slashing the Gordian knot of complex problems with brilliant rhetorical affirmations. Indeed, one of them, Georges Duthuit, roused to fury by Malraux's alleged blunders, has gone so far as to write a three-volume riposte, illustrated with almost as many plates as the original, and ironically

---

[1] There have also been rumours of a projected *Musée imaginaire de l'art fantastique*.

entitled *Le Musée inimaginable*.[1] What practising artists think of
Malraux's work, however, we have yet to discover. In Britain
Malraux's most incisive critic has been Professor E. H. Gombrich,
who has made some effective attacks;[2] on the other hand he has
received much more sympathetic treatment in Mr. Righter's
essay.[3]

One principal idea underlies *Les Voix du silence*: the belief that
in a world without religion art is the supreme *anti-destin*. Here
Malraux is going back beyond *Les Noyers*, where art and intellectual abstraction are swept aside by Vincent's intuition of the
beauty and value of simple rustic life, formed by centuries of
human effort and close contact with nature, to a position very close
to that in *La Condition humaine*, except that other forms of *anti-
destin*, such as mythomania, revolutionary action, or thirst for
power, are now ignored. Indeed Malraux, at the end of *Les Voix*,
gives the dates of composition as 1935–51; and, apart from hints
and remarks in his novel which betray the same preoccupations,
the basic conceptions of art as *anti-destin*, of 'metamorphosis', and
of the imaginary museum are directly expressed in an article published in *Commune* in 1935.[4]

The idea of art as *anti-destin*, as self-affirmation and self-transcendence, is, however, not as original as some critics have

[1] Paris, 1956.
[2] E. H. Gombrich, 'André Malraux and the Crisis of Expressionism', review of
The Voices of Silence, in *The Burlington Magazine*, 1954, reprinted in *Meditations on
a Hobby Horse*; and review of *The Metamorphosis of the Gods*, *The Observer*, 9 Oct.
1960.
[3] W. Righter, *The Rhetorical Hero*.
[4] 'L'Œuvre d'art', *Commune*, no. 23, July 1935, pp. 1264–6. Cf. also 'La Psychologie de l'art', *Verve*, Dec. 1937, pp. 41–8; and R. Girard's article, 'Les
Réflexions sur l'art dans les romans de Malraux', *Modern Language Notes*, 1953,
pp. 544–6. Malraux's interest in art obviously goes back much further than 1935,
indeed, right back to his early youth (although the story that he himself was painting in the style of Kandinsky about 1920 may, *faute de preuves*, probably be rele-
gated to the frothier part of the legend). But there is a qualitative difference from
about 1935 on: witness another *Commune* article (July 1934, pp. 68–71), 'L'Art est
une conquête', where Malraux mixes germs of later ideas with fulsome eulogy of
Soviet methods—'A la bourgeoisie qui disait: *l'individu*, le communisme répondra:
l'homme'; 'vous [les communistes] faites surgir ici la civilisation dont sortent les
Shakespeare . . .'. By 1935 Malraux's faith in Communist art, if not politics, was
evidently already fading.

thought:[1] it corresponds very closely to Nietzsche's main thesis in *The Birth of Tragedy*, and in fact much of Malraux's book can best be described as an application of this thesis, not to music and tragedy as in Nietzsche, but to the plastic arts. (The close parallel between *La Tentation de l'Occident* and *Les Voix*, remarked by several critics, is the result of their common Nietzschean source.) Through Nietzsche, leaving on one side his debt to Wagner and to the Hegelian dialectical triad of Dionysian, Apollinian, and Greek tragedy as synthesis, on which his argument is patterned, the idea goes back to the Romantics. The supreme status of the arts and the claim of the artist to be priest or prophet are central Romantic attitudes, directly consequent on the loss of religious belief among most of their number; the everyday world, without God, being unsatisfactory to them, they attempted to create a world of art as a rival to it, thus bringing into being the dichotomy between everyday life and art which has, for better or worse, been a fundamental factor in European aesthetics ever since.

The close parallelism with Nietzsche is illustrated clearly in the last section of Malraux's book, devoted to a lyrical elaboration of the vision of art as *anti-destin*, which he begins with a definition of Greek tragedy in Nietzschean terms: 'la conscience simultanée de la servitude humaine et de l'indomptable aptitude des hommes à fonder leur grandeur sur elle' (p. 628). This derives closely from Nietzsche's dictum, 'Only as an aesthetic product can the world be justified to all eternity',[2] and the idea of tragedy as 'metaphysical solace': 'With this chorus the profound Greek, so uniquely susceptible to the subtlest and deepest suffering, who had penetrated the destructive agencies of both nature and history, solaced himself.'[3] Thus the chaos of life can be redeemed by the heroic

---

[1] To take merely one example, Somerset Maugham in *The Summing Up* (1938): 'To [the author] life is a tragedy and by his gift of creation he enjoys the catharsis, the purging of pity and terror, which Aristotle tells us is the object of art . . . everything is transformed by his power into material, and by writing it he can overcome it. . . . The artist is the only free man.' (Penguin edn., 1963, p. 125.) No doubt Maugham would scarcely have claimed profound originality for this statement, verging as it does on cliché. But Malraux, despite his superiority of expression, is using the same basic idea.

[2] *The Birth of Tragedy*, Doubleday Anchor paperback edn., p. 42.

[3] Ibid., pp. 50–1.

achievements of art. Art, then, for Malraux as for Nietzsche, is a triumphant reply to destiny, the highest form of human self-expression: 'l'homme ne devient homme que dans la poursuite de sa part la plus haute; mais il est beau que l'animal qui sait qu'il doit mourir, arrache à l'ironie des nébuleuses le chant des constellations, et qu'il le lance au hasard des siècles, auxquels il imposera des paroles inconnues' (p. 640). This is both the theme and the justification of Malraux's book.

This last passage is one of very many fine examples that illustrate Malraux's style and approach to his subject. This too can be paralleled in Nietzsche; both share a preference for expressing themselves in rhetorical language: aphorisms, epigrams, poetical imagery, bold metaphors—and half-truths. The literary effect is powerful, and correspondingly weakens the rational argument. The fundamental logical defect of this approach is that extremely bold hypotheses are affirmed as fact, rather than put forward as a basis for experimental confirmation: Nietzsche begins *The Birth of Tragedy* with an attack on ascertaining facts, recommending instead direct apprehension of them.[1] This trust in intuition is complete; and Malraux follows him in his rejection of ordinary scholarship,[2] which is to be replaced by the fertile power of myth. As Nietzsche puts it, 'Man today, stripped of myth, stands famished among all his pasts and must dig frantically for roots, be it among the most remote antiquities. What does our great historical hunger signify, our clutching about us of countless other cultures, our consuming desire for knowledge, if not the loss of myth, of a mythic home, the mythic womb?'[3] What else is Malraux's interrogation of history, his dialogue with the artistic masterpieces of the past?

This vision of art as a justification for life immediately places artistic appreciation on a most exalted level, since art becomes a transcendental substitute for religion. This explains why critics of

[1] *The Birth of Tragedy*, p. 19.
[2] Ibid., p. 112: 'Alexandrian man who is at bottom a librarian and scholiast, blinding himself miserably over dusty books and typographical errors'; p. 122: 'Those university teachers who have not exhausted their energies in the emendation of classical texts or the microscopic inspection of linguistic phenomena.'
[3] Ibid., p. 137.

the Catholic persuasion have attempted to argue that Malraux's thirst for the absolute is itself religious, and but a short step from an overtly Christian position.[1] Despite its superficial attraction, this line of thought is in fact an example of what Sir Karl Popper has called a 'reinforced dogmatism':[2] a system of dogma which has a built-in circumvention of all criticism, so that an atheist writer by his very atheism is seen as betraying his fundamental religious quest. (In Malraux's terminology this is 'annexation' with a vengeance.) Simple pleasure in artistic beauty—'délectation'—is also rejected: Malraux exhibits the same contempt for 'art d'assouvissement' as Sartre for 'romans de consommation', and the word 'beauté' rarely occurs in his works.[3] Thus to affirm art as man's supreme metaphysical achievement seems in many ways a typical modern position: the older aesthetic terminology of 'beauty' has very largely been replaced by one of 'significance' in the last thirty or forty years. Yet it is still Romantic in essence: deriving from Burke's distinction between the sublime and the merely beautiful —later a key conception in Romantic aesthetics. It is also a highly intellectualized attitude which, although it corresponds closely to current critical thought, is still not universally applicable as a criterion of artistic appreciation; and, above all, its validity is greatly impaired when it is applied to works of the eighteenth century or before.

There are other important features of Malraux's vision which can be traced back to Nietzsche (and again beyond him to Romanticism). Viewing the world entirely in aesthetic terms, culture becomes directly equated with art. Again, this may be considered a superficially attractive idea; again, on careful consideration, it can only be taken as an inadequate conception of the complex fabric of any society. Any full definition of a culture must include much

[1] e.g. A. Blanchet, *La Littérature et le spirituel*, vol. 1, *passim*; J. Onimus, 'Malraux ou la religion de l'art', *Études*, Jan.–Mar. 1954, pp. 3–16; J. Steinmann, *Littérature d'hier et d'aujourd'hui*, Bruges, 1963, *passim*; among many others. The fascination of Malraux for Catholic critics is clear, and evidently springs from this hope of extracting a Catholic message from his works, particularly the art philosophy.

[2] K. R. Popper, *Conjectures and Refutations*, p. 327.

[3] This point is made by Professor J. R. Lawler in his interesting article, 'André Malraux and the Voices of Silence', *Meanjin*, xix. 282–90.

more than an enumeration of its works of art; Malraux's view implies the Romantic belief (often seen as decadent) that life is part of art, not art an aspect of life. This is leaving on one side two further difficulties: Malraux only deals with the plastic arts, largely ignoring literature and music, which would both present considerable problems if he attempted to fit them into his pattern. In music especially, craftsmanship is clearly a crucial factor; in literature content cannot be ignored, and the use of language focuses attention on communication, evoking highly subtle and complex responses in the reader. Malraux is thus reduced to an equivalence between culture and plastic art. In addition, much art has perished; even when dealing with the art of so recent a period as the Renaissance, we have before us, in Malraux's imaginary museum of photographs, only a part of the full evidence. For the art of thousands of years ago the position is much worse, and he finds himself forced to interpret whole civilizations from a few sculptures alone. It is true that he makes a similar point himself: 'Le nombre des grandes œuvres antérieures au christianisme retrouvées par nous est infime, comparé à celui des œuvres perdues';[1] but this seems later to be forgotten, and, because of the metaphysical overtones of his primary idea, he further limits culture by identifying it with religion, le sacré. Hence Byzantine painting is seen as the direct expression of 'la Présence éternelle qui emplit l'Orient hanté' (p. 203).

Malraux goes further with Nietzsche (and Spengler, who was deeply influenced by the same idea) in equating culture not only with art, but also with style. 'Culture is, before all things, the unity of artistic style, in every expression of the life of a people.'[2] Nietzsche continues to the effect that knowledge and learning are not essential to culture, and may even contradict it, and attacks boasted German culture for not being genuine culture as much as knowledge about culture. The true aim of culture should not be mere knowledge, but the production of genius and the creation of masterpieces. Nietzsche in effect gives art an 'aristocratic' value, contrasting the valuable few (artist-geniuses, and the works they

---

[1] *Les Voix du silence*, Paris, 1951, p. 22. Quotations are from this edition.
[2] 'David Strauss', in *Untimely Meditations*, Section I, i.

produce) with the worthless many (everyone and everything else, including minor artists and their works). Thus the aesthetic field is made subservient to his general ethic of heroism, reversing Schopenhauer's position; Malraux follows Nietzsche in making art the highest expression of will, and in only concerning himself with genius.

The immediate consequence of explaining cultures in terms of will is to make artistic creation a matter of dynamic striving to excel and overwhelm other artistic creation. This is seen above all in Malraux's section entitled 'La Création artistique', where he very forcefully advances the view (again not entirely original, though it is mainly through Malraux that it has become so widely known) that the artist is impelled to create, not through contemplation of reality, but through contemplation of another work of art, which he wishes first to imitate, then to outdo.[1] Art being style, the artist 'naît donc prisonnier du style, qui lui a permis de ne plus l'être du monde' (p. 314), bringing us back to the Romantic dichotomy between life and art. In rebelling against existing styles, he creates his own:

L'art naît précisément de la fascination de l'insaisissable, du refus de copier des spectacles; de la volonté d'arracher les formes au monde que l'homme subit pour les faire entrer dans celui qu'il gouverne. L'artiste pressent les limites de cette incertaine possession; mais sa vocation est liée, à son origine puis à plusieurs reprises avec moins d'intensité, au sentiment violent d'une aventure. (p. 318)

The violent nature of artistic creation is well symbolized by Malraux's choice of terminology. Words like the following occur again and again: *arracher, écraser, conquérir, amputer, annexer, lutte, affronter, victoire*. Even milder words such as *dialogue* or *métamorphose* betray the same dramatic origin. We may, if we wish, express this dynamic view of artistic development in dialectical terms: one artist's work, or his style (thesis) produces by rivalry another style (antithesis), and a third style then arises (synthesis);

[1] It is interesting to find a very similar idea in an undelivered lecture by Gide, 'Les Limites de l'art' (1901), printed in *Prétextes* (1963 edn., pp. 22–8, especially pp. 24–5).

though whether much is gained by formalizing this view of constant artistic development is another matter—except that its Hegelian origin is thus made apparent. Malraux has, in fact, taken over from Hegel, via Nietzsche, a serious contradiction which vitiates his entire line of argument. On the one hand, we have this dynamic view of artistic creation, in which all artists are rivals; on the other, art is culture, a conception about which Gombrich is surely correct in saying that it depends on the Hegelian idea of 'a spirit of the age'.[1] If we examine any given 'age', we find, instead of a unifying spirit which inspires and explains its various manifestations, nothing but endless strife, since for Malraux no true artist can simply accept, much less imitate, existing forms, without creating his own distinctive style. He is quite formal on this point: 'J'appelle artiste celui qui crée des formes, . . . et artisan celui qui les reproduit' (p. 308). Culture, therefore, is rivalry and struggle.

Of these two conflicting notions, the dynamic conception of artistic creation is perhaps more acceptable than the identification of art with culture. Certainly Malraux's view fits a good deal of contemporary art fairly well, with its enormous premium on originality, and the relative lack of importance of technical ability and craftsmanship. This is in fact another typically Romantic attitude: inspiration as the essence of art, rather than execution. Whether the dynamic view is universally true is more doubtful; once more Malraux is generalizing from his own subjective tastes, which are indeed typical of contemporary art critics: for example, medieval art, Piero della Francesca, El Greco, Rembrandt, Vermeer, Goya, Van Gogh. It has, indeed, been maintained that his art philosophy is very much a justification of contemporary taste, and an attack on the Classical tradition and above all on nineteenth-century bourgeois values.[2] Certainly Malraux seems to lack a comprehensive theory of value, merely accepting or affirming masterpieces, without demonstrating why they should be accepted as such. Further implications of the dynamic view, together with

[1] Gombrich, *Meditations on a Hobby Horse*, p. 79.
[2] R. Ergmann, in his most sensible article, 'André Malraux reste un romancier', *La Nef*, Mar. 1958, pp. 67–74.

Malraux's insistence that simple representation of reality has nothing to do with true art, are much more debatable. Above all, separation between form and content becomes inevitable; and since style is equated with form—'à "Qu'est-ce que l'art?" nous sommes portés à répondre: "Ce par quoi les formes deviennent style" ' (p. 270)—content has to go by the board. Now few would dissent today from the belief that beauty is in the painting, not in the object represented, and, as Gombrich has pointed out, 'the idea that art is "creation" rather than "imitation" is sufficiently familiar' as well, dating back at least as far as Leonardo.[1] On the other hand, Malraux tends in his enthusiasm to equate style with stylization and even with the artificial. But in itself this can be no guarantee of quality; mannerism may well have a fashionable success, but it has rarely gained the full approval of posterity. Stylization, it can be argued, only too easily becomes a learnable idiom, almost an automatic trick; it usually involves simplification, rather than greater complexity, and therefore greater crudity of response.

The assimilation of all culture to plastic art is the weakest point in Malraux's chain of ideas. Malraux has no patience with the slow collection of evidence through archaeological methods, and ignores the mass of accredited material which is available in discussing knotty points, such as the art of Gandhara. The evidence of history tends also to be largely shrugged off, which does not prevent him from using even the most suspect historical anecdotes when they allow him powerful formulations. In the end this attempt to reduce culture to art alone must inevitably fail. Without a minimum of historical knowledge Malraux could not even begin to treat modern, much less antique, art; given nothing more than, say, a set of antique statues, without any knowledge about them whatever, he might be able to separate them stylistically, but would be completely unable to define their cultural background. Ultimately his arguments depend on documentary evidence about the works he treats, and therefore not on the works themselves, but on a context of *intellectual* knowledge about them; and this being so it is somewhat perverse to ignore detailed

[1] Gombrich, op. cit., p. 3.

archaeological evidence. As it is, his criterion of style allows him
to reject representational art, but gives him no means of evaluating different styles against each other.[1] The final result is enormous
over-simplification of the issues. This is, in fact, what one would
expect if one applied the idea of 'the spirit of the age' to our present
society. Whatever we take as the unit of contemporary society,
say Western European society—and any demarcation at all is
somewhat arbitrary and questionable—the overlapping complexities which we discover in it are certainly irreducible to one 'spirit'.
The same is true of any past society, or for that matter contemporary primitive society; if less complex than our own, they are still
complex enough to defeat any attempt at understanding them by
one single intuitive sweep, which would be possible if any
genuine 'spirit of the age' were present and identifiable.[2] The expression is essentially nothing more than a metaphor, and with its
all-or-nothing implications is not really acceptable as a serious
instrument of comprehension.

If art as 'metaphysical solace' is Malraux's central idea, the
presentation of the 'imaginary museum' is his most important
methodological aid, and it is with this that he begins *Les Voix*. The
formal pattern of the book has aroused criticism for being dis-
jointed; yet a design is there. Malraux clearly wishes to end on a
deeply moving note with his evocation of the tragic power of art;
although this is the major premiss of his work, he has a perfect
right, given his rhetorical treatment, to work up to it as a climax.
He therefore begins with a fairly sober discussion of his method,
the imaginary museum; proceeds to examples of 'metamorphoses',
the transformation of Greek coins at Celtic hands, and the change
from Greek statues to Buddhas; argues from these examples
towards his dynamic view of artistic creation; and thus leaves

---

[1] Any religious criterion of value will equally be unable to make artistic dis-
tinctions. The only saving grace, artistically, of the average *ex-voto* is its obvious
sincerity.

[2] An interesting passage in Simone de Beauvoir's memoirs describes a bitter
argument with Sartre precisely because he claimed to have got to 'know' London
integrally during a short visit. On her side she refused to accept the possibility of
thus being able so quickly to 's'approprier les choses'. The parallel between
Sartre's intuitive approach and Malraux's methods is striking.

himself scope for his moving peroration. In some ways the idea of the imaginary museum is the most fertile of the whole work; if not fully original, again it is Malraux who has given the idea its widest currency.

Les Voix begins by a consideration of the institution of the museum. Malraux points out that, although museums are crucially important in Western appreciation of art, the whole idea is less than two centuries old, and purely European. Its importance is that it has 'imposé au spectateur une relation toute nouvelle avec l'œuvre d'art' (p. 12), in removing individual works from their functional context, and placing them next to each other as 'works of art'—objects of admiration, no longer of use: 'Le musée sépare l'œuvre du monde "profane" et la rapproche des œuvres opposées ou rivales. Il est une confrontation de métamorphoses' (p. 12), as Malraux puts it in characteristically 'dynamic' terms. This has made art appreciation a more and more intellectual operation, replacing the connoisseur's former simple pleasure of contemplation. But the institution of museums alone could not complete this process; Malraux shows how little contact with works of art the great critics actually had in the nineteenth century, because of the purely practical problem of the amount of travel involved. At the present time, with photography and reasonably adequate colour reproductions, plastic art is immeasurably more widely diffused, and almost the whole of world art is at the disposal of the viewer: 'un musée imaginaire s'est ouvert, qui va pousser à l'extrême l'incomplète confrontation imposée par les vrais musées: répondant à l'appel de ceux-ci, les arts plastiques ont inventé leur imprimerie' (p. 14).

The idea of the imaginary museum presents in a striking way one of the most important features of contemporary cultural diffusion. A complete sociology of contemporary culture has yet to be written; but certainly Malraux has pinned down one of its most significant elements.[1] At the same time, Malraux's idea has

[1] Another is the diffusion of music since the invention of the gramophone, radio, and, above all, the long-playing record. A third, perhaps minor, point worth studying would be the enormous success of popularized archaeology. Whether or not this depends on a gratuitous fashion, on the glamour of discovered treasure or of solving intricate problems, or on a metaphysical urge to

implications which he himself perhaps tends to ignore. Certainly the contemporary critic has at his disposal much more direct contact with art than his nineteenth-century colleague, equipped only with a few fleeting memories and inaccurate engravings in black and white. But this is knowledge of art, not necessarily appreciation of it (Malraux makes this point, but later appears to forget it); and reliance on photographs leads to neglect of not only the cultural setting of the individual work of art, but also the work itself, less easily accessible than its photographic reproduction. M. Ergmann notes that at least one of the statues which Malraux discusses in *La Métamorphose des dieux* had not left the cellars of the Athens Museum for the previous fifteen years;[1] and there must be other cases where Malraux's familiarity with his examples has not reached first-hand contact. Photographs can, in fact, be used to support arguments both good and bad. With the enormous number at Malraux's disposal he can select series which would tend to support almost any line of development; and in fact some of his juxtapositions are brilliantly elucidatory, while others might be claimed to be merely arbitrary and perverse. Enlargement and reduction enable him to compare works of widely different size, again with varying success. In the end, however, Malraux seems to be taking as an infallible method of cultural inquiry what is surely no more than an ancillary aid; and one, moreover, which provides him with little defence against the counterfeit. Detection of skilful forgeries needs scientific examination, not merely inspection of photographs. Books on art, certainly, are unthinkable today without the lavish use of photographic illustrations, which is possibly why critics such as Ruskin or Fromentin have acquired such an archaic flavour, since they had to assume that their readers had no reproductions in front of them and spent much time on purely formal description. But what matters is always less the photographs than the original.

Malraux's method leads to a double abstraction. First, individual works of art are taken from their context and placed in a museum;

'interrogate the past' is difficult to say, but it nevertheless remains a striking cultural fact.
    [1] Ergmann, art. cit., p. 74.

then they are removed from their physical body and reduced to two-dimensional photographs of similar size, and it is these which are Malraux's working material.[1] As Duthuit comments, plastic art is thus freed from both time and space; while architecture, where function cannot be denied, is significantly excluded from Malraux's book.[2] Ernst-Robert Curtius, writing just before Malraux, has, moreover, made a good case for the primacy of literature in understanding past cultures: 'In the book, the poem is really present. I do not "have" a Titian either in a photograph or in the most nearly perfect copy. . . . With the literature of all times and peoples I can have a direct, intimate, and engrossing vital relationship, with art not. Works of art I have to contemplate in museums. The book is more real by far than the picture.' 'Were Plato's writings lost, we could not reconstruct them from Greek plastic art.'[3] Curtius is surely right. Man's greatest intellectual creation has been language, rather than art; and when Malraux's interpretations of Greek or Gothic art are not based on documentary, therefore linguistic, evidence, they are often purely subjective. The weakness here is again the uncritical identification of art and culture. Art then being identified with photographs, we have the more obviously untenable position that culture is identified with photographs. Moreover, in one respect Malraux's entire argument seems to be self-refuting: if art alone provides the

[1] Cf. E. Wind, *Art and Anarchy*, p. 77: 'What has been optimistically called the "museum without walls" is in fact a museum on paper.' Mme C.-E. Magny, in her *Esprit* article of 1948 (reprinted in R. W. B. Lewis (ed.), *Malraux*, pp. 117–33), also makes some stringent comments on the imaginary museum. 'The method used . . . is questionable. It exudes an odour of death, of catacombs filled with this accumulation of fragments. . . . It makes one think of a Buchenwald of plastic arts: in this spot gold teeth are standing in a huge pile, over there the corner for tattoos . . . an immense cemetery into which sank five continents and fifty centuries of tender, living, and *human* creation . . .' (pp. 126–7). Mme Magny, irritated no doubt by Malraux's confident assumption of omniscience and infallibility, could scarcely be more cruel. Although she is not altogether fair, her strictures contain a good deal of justification.

[2] Duthuit, op. cit., vol. I, p. 23.

[3] E. R. Curtius, *European Literature and the Latin Middle Ages*, 1948 (English trans., London, 1953, pp. 14 and 6 respectively). Curtius's introductory chapter, despite weaknesses such as an uncritical acceptance of Toynbee's theses, provides a careful justification of the sober study of philology and literature on liberal principles, as a key to cultural understanding.

means of intuitively grasping man's tragic destiny, why does he himself use language, not art, to make this point clear?

Ultimately, in removing simple 'plaisir de l'œil' from the sphere of permissible reactions to art, Malraux may be over-intellectualizing it. As Duthuit remarks, Malraux, in commenting that in Asia 'contemplation artistique et musée sont inconciliables' (p. 12), gives away his own case; but instead of examining more critically the idea of the museum, which has, as he himself indicates, divorced art from the rest of life, Malraux simply dismisses the idea of aesthetic enjoyment.[1] This aspect, although in line with the general asceticism of Nietzsche—and his own, as far as can be judged from the novels—is nevertheless highly subjective. Simple appreciative pleasure has been as evident in the West as in the Orient, in both classical and modern times; and, if it is objected that the state of mind of the medieval worshipper in the Gothic cathedral contained no trace of artistic enjoyment, the answer must be that, though this is probably so, for him art was part of life—the recurrent ritual of worship—and not the other way round, as Malraux seems to suppose. He thus excludes from his work attitudes with which he has no sympathy, rejecting them without attempting to refute them; naturally a somewhat biased and limited approach is the result. An interesting parallel has been drawn here between Malraux and Berenson.[2] Berenson, holding more traditional views, accepted simple aesthetic pleasure as adequate justification for appreciation of art, excluding most other considerations; while Malraux uses art perhaps less as subject-matter than as a starting-point for Nietzschean philosophizing.

[1] Cf. Duthuit, op. cit., vol. 1, p. 20. One might add to this that the entire idea of a huge 'collection' of art is somewhat alien to the Oriental connoisseur, who is usually perfectly happy in the contemplation of a very few works, not necessarily representative. To a great extent intensity is incompatible with quantity: the visitor trying to 'take in' the whole of a big museum or gallery in a short time merely ends up bewildered and weary. Malraux's imaginary museum, with its thousands, even millions, of photographs, is almost certainly too vast for much profit to be gained from it by anyone except the professional. (The whole idea of 'collecting' vast hoards of artistic objects, especially as practised by millionaires, might doubtless be traced back by Freudian methods to not very creditable infantile origins. However, this is another matter.)

[2] B. Halda, *Berenson et André Malraux.* Cf. also Righter, op. cit., pp. 48–50.

Berenson deliberately limited his field to the Classical tradition, culminating in Renaissance art, and refused to consider any non-European art. Malraux, on the other hand, has little sympathy for Classical artists such as Raphael, and accepts non-European art warmly and sometimes uncritically (except for Chinese art, for which he appears to have something of a blind spot). Above all, to Malraux post-Impressionist art is a triumph (it fits his arguments best), while to Berenson it is a sad decadence (it negates almost all his values). To sum up, Berenson is a typical representative of Classical values, Malraux of Romantic, or, better, Expressionist ones; the difference might also be expressed in terms of Apollinian and Dionysian. Berenson's overriding criterion of life-enhancement gives primacy to life over art; Malraux reverses the order. This contrast brings out the essential subjectivity of Malraux's—and of course Berenson's—tastes, and he is, like all critics, much more convincing when writing about works he appreciates than about those he dislikes. (Even Malraux's intellectual attitude, incidentally, could still be called a kind of enjoyment; he slams the door on aesthetic pleasure only to find it returning through the window disguised as metaphysical sympathy.)

The question of the subjectivity or the relativity of tastes is obviously crucial in any general theory of aesthetics. Malraux's attitude on this point is ambivalent. Frequently he appears to accept the Spenglerian thesis that past cultures—and therefore their art—are irremediably alien to us: 'Toute œuvre d'art est amputée, et d'abord de son temps' (p. 63). We are therefore thrown back on our own resources, necessarily subjective, when considering such works: 'le chef-d'œuvre ne maintient pas un monologue souverain, mais un invincible dialogue' (p. 67). Having said this, however, he proceeds to develop his own interpretation of the past and its art as if he were establishing incontrovertible fact, in a tone which brooks no argument. In fact, as Gombrich has drily commented, he wants to have his cake and eat it;[1] he wishes to sweep away any existing interpretations, on the grounds that knowledge

---

[1] Art. cit., *The Observer*, 9 Oct. 1960. The uneasy equilibrium between these two ideas is sometimes betrayed by Malraux's terminology, e.g. 'Le *mythe véritable* de l'art grec . . . ' (p. 83, my italics).

of the past is closed to us, and then insists on the correctness of his own. How else can he be so sure that Byzantine art typifies the art of the whole Orient in expressing *le sacré*? It is difficult not to accept Gombrich's sober solution, once Malraux's 'all-or-nothing' attitude has been cast aside:

> To the question whether we can understand the art or mentality of other periods or civilizations, or whether all is 'myth', the answer of common sense is surely that we can understand some better, some worse, and some only after a lot of work. That we can improve our understanding by trying to restore the context, cultural, artistic, and psychological, in which any given work sprang to life, but that we must resign ourselves to a certain residue of ignorance.[1]

In short, that myth is no substitute for knowledge, and that we must rely on normal historical and archaeological techniques, however dull and unglamorous they may appear. Malraux's interpretation of art in terms of expression of personal transcendental feeling must remain not proven. It is fairly widely accepted today that the ultimate origins of art are religious in nature, an integral part of ritual and ceremony (Malraux is on well-trodden ground here, just as he is flogging a dead horse in attacking an aesthetic of representation, which has really not been held by any serious artist or critic for the past fifty years). Primitive art has, it is true, nothing to do with entertainment; nor need it have to do with self-expression, as Malraux appears to suppose. Self-expression is a highly Romantic phenomenon, essentially individualistic; while primitive religion is entirely social.

The key word in Malraux's use of myth to interpret works of art is *métamorphose*: the 'dialogue' between works and successive generations of beholders, all reading their own 'myths' into them, results in a series of metamorphoses. But the term 'metamorphosis' is used in more senses than one. It is not only the different effect of the same work on different viewers; at other times it may mean the development of forms, or styles, within a culture; and also the diffusion of forms, or styles, between cultures. Since Malraux nowhere makes any attempt to define or to analyse his concept,

---

[1] *Meditations on a Hobby Horse*, p. 84.

frequently these senses run together, and the result is a certain confusion of argument. The second main section of Les Voix, entitled 'Les Métamorphoses d'Apollon', uses the term in the latter two of the three main senses, with varying degrees of effectiveness. Malraux's main concern here is to explain the course of art from the Greek world, through the Roman and Byzantine empires, to the flowering of Gothic painting and sculpture in the Middle Ages; and, above all, to refute the idea that there was a 'regression' from accurate representation to the 'primitives' of the Dark and Early Middle Ages. He makes many interesting suggestions, but methodologically his procedure is weak, since he starts off with his hypothesis of art as metaphysics, and merely searches for evidence which appears to fit this line of thought. He has only moderate sympathy for Greek art of the Classical period, where the divine element is clearly weaker; and none at all for Roman art, especially portrait sculpture, irredeemably representational. On the other hand, post-Roman art, beginning with the Christian art of the catacombs, and passing through Byzantium to the Gothic, he views as progression, not regression: it has, he states, freed itself from representation and developed style, or rather a succession of styles, and its metaphysical connotations are clear. Here again, the individual elements in Malraux's wide sweep are not original. He shows familiarity with, and uses, the ideas of Henri Focillon (himself influenced by Spengler's 'organic' concepts), Élie Faure, Émile Mâle, and Wilhelm Worringer, among others, while much of what he says, especially about the supposed lack of skill of the 'primitives', had been in the air for many years.[1]

This section of Malraux's book, where he is most closely attempting to make definitive judgements in the fields, not of general aesthetics, but of art history, can best be left to the professionals to judge. Some of Malraux's aperçus have received qualified, occasionally grudging, approval; others scathing criticism. Methodologically, his greatest weakness, as always, is his tendency to over-simplification, to reduce long-argued issues to

[1] To take only one example, we find Naphta in Thomas Mann's Magic Mountain declaring, against Settembrini's belief that medieval art implied lack of skill, that it in fact proves emancipation from the natural (Penguin edn., 1960, p. 395).

one vivid antithesis or metaphor. (Because his work is clearly not analysis, some critics have assumed that it must therefore be synthesis. This is not so, since synthesis can only develop from mastery of all available material. Malraux's method is neither analysis nor synthesis, but accumulated hypothesis.) Two examples will illustrate this method. Malraux compares the design of Hellenistic coins and their transformation at the hands of barbarian tribes who were nominally copying them. What was originally a head now becomes mere pattern, with all trace of human features lost. For Malraux this proves that the barbarians were rejecting classical representation in favour of abstract ornament. Gombrich, on the other hand, apart from showing how the argument goes back some fifty years, states that this particular 'metamorphosis' was more probably the result of copying and recopying the image until it had evolved into craftsmen's schemata.[1] For the layman it is impossible to decide issues such as this, though Gombrich's view perhaps seems more plausible, since it does not have to depend on any ultimately metaphysical belief among these tribes in art as *anti-destin*.[2] Malraux's main virtue in introducing this problem of the Celtic coins is not that he has solved it, but that he has made it known to a much wider readership than a limited circle of numismatists.

The art of 'Gandhara'—the most easterly marches of Alexander's empire, lying astride the present-day frontier of Pakistan and Afghanistan—provides Malraux with an even more striking series of metamorphoses. In this region sculptures of recognizably Hellenistic style continued to be produced for some eight centuries, and are often known as 'Graeco-Buddhist'. Malraux, here enthusiastically following the lead of René Grousset, claims that these sculptures not only gave Buddhism its first representation of the Buddha—which is a fairly widely accepted point of iconography—but also acted as a link between Greek art and that of both China and India, which thus become dependent on the West. This is an

[1] Op. cit., p. 81.

[2] A similar problem, of wider scope, would be the development of the Chinese character from simple pictogram to its present highly formal state: how far does this development depend on rejection of representation, or on simplification for ease of writing, or on other factors altogether?

exciting claim; as usual Malraux accepts the most dramatic theory because of his dynamic conception of art. In making all oriental art depend on Western—with only a handful of references or illustrations to back up his claims—Malraux further irritates the specialists: Duthuit dismisses the whole section in scorn as 'le coup du Gandhara'. And again the layman cannot judge—especially when he reads Sir Mortimer Wheeler on the subject:

in the aggregate one of the most notorious and intriguing problems of art-history. . . . Its literature is immense and growing. The absence of an objective chronology has facilitated an infinite manipulation of the evidence in accordance with taste and theory, and until modern methods of excavation are applied to Buddhist sites far more rigidly than they have been in the past this source of doubt and disputation will remain.[1]

And once more Malraux, in substituting myth for exact historical fact, confuses the two and presents his view as if it were incontrovertibly established. His section on Gandhara is most valuable, not as a contribution to knowledge, but because it presents the issue dramatically to readers who have never previously encountered it.

Malraux's other art books add details to the vision of art put forward in *Les Voix*, but do not introduce any radical changes. *Saturne* provides an expressionist interpretation of Goya's works: Goya fits Malraux's metaphysical view of the artist perhaps better than any other, and stands out as the tormented challenger of destiny. 'Bientôt les peintres oublieront au prix de quelle angoisse cet homme avait dressé contre toute la culture dans laquelle il était né son art solitaire et désespéré.' 'Goya n'est pas parce qu'il figure les tortures, le rival du dieu qui les permit; mais parce qu'il fait de chacune d'elles un cri du hululement nocturne de Prométhée.'[2] The study of Goya is in fact contemporaneous with *Les Voix*, and

[1] R. E. M. Wheeler, *Rome beyond the Imperial Frontiers*, Pelican edn., pp. 195–6. Wheeler, incidentally, sees Gandharan art as essentially Romano-Buddhist, not Graeco-Buddhist at all; although it is only fair to note that some of the most recent archaeological evidence tends more towards Malraux's views. A full account of Gandharan art, with an extensive bibliography, is contained in *Encyclopedia of World Art*, vol. 6, London, 1962. Cf. also its comment: 'after more than a century of investigation and almost seventy years of historical research, the art of Gandhara presents an unusually inchoate balance sheet' (p. 25).

[2] *Saturne*, Paris, 1950, pp. 177 and 156 respectively.

naturally adopts the same tone and reflects the same preoccupations: Goya as the exemplary metaphysical artist. The collections of Vermeer and Leonardo are excellent art books of the conventional type, each containing the complete paintings of the artist finely reproduced in colour, with texts by numerous critics, and a normal scholarly documentation (not by Malraux himself). They are, indeed, products more of Malraux the publisher than Malraux the writer; distinguished contributions to the imaginary museum. So also are the three volumes of *Sculpture mondiale*, each prefaced by an essay by Malraux, again with documentation by other hands. Here much of the world's sculpture is collected and strikingly juxtaposed; though it is a fair criticism that Malraux's own essays are too far removed from the individual photographs to achieve the same impact as *Les Voix*, where text and images are much more closely integrated. Finally—so far—there is the initial volume of *La Métamorphose des dieux*, which takes up again the question of art as the expression of religion. Although this preoccupation with religion has seemed to some critics a presage of Malraux's conversion to Christianity, such an interpretation is no doubt gratuitous; and he is really no more than extending and deepening the observations on 'metamorphosis' contained in the second section of *Les Voix*. It is a book which can best be approached after a careful reading of *Les Voix*, on which it closely depends, and—up to now—has yet to achieve the latter's great popularity.

What, in the end, does Malraux's art philosophy amount to? Certainly he has succeeded in bringing his ideas home to a wide audience, and despite serious attacks on it critics of all opinions think it worth while to make reference to Malraux in their books. Even M. Duthuit, opposed to it root and branch, obviously thought it worth combating or he would have scarcely devoted three volumes to this task.[1] Extravagant praise from some quarters has possibly done Malraux disservice, since those responsible seem largely unaware that Malraux's ideas are not, for the most part, original, and that the central vision of art as metaphysical

---

[1] Duthuit's attack would perhaps be more effective if his language were more moderate. In attempting to use Malraux's rhetoric (strongly laced with sarcasm) back on him, he often merely strikes a somewhat hysterical note.

solace derives directly from Nietzsche. In their enthusiasm for
Malraux's lyrical proclamation of the autonomy of art, they have
tended to ignore the inconsistencies in his arguments (and even
automatically to accuse those who point out these weak elements
of having 'failed to understand' his views). Yet wide popularity
does not necessarily imply lasting importance, whatever the interest focused on Malraux's ideas now—and this interest itself is
undoubtedly part of the general appeal of 'philosophies of man' to
the contemporary reader.[1] Malraux's aesthetic can rightly be called
an Existentialist one. His subjective, intuitive approach can equally
well be called phenomenological (or vice versa); and his deliberate
attempt to replace objective knowledge or art by a myth depending ultimately on the individual observer is entirely in accordance
with the Existentialist position of the individual giving the world
the meaning he wishes it to have. But he also shares the Existentialist
inability to escape from this fundamental subjectivity. No one will
deny Malraux his right to his view of art as *anti-destin*; but he
merely asserts this position without attempting to prove it. It is
subjective, descriptive of his own reaction to art, not prescriptive,
and he has no reason to assume that it will be universally shared.
There are other means of appreciating art—such as Berenson's—
which are equally legitimate.

Malraux's method, the attempt to grasp the whole of art in one
intuitive movement, implies a single source of artistic creativity.
Art for him is the highest expression of the meaning of life. This
not only closely follows Nietzsche, but is also a common Romantic position (and it is in his substitution of art for religion that
Nietzsche most clearly shows the Romantic sources of his
thought). Transcendental value had been given to art by the
earliest Romantics, particularly in Germany; and art as a justification for life is a typical position of many post-Romantics—in
France alone we can instance Flaubert, Mallarmé, Proust, and
Valéry, among many others. There is a difference of degree—
Malraux emphasizes the metaphysical, rather than the aesthetic

---

[1] The enormous current popularity of Father Teilhard de Chardin is a case in
point. Like Malraux he has received short shrift from the professionals, while being
eulogized by more purely literary critics.

aspects—but the principle is the same.[1] Substituting transcendental art for transcendental religion has one immediate consequence; it prevents full acceptance of ordinary life—indeed, to some extent implies a refusal of life, or even escape from it. Writers such as Ortega y Gasset have fastened on this point, and have taken a view completely opposed to Malraux's. For Ortega, who devoted his book *The Dehumanization of Art* (1925) to this topic, art should serve life, and he criticizes twentieth-century art (and literature) precisely for the qualities that Malraux seems most to admire: their tendency to rid themselves of human content and to imprison themselves in style. Where Malraux sees man's challenge to destiny, his rivalry with the world, as humanism, Ortega sees it as the opposite.[2] Ortega's view is no more—if no less—subjective than Malraux's. Certainly many people who can appreciate the art of the past are genuinely bewildered by the multiplicity of the styles of the present; and, although Malraux's 'dynamic' theory helps to explain the artists' desire to develop an individual style, it does little to help appreciation of it. Many professionals, such as Gombrich—quite apart from pure amateurs, such as myself— follow Ortega in feeling that abstract art is lacking precisely because the human element has disappeared from it. It may remain pleasing as pattern, but is this not merely decorative? At any rate it is arguable that the attempt to separate form from content, and base art merely on form alone, ends simply by impoverishing artists, who have little with which to replace the older traditions, now broken up into a welter of mannerisms. Complete freedom is impossible for them, since some limiting choice must always be made; while the security of a solid tradition has been lost. Artistic creation seems, indeed, usually to have resulted from a complex interplay of originality and tradition; both factors being essential to fruitful development.

[1] This affiliation has been strenuously denied by favourable critics, who have affirmed a qualitative difference between the ideas of Malraux and the others named. I find that I am unable to accept their arguments, despite Malraux's greater sophistication.

[2] Cf. also Bernard Dorival, a leading historian of modern art, who has described twentieth-century non-realistic aesthetics as 'ahumanist' (*XX Century Painters*, English trans., vol. 2, p. 5).

The psychology of artistic creation, as Malraux sees it, is no less one-sided—and again Romantic. For him the artist is the hero, challenging destiny and rivalling God by creating his autonomous world. Yet there is an equally plausible approach—perhaps equally one-sided—from the Freudian side. Without going so far as to claim that artists are 'really' trying to take over their father's role of (pro)creator, there is much in Freud's view that the artist is a man who, far from dominating reality or life, is unable to come to terms with it, and retreats into a private world of his own creation. On this view, art must always be a substitute for life, if a sublimation of it, and the heroic posture of the artist naturally vanishes. Malraux, it is true, rejects the subconscious, since for him will is the basis of artistic endeavour, but he nowhere really comes to grips with the Freudian theory. It is not necessary to declare on this issue, since both views suffer from the same defects of one-sidedness and over-simplification; although Freud's additional explanation of appreciation of art—in which he maintains that spectators or readers themselves to some extent share the neurotic traits of the artist—possibly gives him some advantage over Malraux, who never properly tackles the problem of communication, and does not seem to differentiate between the effect of a work of art on the individual himself, or on the members of a society generally.[1] The truth is surely that the psychology of the artist needs much more analysis than either Malraux or Freud has given it; to begin with, to talk of 'the artist' is already an abstraction; there are only individual artists, and to unravel the different factors which underlie their adoption of an artistic career, and the exact impulses behind each individual artistic work, is not something that can be done by theory alone, by simply stating that art is will, or neurosis, without careful examination of the man or works in question. In most cases, where the artist is dead and has left no record of his intentions and preoccupations, we shall never know.

From the point of view of exact historical knowledge, then, Malraux's contribution is doubtful. As a system his work is

[1] This is the burden of Merleau-Ponty's criticism of Malraux's views, in 'Le Langage indirect et Les Voix du silence', reprinted in Signes, Paris, 1960, pp. 49–104. Cf. also E. Kaelin, An Existentialist Aesthetic, especially pp. 272–9.

unacceptable, despite the validity of many individual insights. Above all his tendency to force everything into a unitary mould, piling generalization on generalization, setting sweeping antitheses against each other—even when sometimes contradictory—naturally leads to over-simplistic views, and especially to excessive abstraction. An example is his dictum: 'Tous les grands arts du passé sont religieux.' This may appear to be an empirical statement, though in fact it is merely a definition: to any art in which Malraux cannot discern religious qualities, such as Roman, he simply refuses greatness. In addition, even if this definition is accepted, it still begs the question of the differences between various forms of religious art, and, indeed, between religions themselves. We have seen that metamorphosis is at best an ambiguous concept; so is style, which may equally well imply the general manner of an epoch, the particular individuality of one artist, or, often, stylization. Malraux's attempt at resolving this problem of style never reaches anywhere near the level of analysis of Wölfflin in his *Principles of Art History*—to mention only one of Malraux's predecessors. Practically all the principal terms with which Malraux operates are no less ambiguous: even the concept of originality,[1] let alone the idea of destiny which has also suffered radical debasement through excessive use by, for instance, Napoleon and Hitler. 'Culture' too, when translated into *Kultur*, is a word with suspicious associations.[2] Too often Malraux fails to define his terms at all; when he does he leaves himself little scope for nuances of middle terms. Taken as a lyrical and imaginative, rather than rational, expression of one brilliant man's reaction to the world of art, *Les Voix* can be accepted much more positively. Now the abstract concepts, too often insufficiently defined and therefore ambiguous or confused, assume great emotive strength. The violent vocabulary of conquest—which, incidentally, is

---

[1] Cf. L. Venturi, *Modern Painters*, English trans., p. 112: 'Originality so-called is an abstraction from the taste and tradition of the time, an act of controversy, of an intellectualist character.'

[2] Malraux follows Spengler in regarding culture as 'higher' than civilization, thus reversing the usual anthropological interpretation of these two terms, which regards all human life as culture, whereas a higher degree of social organization is necessary for culture to become civilization.

curiously negative, even destructive, and out of harmony with the patient craftsmanship and gradual progress towards achievement that is the hallmark of much though not all art—can be appreciated for the enthusiasm it generates. Malraux's art philosophy shares this quality with most Romantic literature: it may produce passionate agreement or bitter dissension, but it leaves few readers cold.

Whether Malraux himself would accept the view that *Les Voix* 'is essentially a grandiose poem of a new kind',[1] rather than a serious philosophical work, is another question. It seems likely that he intended much more than poetic value; and in any case, even viewed entirely on the lyrical plane, as a hymn to human dignity and grandeur, his work has definite weaknesses. Many—most—of the rhetorical passages, particularly towards the close of the book, produce a fine effect, taken individually. Cumulatively, however, there is perhaps a little too much of them; rhetoric, to the contemporary ear, tends to cloy, and Malraux's insistence on certain points, such as the non-representative nature of art or the artist's rivalry with the world, means that his work suffers from stridency and repetitiousness. It is not, perhaps, too imaginative to see something Wagnerian in *Les Voix*. Beneath the rhetoric some of the ideas are almost trite: 'Ce qui est en train de disparaître en Occident, c'est l'absolu' (p. 479); at other times rhetoric degenerates into play on words: 'Chardin, désormais, ne combattra plus Michel-Ange désarmé' (p. 28). Perhaps naturally, the rhetoric itself further underlines the Romantic nature of the book; there is a savour of Hugo or Chateaubriand in many of Malraux's periods, accompanying his distinctive imagery: 'Rien ne donne une vie plus corrosive à l'idée du destin que les grands styles, dont l'évolution et les métamorphoses semblent les longues cicatrices du passage de la fatalité sur la terre' (p. 44).

In the end, then, *Les Voix* seems a rather disappointing work when compared with Malraux's novels; and it is difficult not to regret that he did not continue to work in the purely fictional field. As a philosophical poem the work is not fully satisfactory, despite its qualities; its insights do not entirely outweigh its flaws. It can,

---

[1] Lawler, art. cit., p. 290.

of course, legitimately be viewed as one of the most subtle and extended developments of the Romantic viewpoint in aesthetics, with both the limitations and confusion of that attempt at seeking salvation no longer through rationality, but through art. Probably the most useful way of evaluating Malraux's art philosophy is to examine its results. These are undeniable: Malraux has certainly succeeded in popularizing certain ideas on art, some of which have in fact become clichés of contemporary criticism, as well as in popularizing little-known aspects of art. How many of Malraux's readers had as much as heard of the art of Gandhara before opening *Les Voix*? And perhaps he has even popularized plastic art itself, as a cultural form, leading to a serious interest in art large numbers of readers who might otherwise have scarcely come to know it. This, to my mind, is Malraux's greatest achievement in aesthetics; and to do this the tone of passionate enthusiasm which inspires Malraux's pen was doubtless necessary, however irritating to the initiate: *Les Voix* is in many ways a dramatization, in which footnotes would be as out of place as in a stage play. So we are thrown back on the idea of *haute vulgarisation*. A comparison may be made with Spengler's *Decline of the West*—a book which undoubtedly influenced Malraux not only by its ideas, but also by its form and ambitions. Not many readers today accept Spengler's main thesis that cultures are organic, doomed to eventual decay in a rigid cycle, and that they are mutually incomprehensible. In the end *The Decline of the West* cannot be said to depend on anything more than 'biological metaphor',[1] and it is poetic quality as much as factual truth which is the source of any lasting value in the work. At the same time it is impossible to read the work without profit—and enlightenment—, if only from the many historical details unfamiliar to the non-professional reader. The weaknesses of this approach are shared by Malraux: like Spengler—and Nietzsche—he tries to get far too much into his book, making mistakes from time to time, and following their blind spots or prejudices, such as a dislike of Rome and a tendency to group the whole of Asia, from Byzantium to Japan, in one indivisible unity.

[1] S. Hughes, *Oswald Spengler*, p. 10. Professor Hughes's book provides an excellent critical introduction to Spengler's work.

However, one could scarcely expect Malraux to be content with this achievement: having helped to broaden and deepen general artistic appreciation among the educated lay public, and having produced one of the most distinguished of the many works of *haute vulgarisation* of the last decades. Nevertheless, it seems to me that this is the essence of his work on art. Like those of other poets and novelists before him who have ventured into the world of aesthetics—Diderot, Baudelaire, Proust, or Claudel—his art works are read primarily because of his existing prestige as a writer. They are a pendant to his novels, not the culmination of them; and if art is the small change—*la monnaie*—of the absolute, Malraux's art philosophy is the small change of his reputation and ability as a novelist.

9

CONCLUSION

ALTHOUGH it is obviously too early to attempt a definitive
estimate of Malraux's work (and one hopes there are more
books of his to come), certain profitable comparisons can
be made with both his predecessors and his contemporaries. In the
first place, he clearly belongs to the 'heroic' tradition in French
literature, running from Corneille through Stendhal and Barrès to
the present, with its roots in epic, and powerfully reinforced in the
nineteenth century by the symbol—or the legend—of Napoleon.[1]
This is obvious enough: taking only one example, Saint-Just,
about whom Malraux himself has written as an exemplary figure
of will and energy,[2] we find in his posthumous notes: 'Je méprise
la poussière qui me compose et qui vous parle; on pourra persé-
cuter et faire mourir cette poussière; mais je défie qu'on m'arrache
cette vie indépendante que je me suis donnée dans les siècles et dans
les cieux.'[3] The comparison with Malraux is astonishingly close,
since even the vocabulary is similar—'arracher', 'les siècles': for
Saint-Just, too, life is a vain struggle against destiny, yet he will
have left his scar on the map.

Stendhal is a direct antecedent of Malraux the novelist. The
main link is still energy, or the quality which since Schopenhauer
and Nietzsche has usually been called will; and its expression in
fictional terms, the theme of ambition, in which the protagonists
test their energy in a situation involving struggle. In Malraux's
case the ambitions are much more grandiose than the usual purely
social aims, metaphysical in their challenge to destiny or world-
shaking in their attempt at political revolution; yet ambitions they

[1] Cf. the extensive and useful treatment of this theme in P.-H. Simon, *Le
Domaine héroïque des lettres françaises.*
[2] Preface to A. Ollivier, *Saint-Just ou la force des choses*, Paris, 1954, pp. 11–29.
[3] Quoted in Simon, op. cit., p. 289.

remain. But, above all, both men try to create their own fictional
world; as Malraux himself has claimed, the artist 'doit créer un
monde cohérent et particulier, comme tout autre artiste. Non
faire concurrence à l'état-civil, mais faire concurrence à la réalité
qui lui est imposée, celle de "la vie", tantôt en semblant s'y
soumettre et tantôt en la transformant, pour rivaliser avec elle.'[1]
Thus the novel is seen as the expression of the novelist's *Weltanschauung*, and will inevitably have a very personal flavour. Yet because of the fundamental belief in energy there are many parallels
between the two: their exoticism, their fascination with political
intrigue, in which Stendhal's professed liberalism seems as out of
place as Malraux's belief in *fraternité*; Stendhal's belief in privileged moments, equalled by Malraux's moments of insight; the
combination of the novel of adventure and the psychological novel
in the alternation of action and self-analysis (there is much of
Julien Sorel and Fabrice del Dongo in most of Malraux's characters; and if most of Malraux's characters are projections of himself, so are most of Stendhal's). There are also minor parallels: the
quest for the father-figure, possibly to be explained by both men's
attitude to their own parent; and the fascination with the prison
cell. The parallel even extends to critical reactions, which in both
cases tend to be passionate, for or against: in one way Stendhal's
work is still for 'the happy few', since some readers reject his
private world root and branch, and this applies to Malraux as well.

The creation of a personal fictional world is the link in common
between Stendhal, Malraux, and Dostoevsky, who can probably
be regarded as the strongest fictional influence on Malraux.[2]
Dostoevsky's characters are also largely projections of his own
personality, and his novels add up to a vision of the world, not an
attempted copy of it (and, once more, some readers refuse the

[1] Marginal comment in G. Picon, *Malraux par lui-même*, p. 38.
[2] Cf. R. W. Mathewson's interesting article 'Dostoievski and Malraux', *Slavic
Printings and Reprintings*, xxi. 211–23. Rachel Bespaloff, in *Cheminements et
carrefours*, also makes a sustained comparison between Malraux and Dostoevsky;
while Malraux's own essay on Laclos makes clear the line of affiliation from
Raskolnikov through Julien Sorel back to Valmont, the link being conceived in
terms of will. Malraux's interest in Dostoevsky may originally have been kindled
by both Suarès and Gide.

vision utterly, in the belief that human beings are just not like Dostoevsky's vision of them). But whereas Stendhal's writing is constantly shot through with irony, both the other men are writing at a high pitch of seriousness and self-consciousness from which irony and humour of the normal kind are usually absent.[1] It is this frenetic intensity which unites Malraux most closely with Dostoevsky, together with treatment of characterization, in which there is little psychological analysis of the traditional type, but instead ample illustration of psychology in action, if possible violent action; that is, insights into human behaviour rather than explanation of it. Also dialogue is the favourite narrative mode of both men, while they each use imagery in the same way, to intensify emotional appeal; much of the content of the imagery—insects and reptiles, inspiring horror and disgust—is also similar.[2] There is something of Dostoevsky in Malraux from the mid 1920s onwards—the theme of an exhausted Western material civilization in need of spiritual regeneration in *La Tentation de l'Occident*—but the influence becomes overt in *La Condition humaine*. Malraux might not have imagined Tchen's murder of the go-between without the model of Raskolnikov (although its use as a dramatic opening to the novel is original); and in addition to this conception of murder without guilt, the novel is full of Dostoevskyan echoes. Clappique, the mythomaniac and buffoon, seems a deliberate attempt at a 'Dostoevskyan' character: he may have had a model in real life, but he also recalls General Ivolgin, another mythomaniac, in *The Idiot*, and in his function in the novel can be compared with Marmeladov in *Crime and Punishment*. Katow quotes—or rather misquotes—*The Idiot* at the moment of death,[3] and the scenes of interrogation recall Porfiry and Raskolnikov, while there is a clear parallel in the systematic use of pride and humiliation as dynamics for action. (How far Malraux has captured the authentic Dostoevskyan note can perhaps be illustrated by

---

[1] The treatment of the *colloque* in *Les Noyers*, and other occasional passages, such as Claude's interview at the French Institute, are exceptions, but this is generally true.

[2] Cf. R. E. Matlaw, 'Recurrent Imagery in Dostoevskij', *Harvard Slavic Studies*, iii, 1957, pp. 201–25.

[3] Mathewson, art. cit., p. 220.

comparing his novels with *Les Caves du Vatican* or *Les Faux-Monnayeurs*, where Gide was equally concerned, under the Russian's influence, with irrational violence and crime without guilt. But his work is much less intense, more artificial and 'literary'.)

In both men too we find a preoccupation with the metaphysical; characters and situations are often no more than means of expressing this higher significance. As an American critic has put it, 'there is present the same brooding sense of metaphysical terror, the same feverish speculation about matters of ultimate concern, the same desire to penetrate regions of awareness inaccessible to the "normal" self'.[1] But these metaphysical yearnings, set at a high pitch of nervosity—'anguish'—, this search for a transcendental reality, an 'absolute', end very differently. Dostoevsky plunges himself into a mystical blend of Orthodox Christianity and re-actionary Slavophilism, having developed his own conception of Nietzsche's 'God is dead', only to reject it as intolerable; Malraux, on the other side, has no Christian bias, and his ethical conclusions are entirely non-religious: man must affirm his own values, with no help from the divine. It is, then, only the premises which are shared: the lack of belief in progress, or in reason and science as providing a satisfactory explanation of mankind, the thirst for the absolute, and the conception of the novel as a spiritual adventure. Tchen's murder is a case in point: Raskolnikov plans a murder without any sense of sin or guilt, and the action of the novel after this initial act is largely a demonstration of their development within him, despite himself. In Tchen, on the other hand, there is no guilt, no necessity for atonement beyond perhaps the desire to confess to Gisors: from the act onwards he is isolated from other men. This is generally true in Malraux: we certainly find his themes dealt with in terms of pride and humiliation, but humiliation does not imply humility; the plane of his works is more heroic than that of the Russian, self-abasement is replaced by virile fraternity, and humiliation immediately contrasted with dignity. Katow, it is true, is a lay saint, but his attitude, although genuinely humble, remains one of quiet dignity, and there is nothing of the

[1] C. I. Glicksberg, *The Tragic Vision in Twentieth-Century Literature*, p. 138.

'divine idiot' in him. Again the exception is *Les Noyers*, but despite the retreat from heroism in this novel, it is the least Dostoevskyan of all Malraux's works.

Dostoevsky first gained a really appreciative audience in France just before the First World War; after the critical studies by Suarès, Gide, and others, it was very natural that Malraux should admire him. The parallel with Barrès, noted by many critics, is a little more complex, since by 1920 Barrès was already regarded as somewhat out of date, especially by the Dadaist–Surrealist group, on the fringe of whom Malraux moved. As an adventurer he had been eclipsed by others, notably by d'Annunzio whose career was then at its apogee; and as a pillar of established institutions he had little appeal to the rebellious young. But beyond the basic attitudes of the Surrealists stands the *culte du moi* just as much as Nietzsche's Superman; indeed, since Nietzsche was hardly known in France until the early 1890s, when the first translations began to appear, and when Barrès was already a national figure both as writer and as politician, the popular influence of the two men ran together in France in one stream.

The literary relationship between Barrès and Malraux is perhaps a parallel, rather than an influence, although Barrès may well have acted as an exemplary figure to the young man of 1920. Both shared an enormous ambition: not merely for literary or political success, but to become a *grand homme* on the national plane. To accomplish this much of Barrès's life was a deliberate, often self-conscious, pose, and Malraux has followed the pattern. From an initial attitude of revolt, against what was seen as contemporary decadence, mixed with a supreme self-confidence and even a certain arrogance in the process of self-launching, we can see in both a gradual transition, marked by what one might call grand opportunism, to the established national figure, man-of-letters-cum-politician. (Malraux's political career has, of course, been a good deal more successful than Barrès's; no doubt partly because de Gaulle is an incomparably more formidable figure than Boulanger.) Barrès took up Stendhal's *égotisme* and energy as the basis of the *culte du moi*, and it is this which Malraux primarily has in common with other writers influenced by Barrès, such as Drieu

La Rochelle and Montherlant; a French critic has noted the similarity between Malraux's formulation in *L'Espoir*, 'transformer en conscience l'expérience la plus large possible', and Barrès's 'sentir le plus possible en analysant le plus possible'.[1]

The parallel may be taken further. Barrès too, between the death of Boulanger and his anti-Dreyfus stand, flirted with Jaurès and socialism; while his final nationalism could no more be rationally justified than can Malraux's; indeed, the fundamental approach of both men is throughout anti-rationalist. Both share the traditional Romantic attraction to the exotic, inseparable from the erotic, and the equally Romantic fascination with death; while Barrès's acceptance of Christianity without real faith, as a 'force spirituelle', is a defiant affirmation of values comparable with Malraux's affirmation of the creative power of the artist. But there is a great difference in intensity between the two: Barrès's interest in art, his indulgence in the macabre, or his conception of sexual love as conquest and development of personal *gloire*—an attitude steeped in misogyny, with genuine shared love seen as humiliation—all are coloured by an ultimately enfeebling aestheticism. Barrès was never truly a participant: as Montherlant has put it succinctly, if maliciously, 'voyeur de la guerre, voyeur de la religion, voyeur de l'amour'.[2] Malraux has, in every field, attempted to turn the vision into a reality; despite the exaggerations of the legend, his life has been very much one of genuine action and participation.

Barrès, perhaps also d'Annunzio, even Péguy, and other figures such as Gobineau—and Georges Sorel, whose works contain both belief in violence as a positive virtue, and a conception of dignity to some extent resembling Malraux's own—are joined by another exemplary figure, still more important: T. E. Lawrence. I have suggested earlier that Malraux's journey to the East may well have been in emulation of Lawrence; but later Lawrence gained still more importance for Malraux, so that one may even speak of obsession. From the prototype of the adventurer he becomes the model of the writer: the adventurer who succeeds in turning the

[1] Quoted in J.-M. Domenach, *Barrès par lui-même*, p. 23.
[2] Ibid., p. 86.

account of his actions into one of the greatest epics of the age. Lawrence's aim in *The Seven Pillars of Wisdom* was to create a book which would stand up against the finest works of literature in the West: he himself named *Moby Dick*, *The Brothers Karamazov*, and *Thus Spake Zarathustra*. The relevance of the latter two to Malraux's own work needs no stressing, while *Moby Dick* is essentially an epic poem, a struggle by the hero against his destiny, pre-eminently the novel as an autonomous world. This literary influence of Lawrence can be perceived, as we have seen, in the title *Les Puissances du désert*. Again, Lawrence's attachment to the Hashemite cause is paralleled by Malraux's adherence to the Communists: the individual will seeking communion with an ideology. The spiritual quest of both men might be summed up in the phrase *le démon de l'absolu*: which was in fact the title of Malraux's proposed book on Lawrence. By then Malraux's development, in the spheres of both intellect and action, had surpassed Lawrence's, and we find him not so much identifying himself with Lawrence as assimilating Lawrence to himself. He makes Lawrence into a symbolic figure, a forerunner of his own vision of man's tragic fight against his fate and struggle for self-transcendence. The result is perhaps less a realistic reconstruction of Lawrence the man than an abstract figure rather like Valéry's M. Teste. Taking Lawrence at the crucial point in his life, after his resignation from the Colonial Service in 1922, before his plunge into the R.A.F., as he re-reads the proofs of *The Seven Pillars*, he sees his task as being to 'transformer une fois de plus en lucidité la confusion de ce qui avait été jusque là son destin'.[1] Describing Lawrence's need of a lyrical style, the necessity of rendering action as a dramatic present, framed by dialogue and atmosphere, Malraux is analysing his own life and works as much as Lawrence's. The latter's basic artistic urge is seen as the escape from the absurd, and his attitude one of 'la lucidité empoisonnée de l'athée de la vie'.[2] In thirsting for the absolute, Lawrence is seen as religious—'si l'on entend par esprit religieux celui qui ressent jusqu'au fond de l'âme l'angoisse d'être homme'—and at the same time deeply tragic: 'L'absolu est

[1] 'N'était-ce donc que cela?', p. 12.
[2] Ibid., p. 18.

la dernière instance de l'homme tragique, la seule efficace parce qu'elle seule peut brûler — fût-ce avec l'homme tout entier — le plus profond sentiment de dépendance, le remords d'être soi-même.'[1] To use Malraux's own term, his 'annexation' of Lawrence is complete.

The greatest individual influence on Malraux's life and work has been Nietzsche; from *La Tentation de l'Occident* onwards the idea of will pervades his writings, and, indeed, his whole life is a brilliant example of Nietzsche's ideal of 'giving style to one's character', and of heeding Nietzsche's call: 'Dare to lead the life of tragic man, and you will be redeemed.'[2] We learn from Clara Malraux that he was 'hanté par Nietzsche, bien entendu' even before they met,[3] although we do not know exactly how well he knew the German philosopher at that date. Perhaps a caveat about Malraux's use of ideas should be entered at this point. He has been widely taken by enthusiastic critics not only as an original philosopher, but also as a man of encyclopedic and exact knowledge in the field of history of ideas; and he has not disclaimed this.[4]

In fact it is unlikely that he has ever made a detailed study of any philosopher; without going as far as Gombrich, who in connexion with *Les Voix du silence* comments a little tartly that 'there is no evidence that Malraux has done a day's consecutive reading in a library or that he has even tried to hunt up a new fact',[5] it seems clear that Malraux's gift is for seizing on individual ideas and expressing them in dazzling formulae, rather than for systematic study and analysis. His life, moreover, quite apart from his temperament, could have left him little time before the Second World War at least for contemplation and reflection; while a certain contempt for professional scholars emerges from his works, above all *Les Noyers*. It is, indeed, exceptional for any novelist to be

[1] Ibid., p. 23.
[2] *Joyful Wisdom*, Ungar paperback edn., section 290; and *The Birth of Tragedy* p. 124.   [3] C. Malraux, *Apprendre à vivre*, p. 274.
[4] No man minds being thought a mighty brain, or a repository of wisdom and knowledge; and it seems possible that literary-minded critics have been impressed by Malraux's ideas in art and anthropology in inverse proportion to their own knowledge of these fields.
[5] E. H. Gombrich, op cit. p. 78.

influenced by careful study of ideas; usually intellectual influences pass by less direct means, through conversation, and simplifications or popularizations in newspapers or reviews. The novelist's concern is with the use of ideas, not the justification of them; within the context of the novel, philosophical themes are no more than artistic insights, and their truth is unverifiable. They are aesthetically on the same plane as insights into character, behaviour, setting, or anything else, and they are subject to the same criteria of plausibility. Or, to put it another way, a novel may illustrate a philosophy, but it can never demonstrate it.

Malraux is not a professional scholar. Although he uses ideas extensively, there is sometimes some doubt whether he really understands their full implications. We may instance his use of Frobenius in *Les Noyers*, where he is obviously struck by certain brilliant arguments and examples, but appears to know little about the anthropological background of Frobenius's work, in particular the disagreement between evolutionists and diffusionists. A clue to Malraux's contact with German ideas is given by his friendship, from the middle 1920s, with Bernard Groethuysen. Groethuysen, a historian of philosophy with Marxist leanings, considerably older than Malraux (he lived from 1880 to 1946), seems to have been a model for old Gisors; but, much more important, he acted as an interpreter of German thought to the younger Malraux. His own works included an *Introduction à la pensée philosophique allemande depuis Nietzsche* (1926), an important book on the *Origines de l'esprit bourgeois en France* (1927), and various writings on anthropology; he was also one of the earliest interpreters of Wilhelm Dilthey. There seems every reason to believe that a good deal of Malraux's knowledge of Frobenius and anthropology originated in conversations with Groethuysen; possibly his more detailed knowledge of Nietzsche owed something to the older man as well.[1]

Malraux's treatment of ideas can perhaps best be understood by

---

[1] Cf. also N. Chiaramonte, in R. W. B. Lewis (ed.), *Malraux*, p. 101. On the other hand, Malraux evidently first came into contact with Spengler and Keyserling when his wife Clara bought their works (in German) in Berlin in the early 1920s (*Nos vingt ans*, p. 53).

contrasting him with a writer whose direct influence on him was almost certainly very little: Thomas Mann. Yet there are numerous parallels. Both have a wide interest in culture and things of the intellect, and they share a rather cerebral attitude towards the novel, seen as a vehicle for cultural analysis. If the sanatorium at Davos is a microcosm of Europe in *The Magic Mountain*, revolutionary Shanghai is a microcosm of the whole modern world; while in *Doctor Faustus* Mann makes the figure of the artist and the mystery of his creative powers a central point of his preoccupations. Both make great use of such wide antitheses as Art/Life, East/West, Reason/Irrationalism, and characters often represent ideas: Settembrini symbolizes reason, Ferral power. Mann too was deeply influenced by Nietzsche, to whom he added Schopenhauer and Goethe as against Malraux's Dostoevsky and Stendhal. *Les Noyers*, as it stands, has to be judged as an intellectual *Bildungsroman*, and the basic antithesis around which it is constructed is not very far from Mann's Art versus Life. Mann too has been taken as 'vastly erudite' and as a 'profound and original philosopher', and an American critic has recently gone out of his way to refute this belief, concluding with the remark that 'Mann will stand or fall as a master of prose fiction, not as a philosopher, political scientist, or essayist'.[1] Mann, in fact, used all sorts of material in his novels, which are packed with ideas to the point of producing a slightly didactic tone offensive to some readers; but little of this material was original, and all of it was a means to an artistic end.[2] This is generally true of Malraux also; his gift is for what one can only call a poetic use of ideas, neat formulations, and transposition into images. One might even go so far as to say that he uses ideas more effectively in the novel form than in his essays. In the novel they are not so direct, and can be put into perspective, criticized, and modified by the use of dramatic dialogue. Malraux seems to have felt this in *La Tentation de l'Occident*—why else use the form of an

---

[1] H. Hatfield, in *Thomas Mann*, pp. 5–6. This is why attempts to extract a complete (Existentialist- or Phenomenological-type) metaphysic from Malraux's works, such as J. Delhomme, *Temps et destin*, interesting though they may be, are ultimately of small help in an appreciation of the novels.

[2] Cf. also Mann's remark to Arthur Koestler: 'If you know too much about a subject, it cramps you' (A. Koestler, *The Invisible Writing*, London, 1954, p. 372).

exchange of letters?—but in *Les Noyers* the ideas are communicated much more effectively still (it is a measure of Malraux's success that critics have often taken these same ideas to be entirely original). In addition ideas expressed in the novel form, since they are on the plane of art, not that of knowledge, need less defence against criticism, as ideas; used in novels, there are different levels of meaning to be drawn from them, while in essays something more unambiguous is demanded.

Malraux's use of Nietzsche, then, depends less on systematic analysis than on certain key insights, accepted intuitively rather than rationally, and affirmed rather than proved. An example is that the concept of Eternal Recurrence, for Nietzsche himself an essential factor in his philosophy, is largely ignored by Malraux, unless we can detect traces of it in his idea of the eternal metamorphoses of artistic forms. Yet this idea probably came to him through Spengler, together with the 'organic' theory of civilizations growing, decaying, and dying. Nor need this omission surprise us, as the Eternal Recurrence is certainly Nietzsche's most difficult conception. The most important element in Malraux is his firm belief in will as the single dynamic of all human motivation and action. This, as we have seen, links up immediately with the French tradition of energy, and again with Dostoevsky, who had greatly impressed Nietzsche: as Stieglitz says in *Les Noyers*, ' "il n'y a que Stendhal et Dostoievski qui m'aient enseigné quelque chose en psychologie", disait Nietzsche'.[1] Twentieth-century psychology, under the shadow of Freud, has had little time for the idea of will, which has tended to dissolve into no more than the surface expression of unconscious motivation; and, although Malraux pays lip-service to Freud, there is no real sympathy or understanding. How could there be, when the main implication of Freud's work was to destroy the omnipotence of will? In various remarks in *Les Noyers* Malraux even seems to reject Freudian psychology completely, as when Vincent contradicts his uncle,

[1] *Les Noyers*, p. 121. This appears in fact to be a misquotation of Nietzsche's remark in *Twilight of the Idols*, vol. 9, p. 45: 'Dostoievski, the only psychologist, incidentally, from whom I had something to learn; he ranks among the most beautiful strokes of fortune in my life, even more than my discovery of Stendhal' (*The Portable Nietzsche*, New York, 1954, p. 549).

claiming that man is not what he hides but what he does, or as when Thirard says that introspection only reveals the nature of introspective man, not of man generally. The idea of will as the primary psychological dynamic is never fully explained; it remains an intuitive affirmation. Indeed, all Malraux's characters rely on intuition for the values—possibly different, or even contradictory—which they affirm; all they really do is 'think with their blood'. This is evident for Perken, Hong, or Tchen; but even those who appear at first more rational, such as Kyo or Vincent Berger, are ultimately in the same intuitionist position.

The other main idea of Nietzsche's, without which the belief in will would lose much of its strength, is the 'postulatory atheism'[1] of the affirmation that 'God is dead'. Here again, of course, a denial of God had been nothing new even in the eighteenth century, but earlier atheists had tended either to worship some abstraction like reason itself, or to preserve Christian values while abandoning religious dogma. Nietzsche places the emphasis on man himself, who can create his own values without reliance on any external authority whatsoever. Self-affirmation and full realization of all one's potentialities form the Pindaric motto: 'Become the man you are!' This cry lies at the base of Malraux's entire life, as well as being the essence of his characters and the central feature, as we have seen, of his art philosophy. But a distinction immediately follows from it, as Nietzsche saw: between the outstanding individual, who has achieved his true self, and the mass of men, in whom 'the intellectual conscience is lacking'.[2] This distinction is quite openly described as that between noble and ignoble, and its influence on Existentialist thought, as well as on Malraux, with the distinction between authenticity and *mauvaise foi*, or *être-pour-soi* and *être-en-soi*, is apparent.[3] Immediate consequences, apart from a ferocious egoism, since other

[1] Cf. A. Espiau de la Maëstre's interesting article, 'André Malraux und der "postulatorische Atheismus"', *Stimmen der Zeit*, clxvii (1960), pp. 180–9. (The term 'postulatory atheism' actually was first used by Max Scheler in 1928.)

[2] *Joyful Wisdom*, section 2 (p. 35).

[3] Ibid., section 3 (p. 37). Cf. W. Kaufmann, *Nietzsche*, p. 135: 'Man's task [for Nietzsche] is simple: he should cease letting his "existence" be "a thoughtless accident".'

men become merely means to an end, or even obstacles, are contempt for conformity and mediocrity. Prometheus is the symbol
of the superior man, and heroism the expression. Pleasure and
happiness are rejected as adequate human goals; instead an ascetic,
belief in self-sacrifice is substituted. For Nietzsche the highest
affirmation of the will to power is seen in the ability to dominate
oneself and one's own emotions, as well as one's bodily needs;
perhaps this is best illustrated in Malraux by the exemplary death
of Katow, a consummation of his entire existence of self-sacrifice.[1]
A lower form of will to power is seen in Ferral; as we have seen,
he is an Adlerian figure—Adler's indebtedness to Nietzsche is
clear, though he too tried to reconcile belief in the power instinct
with socialist politics—but, incapable of self-sacrifice, Ferral ends
in a situation of utter frustration.

   Nietzsche's influence on Malraux is at its most evident, as we
have seen, in *La Tentation de l'Occident* and the art philosophy, yet
it pervades nearly all his works. And, while it is obviously ridiculous to hold Nietzsche responsible for the excesses of the Nazis, it
remains true that he has always been anathema to genuine liberals
—a further reason why the pre-war Malraux cannot be assimilated to a liberal, but only to an authoritarian, Left. We may even
see a Nietzschean influence in Malraux's style, which certainly
shares with the German certain features, both desirable and otherwise: sharp aphoristic formulations bordering on the poetic (it is
arguable that *Zarathustra* can best be accepted as poetry), a lyrical
rhetoric, often impressive, but at times weakening into inflation,
strident repetitiousness, and cloudy confusion. One might even,
indeed, trace back Malraux's taste for violence to Nietzsche, whose
aggressiveness, denied by favourable critics, is at least a key feature
of the popular view of him; struggle seems cardinal to the basic
attitudes of both. Also the sense of tragedy—Malraux's work puts
fully into practice Nietzsche's dictum, 'The hero of the future will
be a man of tragic awareness'. For both philosophers tragedy
means attitude to life; impatient with rationalism and logic, they
eagerly replace truth by myth, and are fundamentally anti-

   [1] Yet an ethic of self-sacrifice, it may be commented, is much nearer the
Christian ideal than Malraux—or Nietzsche—supposed.

scientific. Both also display a certain negativity: Zarathustra speaks mostly of what he is against, like Garine and Malraux's revolutionaries, and the Superman is determined by his contempt for mediocrity very much more than by definite positive qualities.

Ultimately Malraux's adherence to Nietzschean attitudes may prove to have been a mixed blessing. The German's ideas have in the past proved more dazzling to the young than seductive to the mature, and it is possible that Malraux, while owing much of the intellectual and metaphysical weight of his earlier novels to him, has remained too close to Nietzsche to progress artistically much beyond the attitudes of his twenties and thirties. Whereas Stendhal and Dostoevsky primarily inspired Malraux to create novels, Nietzsche's influence seems to have made him want to cast himself in the role of sage, seer, and philosopher, without his having the full equipment—or originality—to succeed in it. In my own view, at least, Malraux's best work is in his novels, and when ideas have become ends in themselves, rather than creative material like any other, the final impact of Malraux's work is weaker.

Nietzsche's influence on Malraux has been reinforced by several other German thinkers. There is first the figure of Hegel, who is mentioned directly on occasion, and who, as we have seen, lies beneath Malraux's 'dynamic' theory of artistic development, as well as his equation of culture with plastic art. But this influence comes really via Nietzsche, perhaps also through Spengler: there is no evidence that Malraux has studied Hegel in any detail, and no overt use of the dialectical method (in contrast with Sartre, whose concepts of *totalisation* and *détotalisation*, in *La Critique*, are openly dialectical). Nor does Malraux make open use of the idea of historical inevitability: even in its Marxist form this conception clashes strongly with belief in individual will, and although at times the idea of 'destiny' seems to imply some degree of inevitability, Malraux's use of it is metaphorical, following Spengler rather than Hegel. In *Les Noyers* the manuscript which Möllberg destroys, *Civilisation comme destin et conquête*, is fairly obviously a Hegelian synthesis, but Malraux is much more interested in Möllberg's rejection of his earlier ideas than in the

ideas themselves, and in the Spenglerian belief in the absolute
hermeticism of different cultures. Hegel has had his influence on
Malraux's intellectual development, but it has been chiefly at
second hand.

Many of the ideas used in *Les Noyers* were, as indicated above,
taken from the works of Leo Frobenius. On the other hand,
Möllberg's final position is that of Spengler, even if the evidence
he uses to justify it is borrowed from Frobenius. And, taking the
art philosophy, there is little in it of Frobenius, but a great deal of
Nietzsche and Spengler. The conclusion must be that Frobenius
provided Malraux with material rather than major premisses, and
his influence is correspondingly small. Hermann, Count Keyserling, should also be mentioned here, especially as Malraux reviewed
very favourably his *Travel Diary of a Philosopher* in the *N.R.F.* in
1929, declaring that he preferred it to all Keyserling's other books
(which, by implication, he must have read, or at least known).[1]
Keyserling, indeed, shares certain features with Malraux: the belief in development of personal ego by means of will, intuition as
the chief means of cognition, the equation of philosophy with
Weltanschauung, and the indulgence in broad generalizations and
antitheses about East and West, love and sex, religion, history, and
culture. On the other hand, Keyserling is essentially anti-action,
and here Malraux is at the opposite pole; and Malraux entirely
lacks the other man's snobbery, if not altogether his assertive
complacency.

It is, however, in Spengler that we find, after Nietzsche, the
closest parallel with Malraux, both in thought and in temperament. The whole intuitive concept of destiny, and of the temporal
contingency which engenders Malraux's 'cosmic' images, can be
found in Spengler's work. The influence grows stronger in
Malraux's novels through the 1930s and, after providing the
essence of the intellectual position of the Altenburg colloquy,
underlies much of the art philosophy. Many of the Spenglerian
concepts which Malraux uses do, indeed, go back to Nietzsche:
the conception of the organic growth and decay of mutually incomprehensible civilizations, which forms the basis of Möllberg's

[1] *N.R.F.*, June 1929, p. 886.

final beliefs, as we have just seen, is a case in point. Spengler's method, intuitive and assertive, foreshadowed Malraux's own; and it brought similar attacks from professional scholars.[1] His belief that thought proceeds through flashes of perceptive insight allows Spengler to treat history not merely as a succession of events, but also as an endless source of symbols. Rejecting logical and causal analysis, he is enabled to posit a destiny which must be understood for his work to be understood, without providing a comprehensible definition of it: 'Destiny is an *Idea*, an idea that is incapable of being "cognized", described or defined, and can only be felt and inwardly lived.'[2] Malraux's use of the concept of destiny depends on exactly the same intuitive grasp of 'inner meaning'.

There are many other points in common. Spengler's 'Faustian' vision of modern European culture, with its constant restlessness and dynamic striving, closely resembles Malraux's view of incessantly developing artistic creation; and, as we have seen, Malraux adopts Spengler's definition of 'culture' and 'civilization' with the consequent deprecation of the latter. (Malraux's dislike of Roman art is also in tune with this last distinction, and follows Spengler's opinion.) The 'homme fondamental', the eternal and unchanging peasant whom both Vincent Berger and his son discover in the experience of war, seems very likely to be derived from Spengler's 'ahistoric peasant', as Germaine Brée has pointed out,[3] while Spengler's differentiation between these peasants and the privileged group of 'creators', who experience 'destiny' and generate the organic cycle of culture—the Nietzschean 'aristocratic' conception—is also paralleled in Malraux. Malraux's concept of the 'sacré'—the religious spirit which bears down remorselessly, in his view, on the whole Orient, can perhaps be traced to Spengler's Magian culture of the Near East. Again, Nietzsche's

[1] We may contrast Malraux remarking about the close of the Second World War that the most important intellectual task facing Europe was the refutation of Spengler, with Sir Karl Popper, writing about the same time, who dismisses Spengler's work in a footnote as not to be taken seriously. Cf. Frohock, op. cit., p. 151; and K. R. Popper, *The Open Society and its Enemies*, vol. I, p. 231.
[2] O. Spengler, *The Decline of the West*, vol. I, p. 121.
[3] G. Brée, *Camus*, 1961, p. 77.

contempt for the humane, and his belief in violent action, is adopted by Spengler, with the 'tragic' view of life; though the older man's optimism is nowhere recaptured, and Spengler accepts Burckhardt's fundamental pessimism about material progress and moral development alike. Imagination, for both Malraux and Spengler, implies anti-intellectualism: Spengler, despite greater scientific knowledge than Malraux, is not fundamentally any more in sympathy with scientific endeavour; and neither has much interest in sociology, preferring the more colourful and dramatic material to be found in ethnological results. Spengler, then, may be added to Nietzsche as a secondary philosophical influence; himself deeply influenced by the older man, he was an obvious figure to attract Malraux, already under Nietzsche's spell, and *The Decline of the West* can only have powerfully reinforced, and refined, Malraux's existing convictions.

The twentieth-century writer who comes closest to Malraux is, as has frequently been remarked, Saint-Exupéry, his almost exact contemporary. Above all, in combining a literary career with a life of action,[1] though here there is a distinction. Saint-Exupéry was a professional man of action, sticking firmly to his chosen *métier* of aviator, despite all opposition, while Malraux has acted in a large number of different fields, always remaining basically an amateur: no doubt a 'génial amateur' as his first wife has called him,[2] but nevertheless an amateur. But their work has many features in common. Primarily their belief in absolute spiritual rather than material values, in the affirmation of man's grandeur and dignity, to be achieved through action and heroism, and the refusal of weakness: the whole amounting to what André Maurois has called 'héroïsme mystique'.[3] Something of the same kind is to be

[1] An interesting remark in Malraux's discussion with James Burnham casts light on this double aim. 'The idea of an incompatibility between the life of art and the life of action seems to be comparatively recent. After all, Sophocles, Dante, Bacon and Cervantes were men of action, and three of them were soldiers. Henry James and Flaubert do not represent the eternal prototype of the artist' ('The Double Crisis: a Dialogue', *Partisan Review*, Apr. 1948, p. 437).

[2] C. Malraux, *Apprendre à vivre*, p. 274. If anything, publishing has been Malraux's major occupation, from the early days about 1920 with Doyon and Kra, until his resumption of ministerial office in 1958.

[3] A. Maurois, *De Proust à Camus*, p. 230.

found in Conrad, whose characters also tend to seek out extreme situations. This goes together with a certain contempt for the sedentary existence of the bourgeois and the *ronds-de-cuir*. In Saint-Exupéry's group of aviators, dedicated to the almost abstract task of delivering the mails, we recognize something akin to Malraux's virile fraternity; and both men tend to relegate women to the background of their works. *Pilote de guerre* is an *œuvre engagée* as much as *L'Espoir*, if much more directly autobiographical. Saint-Exupéry shows, indeed, no great ability to create plot or character outside his own immediate experience, and perhaps the greatest quality of his work lies in the almost poetic transposition of his own experiences against an exotic background. This too he shares with Malraux, although Malraux's imagery and vision are usually both more distinctive and more powerful. It is curious too that both men should ultimately have turned away from the novel to write a deliberately poetico-philosophical work. Critics have, however, generally felt that Saint-Exupéry's ideas, as expressed in *La Citadelle* and the *Carnets*, without the concrete basis and imagery of aviation, were unsatisfactory: energy and will, even if devoted to ends which can be compared to Malraux's *anti-destins*, are morally neutral qualities in themselves, and when put at the disposal of the absolute ruler in *La Citadelle* immediately seem anti-human, almost Fascist. The same criticism might be applied, as we have indicated, in lesser degree to Malraux.

However, it would be wrong to do much more than to draw a parallel, although it seems likely that in the flying scenes in *Le Temps du mépris* and *L'Espoir* Malraux was deliberately invading Saint-Exupéry's territory; while the emphasis on discipline seems to owe something to *Vol de nuit* in particular. Above all, violence is not as essential to Saint-Exupéry's concept of heroism as it is to Malraux's, while the former's humanism is also more traditional, embodying greater respect for human personality. With his career cut short in the war, it is impossible to say how he would have developed had he survived, although there is a suspicion that he had almost written himself out; at any rate, from the works we have, Saint-Exupéry's certainly appears the narrower talent of the two, not perhaps because of any inferiority in ideas, but because

Malraux's expressive abilities are greater. This comparison again reinforces the point that the essence of Malraux's talent lies less in his thought than in the poetic effectiveness of its embodiment in fiction.

Despite the close affinities with Saint-Exupéry, the French writer of the present century with whom Malraux can most fruitfully be compared is, perhaps, Sartre. Both have been vastly successful as writers, in different ways, though both have striven to be much more than writers. Since 1945 there has been hostility, amounting almost to a feud, between the two, which does neither of them particular credit. Political differences have at the same time accentuated personal jealousies, with a distinct note of sour grapes on Sartre's part, since Malraux has clearly been much more successful in his political career.[1] But in fact the parallel between the two writers is very close, despite disclaimers from Sartre; whether he has developed many of his ideas from Malraux or from elsewhere, the final results have much in common.

Sartre, though only four years younger than Malraux, belongs to a different literary generation altogether, because of his late start; above all, he developed late in political consciousness, and only transformed a vague but powerful hostility towards the bourgeoisie into sympathy with Marxism during the Second World War—ironically, at the same time when Malraux was finally abandoning all Communist sympathies. Sartre's preoccupation with a political stance in the post-1945 era, persisting long after he has lost any chance of playing a useful role, almost certainly has its origin in his unwillingness to be *engagé* politically before the war. The emotional guilt aroused by this failure to act, much more than rational conviction, seems the dynamic of his post-war career. His present intellectual task in the *Critique de la*

---

[1] Cf. Simone de Beauvoir, *La Force des choses*, p. 492. Malraux, after refusing to collaborate in *Les Temps modernes*, apparently managed to have the review turned out of its premises at Gallimard's; after gaining power in 1958, visiting Brazil as Minister of Culture, he deliberately attacked Sartre's works in a speech—an outrageous act according to Simone de Beauvoir: 'un ministre de la Culture insultant à l'étranger un écrivain de son pays, ça ne s'était encore jamais vu'. On the other side, Malraux was cruelly lampooned in Sartre's political satire, *Nekrassov* (1955; published 1956).

raison dialectique, his attempt to reconcile Existentialism—the philosophy *par excellence* of individual responsibility, choice, and decision—with Marxist historical inevitability, was very much Malraux's difficulty in the 1920s and 1930s and possibly explains why neither took commitment to the point of party membership; although Malraux never attempted a systematic synthesis, it is, as we have seen, the tension between the two attitudes that forms the strength of his 'revolutionary' novels.

Sartre, in the 1930s, specifically denied the will to power, and attacked the idea of the adventurer as 'un deterministe inconséquent qui se supposerait libre'.[1] Later, in *La Nausée*, he took a deliberate sideswipe at the Malraux-type hero by making Roquentin a former archaeologist and adventurer in Indo-China and the East, who had come to see the futility of his life there.[2] But *La Voie royale* is Malraux's only novel where adventure is not linked with political action, and Sartre's own later development takes him from the apolitical contemplation of Roquentin who finds, Proust-like, salvation in art by writing a novel, towards the very commitment, and therefore belief in action, which was Malraux's position throughout the 1930s. In *Les Mains sales* the bourgeois Communist, Hugo, has much in common with Garine and Kyo—and for that matter with Jacques Thibault. Sartre seems to draw on Malraux's novels a great deal in this play and also in *Morts sans sépulture*, but without achieving the 'plausibility of events' which marks Malraux's work. This, I believe, is a consequence of the 'open' nature of drama of situation; there is a much greater sense of realism in the *nouvelle*, *Le Mur*, which likewise owes something to *L'Espoir*, than in Sartre's drama.

In both writers we find certain fundamental attitudes, predispositions[3] which perhaps antedated any developed philosophy

---

[1] S. de Beauvoir, *Mémoires d'une jeune fille rangée*, p. 342.

[2] Cf. J. Weightman, in his excellent essay on Sartre, in J. Cruickshank (ed.), *The Novelist as Philosopher*, p. 116; and G. D. Watson, 'Roquentin in Indo-China', *AUMLA.*, no. 22 (Nov. 1964), pp. 277–81.

[3] Cf. Professor W. T. Jones, who, in *The Romantic Syndrome*, The Hague, 1961, develops the idea of pre-rational 'temperamental biases' in every personality (p. 15). This may provide another reason why attempts to furnish a formal exposition of Malraux's ideas are of doubtful validity: they tend to embody

such as, in Sartre's case, his contact with Husserl's phenomenology and Heidegger, and in Malraux's, even his conscious use of Nietzsche. Sartre's Existentialism is basically subjective affirmation of the elements and values of individual experience; the same definition can be applied to Malraux. Both accept the world as *given*, not needing proof, and as *other*: there is a constant dichotomy between the self and the world, on which the self proves its individuality by acting. The self, for Sartre no less than for Malraux, has to be defined in terms of will; both refuse, together with transcendental religious belief, any idea of psychological determinism, and above all the Freudian theory of the unconscious, since this would sap their primary value of individual choice and responsibility. This rejection of determinism is one of the fundamental tenets of any kind of Existentialist philosophy; it can also be found, though in philosophically—if not literarily—rather trivial form, in Gide's *acte gratuit*. It is symptomatic in Malraux and Sartre of a rather impatient attitude towards the whole of natural science,[1] going together with an epistemology which, like Nietzsche's, is pure intuitive affirmation.[2] Truth itself is thus made subordinate to will. There is no need to assume that Malraux had any detailed acquaintance with the work of Heidegger, much less of Husserl—though he may well have known of them, perhaps through Groethuysen—, since, as we have seen, his position can be derived from Nietzsche alone. So might Sartre's, though he took many of his ideas through other German intermediaries, above all his liking for dialectical method and elaborate terminology.

Belief in will implies a strongly Cartesian separation of mind and body, evident in both writers (and again in Nietzsche). This, we have seen, is taken in Malraux to the point where even Claude Vannec's or Perken's body is seen as part of the *other*, to be struggled

rationalization of emotional attitudes, rather than present genuine exposition of rational thought.

[1] C. P. Snow's 'two cultures' are perhaps even more evident in France than in Britain and America.

[2] Cf. K. R. Popper, *Conjectures and Refutations*, p. 194. His epistemological strictures on Heidegger apply equally to Sartre and Malraux; and, indeed, belief in intuitive knowledge is perhaps the chief common fact among Existentialist-type philosophies.

against; and in Sartre almost to the point where illness is merely a failure of will.[1] Emotional and sexual relationships become, on this view, a source of weakness: hence eroticism—sex through the mind, at the service of will, rather than through the body—is the chief sexual relationship we find in Malraux, and in the later novels there are hardly any sexual relationships at all. In Sartre's work there is a distinct note of asceticism and disgust with the flesh, and even dislike of woman as a corrupting influence; the parallel with Nietzsche may once more be noted.

Belief in will also leads necessarily to 'aristocratic' values: a separation of the finer individual, who makes full use of his powers of volition, from the general run of men. For will is not a passive quality, but a dynamic force compelling the individual to action and choice. Like the Cornelian hero, or Perken or Claude Vannec, the man who is *pour-soi* has at all times to reaffirm his will; and this can only be achieved by attacking and conquering obstacles. Since all that is not will is the *other*, these obstacles include other men; and the result is a world of strife and violence. Will therefore makes action the basis of personality, and in his insistence that a man (Garcin in *Huis clos*) is only what he has done, and not what he would like to be, or thinks he is, Sartre is in an almost identical position to that of Malraux's formula that man is the sum of his acts. This attitude is fundamental in Sartre: writing about 1930, Simone de Beauvoir comments: 'Nous mesurions la valeur d'un homme d'après ce qu'il accomplissait: ses actes et ses œuvres.'[2] For Sartre man begins with his existence and has freedom to choose his own essence, and only by choosing does he take on any significance, or 'authenticity': this again is merely Nietzsche's concept of 'giving style to one's life'. But what about the man who does not make 'authentic' choices, and who fails to meet the Sartrian pattern? His responsibility, since both religious and psychological determinism have been rejected, is still complete, and he is therefore in a state of *mauvaise foi*. So humanity is divided into sheep and goats: or outstanding individuals and the common herd.

[1] In *La Force de l'âge* we find him declaring to Simone de Beauvoir that 'si l'on cédait aux larmes, aux crises de nerfs, au mal de mer, c'est qu'on y mettait de la complaisance' (pp. 134–5).   [2] Ibid., p. 48.

And Sartre, trying to escape this difficulty by commitment to Marxism, has the same problem as Malraux creating his *fraternité virile*, which never really rises beyond the level of a passionate ideal. Manuel's development to leadership in *L'Espoir* is marked by a steady decrease of comradeship, and an ever-increasing necessity to use his fellow fighters as instruments rather than as ends in themselves.

This is not the place to launch into a thorough critique of Sartre's philosophy; yet it is difficult not to regard his attempt to build up an entire metaphysic on what is ultimately no more than a subjective affirmation of will as somewhat naïve (despite considerable subtlety in execution) and doomed to inadequacy from the start. Sartre's speculations, indeed, are in many ways metaphysical intrusions into the field of psychology; he presupposes certain psychological facts, such as the existence of human freedom and will, without any attempt at proving their existence. Complete freedom of choice, it might be argued, is in any case a logical impossibility; given an infinite number of things to choose from, choice is impossible, since the process of examination and evaluation would equally be infinite, and therefore never-ending, while if the number is finite restraint has been imposed from outside and the freedom is no longer complete. The very notion of choice thus implies limitation. Quite apart from this, freedom from all restraint is psychologically an intolerable situation;[1] if all habit is to be banned from our behaviour, which is to be entirely based on willed choice, it is not surprising that we will find ourselves in a state of permanent nervous tension, which we may choose to call *angoisse*. And, since our feelings of guilt are immeasurably increased by the sins of omission or of merely passive activity which comprise *mauvaise foi*, the nervous tension mounts still more. Sartre's Existentialism is, in fact, an intellectual construct, based on untenable premisses, and is riddled with confusion between the psychological and the metaphysical. Above all, he tends to universalize individual feelings, and forget the subjective, descriptive

[1] Cf. Gombrich, op. cit., p. 144, who makes the same point about the contemporary artist, who has so great a choice of styles available to choose from that he may not know where to begin.

origin of his idea. For example, Sartre sees viscosity as universally nauseating yet fascinating. Yet surely this is no more than a purely personal feeling, contingent on the individual; I myself find most viscous substances (and is there any such thing as viscosity apart from individual viscous materials?) somewhat repellent to the touch, though not to the eye, nor necessarily to the nose (indeed, often the contrary). Equally repellent I find the scratch of a fingernail on cloth, or for that matter certain music; but this is an entirely personal reaction, probably physiological rather than psychological, and with no necessary connexion with any metaphysical concept-system whatsoever. Similarly Malraux's obsession with humiliation seems to originate in personal psychological experience, morbid in nature.

Sartre's philosophy is, then, largely descriptive; which is why it lends itself to presentation in fictional form. But a single example is only convincing in itself, and universal generalization is a different matter. Thus, in *La Nausée*, Roquentin's feeling of nausea, gradually paralysing his whole life, is perfectly convincing—as a psychological feeling. Roquentin, having cut himself off so much from all social life and activity, is paying the penalty of his egoism and isolation by what may perhaps be taken as the first symptoms of insanity. Or again, Roquentin's hostile attitude to the bourgeoisie of Bouville is vigorously portrayed.[1] But as universal metaphysical attitudes these feelings have no necessary validity at all; and the critical reader may, if he wishes, reverse Sartre's process of universalizing individual feelings, and instead see in his entire philosophy little more than psychological predispositions—or even prejudices, such as hate of the bourgeois *salaud*—blown up into pseudo-metaphysical form. Sartre, in fact, constantly exhibits one of the weakest features of the Cartesian tradition: the unwillingness to temper ratiocination with empirical checks; and adds to it the worst fault of German idealism: the tendency to create concepts, even jargon, and assume, with insouciant metaphysical realism, their meaningfulness and reality.

The importance of a view of personality based on a strict

[1] Much of the value of *La Nausée* is, indeed, in its satirical side; it can be read as a successful comic novel just as well as a metaphysical one.

separation between the self, seen as an active will, and the entire objective world is not so much, in Malraux's case, that it vitiates his philosophy. For he has no explicit philosophy, except of art; attempts to make a general system out of the various ideas presented in his novels have been the work of his critics, rather than himself. The separation, indeed, can immediately be dramatized into 'Man versus the Cosmos', and therefore provides a useful base for the construction of highly dramatic fiction. But at the same time this dichotomy implies an over-rigid psychological framework, and lays both Malraux and Sartre open to the charge that their characterization is weak. Malraux has, it is true, specifically attempted to rebut this charge with references to Dostoevsky and the claim that 'Le roman moderne est, à mes yeux, un moyen d'expression privilégié du tragique de l'homme, non une élucidation de l'individu'.[1] But this is judging in his own cause; and in any case depends on a unified view of man, presuming that the tragic elements of all men's lives are identical—another example of the same over-rigid classification which led to the original criticism. For Malraux's antithesis is false: the truth is surely that even though the metaphysical conditions of human existence are the same for all men—time, solitude, and death—the ways these affect men are different in almost every case, and blend together with the material aspects of individual existence to form the full texture of life. To take the example of Mann again, both *Buddenbrooks* and *The Magic Mountain* are built around the themes of time and death, but at the same time contain portraits of individual human beings far richer than Malraux's.[2] The latter's strength, on the other hand, is his febrile intensity, born of his vision of life as constant tension and struggle; his weakness is the lack of detachment which is the other side of the same coin.

Both Malraux and Sartre lack tolerance in their characterization:

[1] Marginal comment in Picon, op. cit., p. 66.

[2] One might add that in *Doctor Faustus* Mann comes close to achieving the elusive goal of so many novelists: the really convincing portrait of the great artist. Yet Malraux, in his works on art, shows at least as many effective insights into the psychology of artistic creation as Mann; we may well regret that he did not embody them in the novel form, where their *individual* validity would have been unchallengeable.

a certain charity towards human failings evident in novelists such
as Tolstoy, Martin du Gard, or Mann again. Nor is this surprising,
since the belief in the outstanding individual automatically implies
his superiority over the common run of men.[1] Nietzsche made
short work of the Christian idea of compassion, and he is followed
in this by the two Frenchmen (in their writings at least). All ultimately believe that what matters in life is the spiritual dimension,
not the material one, much less happiness. Their values are those of
an *élite*, based on greatness of spirit. Against this one might object
that an attitude of supreme unconcern for the interests of the
majority of men is not likely to make for a good understanding of
them. In Malraux's characters, in fact, as in his own legend, we
find affirmation of an ideal, rather than observation of reality: an
ideal of dominant and egoistic masculinity, excluding all weakness. Above all, Malraux—like Sartre—is weak in portraying
women.[2] In all his novels the only women characters treated in
any detail are May and Valérie in *La Condition humaine*, and there
is something rather masculine about both of these. The attempt at
reconciling Kassner's love for his wife with his political activity is
not fully convincing, and there are virtually no women at all in
L'Espoir and *Les Noyers*; nor do the male characters seem even to
have wives. It is difficult to doubt that this situation is brought
about by a deep-lying misogyny, parallel to that implicit in the
Nietzschean position, in which the superior individual is the one
who controls his passions, and women and love are excluded from
the highest human relationships. It is true that in the early novels,
as well as in *La Tentation de l'Occident*, the preface to the French
translation of *Lady Chatterley's Lover*, and the essay on Laclos,
Malraux has a good deal that is valuable to say on certain aspects of
sexuality, particularly the erotic, or the sexual satisfaction of the
will without emotional involvement with the partner. But these
analyses are narrow (and both less original and less important than
critics such as Claude Mauriac have maintained). Sex, in the

[1] Cf. François Mauriac's comment, in 1937 already: 'Le point faible de
Malraux, c'est son mépris de l'homme' (*Journal*, vol. 2, p. 221).
[2] Mme Magny, who has the right to speak on behalf of her sex, has complained
that Malraux treats them as 'a foreign and incomprehensible race' (in R. W. B.
Lewis (ed.), *Malraux*, p. 132).

widest sense, is a fairly minor element in Malraux's novels; it is
never really a theme at all, but only occurs even in the earlier
books as an illustration of his major metaphysical preoccupations.

A similar criticism may be made about all Malraux's characterization. He almost always confines himself to dramatizing the
reactions of a certain limited type of man—based on his Nietzschean premises—to a certain number of crisis situations; and that
is all. Admittedly crisis situations are unavoidable in the revolutionary novels, but it is perhaps paradoxical that characters whose
ideal is complete freedom should all be so similar, all so highly
self-aware, and classifiable into types, such as the terrorist, the
raisonneur, or the 'organization man'. The reason is, though, that
they are all tied to Malraux's own preoccupations, and their
actions are, in reality, not free at all but rigorously determined.
The ideal of freedom is once more, in practice, self-refuting.
Another criticism which could be raised is that the characters are
not only intellectually conceived, but far from representative, and
therefore fall well short of any degree of universality. Clappique
(and Frantz von Gerlach) are pathological cases in every sense.
Certain relationships receive interesting treatment, especially the
relationship of an older man with a younger one under his aegis,
called by Frohock the 'Neophyte/Initiate relationship'.[1] Thus we
have Perken and Claude, Rebecci and Hong, Garine and the
narrator of *Les Conquérants*, Gisors and several characters in *La
Condition humaine*, Ximénès and Manuel, and even Vincent Berger
and his son. This particular type of relationship is clearly important to Malraux, possibly springing from his own experiences, and
it certainly, like the ideal of virile fraternity, attracts more attention than sexual relationships. Again, he is skilled at the 'thumb-
nail sketch', or brief vignette presenting the minor character who
shows no development: Rebecci again, Hemmelrich, Vologuine,
old Alvear, Leclerc, or the participants in the Altenburg discussions. But in fact, as we have seen, both *L'Espoir* and *Les
Noyers* are very thin in characters who are at all fully developed.
The same criticism has frequently been brought up against Sartre;
and, although there is a considerable body of opinion which

[1] Frohock, op. cit., p. 143.

currently holds that psychological fullness—the traditional gallery of well-drawn characters—is out of place in the twentieth-century post-bourgeois novel, this is not a view which I find myself able to share. Malraux has elsewhere described the present-day trend of the novel as an 'interrogation du destin';[1] but in the fullest sense this has been true of most literature at all times, and the overtly metaphysical interests of Sartre or Malraux could equally well be taken as a comparative failure in clothing ideas with the texture of fiction, an excessive tendency to create abstractions. Tolstoy and Mann again stand as points of comparison.

Another consequence of the philosophy of will is that both Sartre and Malraux tend to a prescriptive, rather than descriptive, view of man: they hold up an ideal, rather than observe reality. (In *Les Chemins de la liberté* by the negative method of presenting unsatisfactory responses to situations. Again, this generalization is less true of *Les Noyers* than of Malraux's earlier novels.) Authenticity, or readiness for action, tends to be equated with virtue, and there is thus an element of moral exhortation in their works. Their intense subjectivism does in fact lead them to create recognizably independent worlds; Malraux's is far more striking because of the unmistakable dramatic quality of his writing, whereas Sartre writes in a flat, even drab, style which perhaps tends to obscure the individuality of his novels. But the creation of an autonomous world is not necessarily enough, since its ultimate success will depend on how far readers can participate in it. Violence is an integral element of Malraux's world: connected with his belief in will and action, which automatically lead to struggle. Indeed, it is difficult to see how he could, with his predispositions, treat a passive, static theme; and this may have some bearing on his abandoning of the novel after *Les Noyers*. It is arguable that public violence has been inescapable in the present century, and even, going further, that the apparently peaceful state of Europe in the nineteenth century was simply the result of warlike energies being expended in imperialist and colonial adventures in other continents. Yet violence has never been a major factor in the main

[1] Preface to M. Sperber, *Qu'une larme dans l'océan*, French trans., Paris, 1952, p. xx.

tradition of the European novel, which has been psychological and social; and in Malraux's own case, as we have seen, there is an obsession with violence even in the early 'Surrealist' works, long before he had any but vicarious experience of wars and revolutions. In his use of violence as a principal theme he is not a Realist so much as an Expressionist, writing about his own personal obsessions.[1] At the same time his works are undoubtedly more effective when he has a realistic setting: the China novels are more convincing than *La Voie royale* (even though personal observation may have been small); and *Le Temps du mépris*, where Malraux has to rely on imagination, is much less assured than *L'Espoir*, where a fair amount of the material was directly observed. This points to a weakness in his theory of the creation of the 'monde cohérent et particulier', which is for him the aim of every artist. When he continues, 'faire concurrence à la réalité qui lui est imposée, celle de "la vie"',[2] one might reply that dependence on reality must always destroy any hope of successful rivalry. *L'Espoir* could not have been written without the Spanish Civil War; but the war could—and did—take its course without heeding Malraux's novel, since its final outcome belied his optimism.

Altogether, then, Malraux and Sartre show unmistakable affinities in their work; and we may surmise that their fundamental emotional attitudes are very close. Sartre's ideal of freedom depends, just as much as Malraux's ideal of action, on will, and neither has any ultimate rational justification. The same is true of their entire ethic: authenticity is not enough to provide a standard of moral judgement, and Sartre's hate of the bourgeois, comparable to Malraux's earlier attitude (in the last twenty years greatly muted) is, as Dr. Weightman has pointed out, perhaps no more than emotional release, purely negative.[3] Nor is *engagement* any

---

[1] The Surrealist fascination with violence has often been noted. Dali and Buñuel are perhaps the best-known examples of this.

[2] Marginal comment in Picon, op. cit., p. 38; cf. p. 205, above.

[3] Weightman, op. cit., pp. 121, 126. It is also arguable that the individual values which Malraux and Sartre affirm are, if not bourgeois in origin, at least most commonly open to achievement in a bourgeois society. Both men (like Nietzsche) came from a bourgeois background; and, despite strong feelings towards it of resentment, hatred, or guilt, have never succeeded in shaking it off.

better, since the ethical question is still left open: joining the French Resistance is one form of *engagement*, joining the Vichy militia another.[1] Neither can be justified except by an appeal to some further system of values; nor can the ethical choices of Malraux's characters. Sartre seems to have realized this, and it may be a contributory reason for his having left *Les Chemins de la liberté* unfinished. Neither Malraux nor Sartre appears to have been able to integrate the experience of the Second World War adequately into the novel form, and it is noteworthy that they have both abandoned fiction. *Engagement*, indeed, apart from being more or less Malraux's *fraternité virile*, must inevitably tend towards propaganda and *bourrage de crâne*, and one might well argue that the great period of *engagé* writers was in the jingoism of the First World War. It is difficult to deny the criticism of Malraux and Sartrian Existentialism alike, that they are basically antiintellectual, Romantic in inspiration, and emotional in appeal.

The parallel between the two men in fact goes further. Both use repulsive images from the animal world to express the inhuman and hostile: Tchen's visions of 'crustacés' recur in Frantz's hallucinations in *Les Séquestrés d'Altona*, both being highly personal in origin. Both too have a keen sense of the contingency of time, and Roquentin at least is brought to see history as an ungraspable reality, since the past is irretrievable. From this it is only one step to the pragmatic view—that history is fruitful myth, which we find in *Les Voix*. Sartre has, indeed, indirectly attacked Malraux's view of art in *Les Mots*, using Malraux's own terms such as *destin*, and claiming that 'La culture ne sauve rien ni personne, elle ne justifie pas';[2] nevertheless he is deeply interested in culture as a human product, and in his work on Tintoretto he has very much adopted Malraux's methods, if not his conclusions. Many, indeed, of Malraux's psychological insights run parallel with the concepts which Sartre has developed at length, such as *dissociation*

---

[1] I have been told of a young French student who, *after* the Allied landings in Normandy in 1944, suddenly joined the Fascist militia and appeared at the Sorbonne in a black uniform. He did not survive August 1944 to explain his motives, but his sincerity and authenticity could scarcely be challenged.

[2] Sartre, *Les Mots*, p. 211.

and *complicité*.[1] The source of Sartre's conceptual system is undoubtedly to be found in Husserl, Heidegger, and the dialectic, but terms such as *angoisse* and *absurde*, even possibly *nausée*, had already been used by Malraux in much the same metaphysical sense. Sartre is certainly the much more subtle mind of the two, and there can be little comparison between their philosophical talents; at the same time, Sartre's fiction, with the exception of *La Nausée* and possibly one or two stories in *Le Mur*, has already worn somewhat thin, and Malraux has presented similar ideas much more effectively in fictional form.

Malraux's relationship with Camus is less close than with Sartre, although Camus has made more use of the concept of the absurd. The main difference between the two men lies in their view of humanism. Camus largely escaped the fascination of Marxism and its radical solutions, and at the same time, in *La Peste*, specifically rejects heroism—with its overtones of heroics—as an adequate attitude, replacing it with *honnêteté*. Lucidity in the face of the absurd, the other fundamental quality of Malraux's heroes, is, however, accepted by Camus: not only in Rieux, refusing to close his eyes to the reality of the plague and calmly facing all its implications and dangers, but also in Clamence, sitting in his bar in Amsterdam. In *Le Mythe de Sisyphe*, too, the adventurer is largely disowned; the effort being more significant than the achievement, and glamour replaced by endless toil. Camus's conception of humanism is the more usual one, almost to be equated with humanitarianism, a mixture of stoicism, compassion, and humaneness, and one which is open to all men, not merely a minority of outstanding individuals. Malraux approaches this position only in *Les Noyers*, where his treatment of German characters may be compared to Camus's tolerant attitude in *Lettres à un ami allemand*; the attitude in *Les Noyers* is an exception. In the bulk of his work he shows little sympathy with qualities of compassion, which, with Nietzsche, he sees as degrading. Yet Camus, while refusing affirmation of will as a satisfactory ethic, seems to have been attracted

[1] Cf. B. T. Fitch's interesting study, *Le Sentiment d'étrangeté chez Malraux, Sartre, Camus et Simone de Beauvoir*, where many detailed points of comparison are indicated.

to it in the sphere of art, and, indeed, to have come fairly close to the idea of art as *anti-destin*.[1] Had he lived he might have developed still further in this direction; and certainly, perhaps like other writers primarily interested in metaphysical themes, he seems to have been turning away from the novel to more direct expression of ideas in his last years. But the real similarity between Malraux and Camus lies more in their starting-point—the apparent futility of a world without transcendence—than in their conclusions, and it is clear that Malraux and his formulation of the 'absurd' played a great part in Camus's early development.

The question of Malraux's humanism is fundamental in an understanding of him: indeed, two recent studies have embodied the term in their title.[2] The aim behind this line of approach is evidently to present Malraux as an exemplary modern humanist, and certainly this claim has been cogently argued. Yet at the same time the claim perhaps seems misconceived, since if it is accepted the whole concept of humanism has to be redefined in such a way as to deprive its more usual meaning of all content. Leaving aside the Renaissance concept of humanism as Classical studies, in the last century the term has come to mean largely the dismissal of the supernatural, and therefore of religion, from human affairs, leaving man to fend for himself with his own resources. But this has immediately been taken further to imply a degree of human co-operation and understanding, hence the 'humane' overtones mentioned above. In seeking to make an exemplary humanist out of Malraux, critics are forced to abandon these last aspects, and to define humanism solely in terms of atheism—or agnosticism—and positivism. This, indeed, is an arguable position, but if maintained it makes a humanist out of, say, Stalin (together with everyone and anyone else who does not possess religious belief). Humanism, on this definition, yields little possibility of differentiating among the many different attitudes grouped together here. Occasionally, even, this type of definition has been broadened to include as a

[1] e.g. 'Le but de l'effort artistique étant une œuvre idéale où la création serait corrigée', 'Remarques sur la révolte' in *L'Existence*, Paris, 1945, p. 22. (Quoted in C. Mauriac, op. cit., p. 156.)

[2] C. D. Blend, *André Malraux, Tragic Humanist*, and J. Hoffmann, *L'Humanisme de Malraux*.

humanist anyone tortured by metaphysical or religious doubts. Yet would one call Pascal a humanist? Scarcely; but he shares many of Malraux's preoccupations—and may well have inspired some of them.[1] For Pascal a world without God would be so terrible that God must exist. For Malraux a world without God is so terrible that man must spend his time restlessly casting round for a means—art, action—to enable himself to face it. Malraux's own definition of humanism, at the end of *Les Voix du silence*: 'Nous avons refusé ce que voulait en nous la bête, et nous voulons retrouver l'homme partout où nous avons trouvé ce qui l'écrase', despite its fine ring, is so vague as to cover almost all possibilities, and to mean all things to all men. Against this Erwin Panofsky's careful definition of humanism is, I would claim, greatly preferable: 'an attitude which can be defined as the conviction of the dignity of man, based on both the insistence on human values (rationality and freedom) and the acceptance of human limitations (fallibility and frailty); from this two postulates result—responsibility and tolerance'.[2] This definition succeeds in excluding from humanism on the one side determinists, such as Marxists, who deny freedom, and, on the other, intuitionists who deny human limitations.

Malraux, on this view, will, in most of his work with the major exception of *Les Noyers*, fall into the second group. He has, certainly, followed Nietzsche in discarding transcendental religious values and in asserting personal values of will in their place, but there is again as little feeling of solidarity with all men or tolerance of them as we find in the German philosopher. Even virile fraternity is an 'aristocratic' conception: a group of superior individuals, bound together in violent action, not a community of men in everyday society. (There is little comprehension of the steady routine of work and leisure which forms the fabric of most men's lives until *Les Noyers*, where Malraux tends to dwell on this

[1] Professor Blend points out (op. cit., p. 110) that Hernandez awaiting execution is an exact transposition of the Pascalian image of life as the condemned cell. The same image occurs with Moreno; with the prisoners in Shanghai; and with Kassner.

[2] E. Panofsky, *Meaning and the Visual Arts*, p. 2. One might also recall Berenson's view: 'Humanism is the belief that life on this planet can be made worth living.'

fact almost as if it were a surprising discovery.) Tolerance is significantly lacking from most of his work, together with much
normal human affection and understanding; this, with the virtual
exclusion of women from importance, makes his novels somewhat barren in what many would regard as a crucial sector, and
the contrast with other novelists such as Duhamel or Martin du
Gard is acute.[1] Suffering, for Malraux, is almost entirely metaphysical, not material or physical; the same contrast can be made.
Again, Malraux's taste for violence, in which there is something
ugly, as well as immature, is hard to reconcile with humanism. It
seems true that Malraux would have agreed with Georges Sorel's
dictum that violence is 'la vertu nécessaire pour animer les autres
vertus de l'homme'. Yet one might well claim that an ethic of
affirmation of will must inevitably prove incompatible with
human solidarity, since unrestrained will immediately impinges on
the will of others, leading to constraint and force.[2] Malraux admittedly is searching for a meaning to life, but, since he presupposes that this can only be found in Nietzschean terms, his
quest ends not far from where it begins. André Blanchet has
shrewdly pointed out that what are by wide agreement some of
the most effective scenes in the novels, such as Katow's gift of the
cyanide or the 'descent from the mountain', are in fact acts of
charity as well as of heroism.[3] But these last episodes, which look
forward to the human solidarity of Les Noyers, however powerful,
are exceptional rather than typical in the earlier novels; more
usually his work has an affirmative, somewhat strident, note which
groups him better, ethically, with such writers as Montherlant or
even Drieu La Rochelle, rather than with Camus or Duhamel.
Perhaps we may detect here a further fruitful tension: between the

[1] The same criticism can perhaps also be applied to the works of Camus and
Sartre. One of the strengths of La Condition humaine is that in it Malraux widens
his focus to treat the father/son and husband/wife relationships.
[2] It is also arguable that the apparent humanism and liberalism of the great
Romantics may in many cases have been incidental rather than real, merely a by-
product of their dislike of contemporary society, which usually happened to be
reactionary. The fundamental egoism implicit in Romantic attitudes is in reality
difficult to reconcile with humanism in the liberal, humane sense: witness Byron,
as autocratic in his private life as he was passionate in his denunciations of tyranny.
[3] A. Blanchet, op. cit., p. 219.

values which Malraux consciously affirms and those which almost in spite of himself come to the fore in these 'exceptional' scenes.

A further point which perhaps requires elucidation is Malraux's relationship to modern tragedy. He himself, notably in the preface to *Le Temps du mépris*, has attempted to assimilate his work to the tragic mode; more recently certain critics have tried to formulate a new definition of tragedy, specifically in terms of man's fight against the absurd, using Malraux as a key example.[1] Certainly, if we define tragedy as man's assertion of his dignity by a necessarily unsuccessful struggle against his destiny in an absurd world, cut off from all transcendental redemption, it is obvious that much of Malraux's work—art philosophy no less than novels—fits very well. Clearly confrontation with the absurd leads ultimately to death, and automatically irony of fate and a kind of tragedy will result. Yet it is just this automatic quality which casts doubt on the definition, and there is a slight suspicion of circularity in the argument. A definition of tragedy is extracted from what we may call the Existentialist *Weltanschauung* of 'man versus the cosmos'—that is, not from life, but from literature; it is then used as a criterion against which to judge works of the Existentialist type, notably those of Malraux, and is, not altogether surprisingly, found to fit closely. Moreover, the definition, like that of humanism criticized above, is too wide, since it covers just about all specifically non-transcendental attitudes, and gives any novel or drama in which the main theme is an unsuccessful search for meaning in life a justifiable claim to tragic effect. Despite the introduction of concepts like those of human responsibility and dignity, there remains a feeling that tragedy has been reduced to a process of the hero vainly beating his head on a brick wall.

The question of the continued existence of 'authentic' tragedy in the twentieth century is one which is far too complex to be treated thoroughly here; there is an equally good claim that widespread loss of transcendental belief has at the same time destroyed traditional tragic effect. If Malraux's works are judged on their

---

[1] Notably Professor Glicksberg, op. cit. Lucien Goldmann, in *Le Dieu caché*, has developed a similar conception of the tragic vision, in terms of refusal to accept a rationalistic, non-transcendental world.

effects, not on their correspondence to a theoretical definition, my contention would be that only *La Condition humaine* comes near to anything properly justifiable as tragic, despite greater superficial pretensions in *Le Temps du mépris*. The fundamental optimism kills the tragic in the later novels, while Perken's death is too melo-dramatic and Garine's situation too confused fully to justify the claim. It is also, perhaps, too easily assumed that the novel is the natural inheritor of the tragic mode formerly embodied in the drama. The belief that the novel should deal primarily with 'metaphysical' subjects, and in particular 'man and his destiny', is currently powerful; but it is none the less a survival of the nine-teenth-century view exemplified in Arnold's literary criterion of 'high seriousness', itself a Romantic survival. It is a tenable position, but is open to the criticism that the novel has not, for much of its history, confined itself to—or even especially interested itself in—'metaphysical' themes; and that, if this criterion is applied now, the novel is restricted to only a part of the full richness of life. This narrowness of scope becomes obvious if we examine the concept of tragic heroism more closely. 'Promethean' is the epithet which has often been applied to works in which a challenge to the gods, or in more modern terms a challenge to death, provides the principal theme. Obviously there is a parallel between Prometheus bound eternally to his rock and Malraux's hero striving to defeat his des-tiny. But it is ultimately little more than a loose metaphor, allow-ing no possibility for the novelist to develop, but merely to repeat the same theme again and again.[1] The penalty of using myth in the novel is that its significance thins out into simple allegory and ab-straction, and it is noteworthy that the book in which Malraux explicitly uses the image of Prometheus, *Le Temps du mépris*, is also his weakest.

[1] Two recent books have gone into the Prometheus theme in some detail: R. Trousson, *Le Thème de Prométhée dans la littérature européenne* (1964); and L. Prémont, *Le Mythe de Prométhée dans la littérature française contemporaine* (1964). What perhaps emerges most immediately from these studies is the sheer number of works which overtly or implicitly have treated the Prometheus theme. It is difficult not to conclude that this interest in many cases may have been the result of a certain barrenness of creative imagination. In addition writers have perhaps too readily assumed that by using the myth their own work would automatically acquire all the aesthetic and emotive force of the original.

It is also perhaps too easily accepted that Malraux's challenge to destiny is the only reaction to the human condition that can affirm man's dignity. There is, however, another tradition which faces up to the problem of a world without transcendental meaning at least as adequately as the heroic challenge: the ethic of work, best presented in *Candide*, but in fact the normal—and for that matter usually the only possible—human reaction. The ethic of work is unappealing to the individualist because it is both unheroic and undramatic, but it could be claimed as a more mature reaction to life, and one which drives away many apparent spiritual difficulties of the *mal du siècle* type. Malraux's conception of heroism depends too closely on violent action—usually occurring in other countries which are originally of little concern to the hero—and begs the question of how the hero is to affirm his challenge in a world at peace. Malraux, as we have seen, has little sympathy for science and technology, or even understanding of them; this is almost inevitable, since his conception of tragedy depends on myth and would be fatally weakened by a matter-of-fact rational approach.[1] The ethic of work, on the other hand, despite its literary unattractiveness, is able to integrate much better the scientific outlook and also Malraux's—and Sartre's—other *bête noire*, the bourgeois way of life. The rhetoric of destiny remains a rhetoric—persuasive rather than conveying absolute conviction.

In rejecting reason, and its chief contemporary manifestation, science, Malraux shows himself anti-humanist again. This particular aspect of his work shows the best way of considering his contribution to twentieth-century literature: not as a humanist, or a tragic thinker, but as a Romantic poet—perhaps the finest contemporary example.[2] The art philosophy is, we have seen, clearly

[1] Even more so by any kind of scientific determinism: but Malraux utterly rejects philosophical just as much as (Marxist) economic determinism.

[2] The older view that Romanticism, as a literary movement in France, died out in the 1840s, is, as far as it goes, unexceptionable. But it is now clear that Romanticism, as an attitude, is a general phenomenon of fundamental importance in European intellectual and cultural history, far surpassing the development of literary movements, and closely connected with the decline of religious faith from the eighteenth century onwards. In France, Baudelaire, Rimbaud, or Mallarmé, to take only three figures, have as good a claim to be called Romantics as the earlier poets; both Surrealism and Expressionism are essentially Romantic movements;

Romantic in essence; and in the novels too the contemptuous rejection of ordinary life and the refusal to allow any sense of limitations to affect the challenge to destiny are equally typical of the
Romantic hero, dividing his life between grandiose and flamboyant gestures and metaphysical introspection. Looked at from a
viewpoint radically opposed to Malraux's own, the whole idea of
anti-destin might be viewed as escapism; and the same might be
said of many other facets of Malraux's work: the exoticism, obsession with mythomania—the Romantic symptom *par excellence*?
—and with revolution and rebellion.

Malraux's philosophy can be called a Romanticism of action,
but it is a Romanticism nevertheless; Edmund Wilson has compared Garine with René and Manfred—'somber, tortured, terrify-
ing, a solitary savage rebel'[1]—and he is also a spiritual descendant
of Lorenzaccio. Indeed, one might well call the thirst for action,
the inability to sit still and lead a tranquil life, the *mal du vingtième
siècle*, if that of the nineteenth consisted of the various forms of
ennui. Like all Romantic attitudes it does not cover more than
limited aspects of human experience; and it is moreover self-
defeating. If to be is to act, then there can be no end to action, no
chance of final achievement, merely an infinite regress of further
action.[2]

Malraux, obviously aware of this aspect of his life and work, has
attempted to defend Vincent Berger against the accusation of
Romanticism: 'Romanesque? A coup sûr; mais les romanesques
ne montrent ni cette précision d'esprit, ni cette maîtrise de leurs
moyens; d'autre part, si mon père n'était sans doute pas indifférent
au pouvoir, il l'était à l'argent. Et n'y a-t-il pas du romanesque
dans toute grande ambition?'[3] But in fact he is giving the case
away, since it is precisely the 'great ambition'—the thirst for
action on the grand scale—which is the touchstone. Nor would

and Romantic attitudes are still enormously powerful today. I propose to develop
these general considerations in a future work.

[1] E. Wilson, *The Shores of Light*, p. 568.

[2] This is, of course, the typical problem that faces the successful revolutionary,
whose dynamic is destroyed by his own success, leaving him with no more than
thirst for continued power.

[3] *Les Noyers*, pp. 63–4.

Malraux's lucidity exclude him from Romanticism; indeed, lucidity is another concept frequently used in connexion with Malraux, but rarely analysed. Lucidity does not necessarily mean detachment: in essence it means little more than the ability to face the prospect of a meaningless universe without taking refuge in religious consolation; in the sense of rigorous and realistic thinking it can scarcely be applied to Malraux's thought, which is, as we have seen, basically intuitive and poetic, and often cloudy or even self-contradictory. The Romantic confusion between the role of the artist and that of the prophet is, indeed, well exemplified in Malraux.

In fact this leads directly to another result. Malraux, like all Romantics, arouses great enthusiasm on first contact, especially in the younger reader: I myself can testify to this effect of the blood sent tingling through my veins as I devoured Malraux in my early twenties. Nor is there anything wrong with this: it is a natural and proper reaction. Yet, again, Romantic poets tend to lose their effect as the reader ages and matures; as prophets they are increasingly felt to be dangerous, and as mentors to be outgrown, as experience and detachment are acquired, and splendour of style ceases to dazzle and numb the critical faculty, but instead begins to cloy. Malraux's quest—the *recherche de l'absolu* which is the fundamental Romantic quest—makes his works perhaps too intense to remain the *livres de chevet* of the mature; with his lack of detachment and self-irony he sometimes seems to take himself a little too seriously. The aesthetic of action and intensity which critics such as Picon, Albérès, and Boisdeffre have developed—largely round Malraux's works—need not be definitive. Malraux's appeal seems, in the main, to spring from the combination of contemporary (political) topics with metaphysical preoccupations; and both may weaken in the future. It is, of course, logically impossible to predict future artistic taste; it is equally impossible—though this is less widely recognized—to predict it empirically with any hope of success, since all the political and technological variables which render impossible any prediction of the future state of world society must be taken into account, together with other aesthetic ones which are purely contingent.

Outside Existentialist writers, and above all Camus and Sartre, the extent of Malraux's influence on later writers is problematical. There are, it is true, novels of action—many of which can perhaps only marginally be considered serious literature—in which Malraux's influence seems obvious. Jean Lartéguy's various war novels, which are in great part thinly romanced *reportage* and tendentious political tracts, clearly derive much from the vignette technique of *L'Espoir*.[1] Equally, Jean Hougron's Indo-China novels, though they contain a better attempt to understand the complexities of the post-1945 situation in Vietnam, are filled with echoes of 'cosmic' imagery and a rather simplistic psychology of will.[2] Other novelists, such as Jean-Louis Curtis in *Les Justes Causes* (1954), appear to have been writing with Malraux—and Sartre—looking over their shoulders; quotations and formulations from Malraux abound in such novels. Yet none of these works has done more than perhaps copy some of the externals of Malraux's novels, the violence and topicality, while the poetry and the metaphysical self-consciousness are largely lacking. (It may be this which has prevented any of them from really being taken seriously.) The art philosophy has impressed later writers: but again largely those whom, like Sartre and Camus, we have already discussed, and whose premises and preoccupations were always very much the same. The *nouvelle vague* seems to have turned away from all three impartially, deserting all human concerns to concentrate on things, on externality and appearance. Of course it is far too early to judge how far this reaction will last; at present all that it is possible to do is to comment that this is at least negative evidence for the view that Malraux lies outside the main tradition of the novel, and that he is a special case, whose work has both personal qualities and limitations to a large extent alien to the main interests, social and moral alike, of both earlier and later European novelists. One might go further and argue that, despite his choice of apparently contemporary themes in his major novels, Malraux is essentially

[1] *Les Mercenaires* (1954), *Les Centurions* (1960), and *Les Prétoriens* (1960) are the best known of Lartéguy's books.

[2] Cf. my essay 'Jean Hougron and *La Nuit indochinoise*', in *France-Asie*, no. 174 (July–Aug. 1962), pp. 489–501.

looking backwards, rather than into the future. He is, with Ernst Jünger, perhaps the best exemplification of the 'Nietzschean' novelist; but, as we have seen, his ideas present no great advance on typical Romantic attitudes, and because of the Nietzschean affiliation he is saddled with a somewhat limited and unsatisfactory set of psychological foundations to his work,[1] together with an almost total lack of interest in the wide stretches of modern life which only a scientific or technological imagination can cover. For better or for worse the future of humanity, and all its concerns, including art and literature, must lie here, rather than in an 'interrogation' of the past. Romantic poets have achieved great poignancy of expression and emotion, but much of the intellectual content of their work—and all great art must, I would maintain, ultimately appeal to the head as well as the heart—is flawed by a peevish attitude to the contemporary world, often ending in a rejection of it which is both practically and emotionally impossible. Malraux shares their merits as an artist, and their vices as a thinker.

Ultimately it is as a poet that Malraux is best considered: a poet in the widest sense. Although he uses ideas extensively, as we have seen, they are, if penetrating, usually not original, and the contrast with Sartre immediately brings out the fact that Malraux is little of the analytical thinker, and that his gift is much more for conveying ideas by pithy—poetic—formulations.[2] What matters is not that he has developed a theory of modern tragedy, based on the necessity yet impossibility of self-transcendence in a godless world; this problem in any case has haunted almost every creative writer since the eighteenth century, and finds its sharpest expression in *The Birth of Tragedy*. Writers such as Flaubert, Turgenev, Tolstoy, Maupassant, Hardy, Chekhov, or Martin du Gard have been just as poignantly aware of the 'tragic' aspects of life as Malraux, and their reaction, if less intense, has not lacked dignity. The question was in any case fully discussed in Unamuno's *The Tragic Sense of Life* as early as 1913; although Malraux men-

---

[1] Cf. Unamuno's devastating criticism that Nietzsche's philosophy is not that of the genuine strong man, but of the weakling who aspires to be strong: *The Tragic Sense of Life*, English trans., London, 1962, p. 65.

[2] A comparison with Valéry might be made here.

tions Unamuno in *L'Espoir*, it is doubtful how well he knew the Spaniard's work. Unamuno writes with considerable emotion and rhetorical power, like Malraux himself, also seeing philosophy as attitude to life and adopting an all-or-nothing point of view, with an ethic of heroism underlying his dictum, 'Spend your life so that you deserve to be immortal'. What matters in Malraux is that he has expressed his own feeling of restless anguish in the face of a meaningless world, in novels which succeed in conveying this powerful vision to the reader. His ideas are less a philosophy than a *Weltanschauung*,[1] and, although this attitude to life may form the basis of his works, their value does not depend on it. To draw another parallel, it is perfectly possible to extract a philosophy of pessimism from Maupassant's stories, and even to attempt to estimate his indebtedness to Schopenhauer—but this has little to do with the reasons why Maupassant's stories are still read. There are plenty of other works which share his rather facile cynicism, and which have sunk without a trace. Malraux, like Byron, has dramatized a mixture of real events and wish-fulfilment; and it is in the dramatic presentation, not the *reportage* or the *Weltanschauung*, that the literary value will rest.

The theory of will as the basic human dynamic cannot, in fact, stand up to careful examination. In completely rejecting determinism it sweeps away even causation, and must inflict full responsibility for their acts on small children (and why not animals?); and it doubtless has a metaphysical origin in the intuitive conception of the self as unmoved mover. Developed into the idea of the outstanding individual, its Romantic nature becomes clear: the theme of the noble individual opposed by the vulgar crowd. But the internal difficulties and contradictions of Malraux's ideas dissolve when he is looked at as a poet. We can compare him, better perhaps than with Byron, with Victor Hugo, whose ambitions and development carried him also into—and out of—some curious political positions in the course of his life. Hugo's 'philosophy' as expressed in *Ce que dit la bouche d'ombre* and *La Légende des siècles*, seen as an adequate explanation of the world, is totally unacceptable, yet the poems which use it as a basis are among the

---

[1] It is of course arguable that all popular philosophy must be *Weltanschauung*.

finest in the French language. Malraux shares other features with Hugo: an extreme egoism and a tendency towards exaggeration and rhetoric, more than redeemed by a gift for brilliant images and striking lyrical passages. Perhaps no contemporary writer, with the possible exception of Curzio Malaparte, has succeeded so well in creating poetic beauty out of scenes of war and death. Lyricism is the keynote of much of Malraux's writing; objectivity is at the opposite pole from his intuitive grasp of reality—which explains why his preference in novels goes to the spontaneity of Dostoevsky rather than the more polished and detached Flaubert. Even when in somewhat elegiac mood, as when he reflects on the strangeness of human existence on one minor planet in the cosmos, at one arbitrary point in eternity—incidentally, a basic Existentialist idea, Heidegger's *Geworfenheit*—, his language tends towards a vigorous accumulation of imagery, usually consisting of directly transposed feelings.

Romantic writers have not, on the whole, been at their best in the novel: a fact doubtless connected with the necessity for sustained effort and with the lack of detachment already noted. (Detachment is a quality much less necessary in poets, where immediacy of effect is usually an advantage.) Romantic novelists have, in fact, excelled in creating exactly those private worlds claimed by Malraux to be the aim of the novelist in general—private worlds either historical or more purely imaginative (like *Wuthering Heights*). Intensity of evocation is the yardstick. Other Romantics have written their best fictional work under tension between Romantic ideals and the real world (as in *Madame Bovary* or *A Hero of our Time*); but in these latter cases it is arguable that the writers are no longer truly Romantic in attitude. (In Malraux, too, this tension is present in *Les Conquérants* and *La Condition humaine*, but missing in the weaker *La Voie royale*.) The novelist who relies on a vision of a private world for his subject-matter will also—unless his vision sharply changes—tend to repeat himself; and in fact there is much in *La Voie royale* and *Les Conquérants* which is repeated in the later novels to little better effect. In addition the private world may lean to the didactic, since the values of that world will tend to be affirmed, and appreciation will to some extent depend on their acceptance. In Malraux these values are heroic, yet sapped by inevitable failure; it may be that the best vehicle for a heroic *Weltanschauung* is epic, not tragedy, and that Malraux's novels fall, at times uneasily, between the two.

Malraux's fundamental concepts, again, are only superficially philosophical. *Destin, fatalité, angoisse, absurde*: all these are poetical concepts, and they owe their power to their emotive, not their rational, implications. It was Malraux who first popularized these words in the French language, long before Sartre and Camus, who are undoubtedly greatly indebted to him for their terminology. He has never precisely defined them, and perhaps because of this, together with over-use in the later novels, they tend to lose their overtones and become almost leitmotivs—in a pejorative sense. His style, indeed, repays careful examination; *Les Voix du silence* can lay claim to being one of the most sustained attempts at high style of the century, with its innumerable ellipses, startling inversions, uncompleted arguments, unexpected juxtapositions, rhetorical questions and concessions, and preference for dramatic verbs such as *arracher, écraser*, rather than abstract forms. From his earliest writings Malraux was a poet; and even his critical articles betray this quality. To take a single, well-known example, the remark in his preface to the French translation of Faulkner's *Sanctuary*: 'c'est l'intrusion de la tragédie grecque dans le roman policier'.[1] This typically flamboyant comment has its effect—which is why it is well known—and illustrates Malraux's ability to bring together dissimilar ideas (novel juxtaposition is the source of all striking imagery); but whether it really adds much to an understanding or appreciation of Faulkner's novel is more doubtful.

When the early novels first appeared they were widely taken as simply autobiographical, and their style an up-to-date brusque *reportage*. Yet in fact their apparent spontaneity conceals careful workmanship. Comparison of the original and post-war editions of *Les Conquérants* and *La Condition humaine* shows that Malraux, even at the height of his career as a novelist, was not afraid to make hundreds of minor stylistic alterations; again, large numbers of changes were made to *Le Temps du mépris* between galley and page

[1] Preface to the French translation of *Sanctuary*, Paris, 1963, p. iv.

proof, and between magazine and book publication.[1] Far from straight *reportage*, Malraux's style is highly deliberate, using the present tense for dramatic effect, and elliptical, even verbless, sentences to increase tension, purposefully alternating between action, dialogue, and reported thought. There is something in it of Martin du Gard's *style notatif*;[2] and one can perhaps also compare it with the work of Ernest Hemingway, an equally conscientious craftsman behind the appearance of naïvety. Hemingway has indeed much in common with Malraux: not least he was another man who deliberately 'gave style to his life'. Violence is equally obsessive in his work throughout his career; and there is a similar somewhat adolescent emphasis on values of physical courage and endurance, which likewise depend ultimately on will. He too can be regarded as fundamentally a poet, rather than a novelist:[3] his heroes are always, like Malraux's, a combination of himself in reality and in wish-fulfilment. As Professor Levin has remarked: 'perhaps [Hemingway] will be remembered for a poetic vision which renews our interrupted contact with the timeless elements of man's existence.'[4] This, I would claim, is also Malraux's greatest gift to posterity.

As it stands, Malraux's work is impossible to assess with any attempt at finality. Even its most ardent champions differ widely about which are the most important books. For myself *La Condition humaine* is Malraux's finest contribution. I find it impossible to see the Surrealist works as other than trivial and imitative; and, although *La Voie royale* foreshadows his later novels, Malraux has

[1] Cf. Frohock, op. cit., p. 94; and my article, 'Malraux—a Note on Editions', *AUMLA*, no. 21 (May 1964), pp. 79–83.

[2] Cf. my *Roger Martin du Gard*, pp. 37–40.

[3] Though Hemingway's famous 'deadpan' style possibly appears to be wearing a little thin, and above all to lend itself too easily to parody—a result of excessive stylization?—, Malraux's mixture of lyricism and staccato dialogue may also date (cf. Yves Gandon's amusing parody of *La Condition humaine* in *Usage de faux*). My own impression is that much of Malraux's writing (like Hemingway's) does not stand up too well to repeated reading, despite its undoubted power on initial acquaintance.

[4] H. Levin, *Contexts of Criticism*, p. 167. Malraux has, indeed, paid generous tribute to the American novelist: 'I consider certain of his novels among the most valuable of our time' (Malraux and James Burnham, 'The Double Crisis: a Dialogue', *Partisan Review*, Apr. 1948, p. 420.)

not succeeded in detaching himself from his subject-matter, which
remains confused, nor in freeing himself from adolescent attitudes.
In *Les Conquérants* the use of the revolutionary struggle gives
him more adequate material to treat, but he is hampered by his
first-person narrator and by the lack of harmony between the comparative success of the revolutionary movement and Garine's personal failure as he sinks into disease and disillusionment. Again,
there is some confusion in the novel and its effect on the reader
tends to be blurred. In *La Condition humaine* Malraux contrives to
integrate a number of different elements, and above all, by choosing a historical episode which inevitably ends in disaster for
nearly all his principal characters, an aura of tragedy is lent to the
novel. As we have seen, Malraux's conception of the tragic side of
life derives largely from Nietzsche, and more generally from loss
of transcendental religious belief; and this modern view of the
essence of tragedy has perhaps nowhere been more powerfully
expressed than in this novel. Elsewhere Malraux tends to use his
novels to affirm values, but here in the various characters—his
richly drawn ones—there is a genuine search for them: a complex
situation is probed for its profound significance, rather than an
artificial one constructed to demonstrate values which precede the
conception of the novel. And also *La Condition humaine* is
emotionally richer than the other novels: the themes of love and
compassion are more sensitively treated. In *Le Temps du mépris* and
L'Espoir political commitment gets the better of this perplexity in
the face of life, and the need to give a positive ending to the latter
novel (however sincere Malraux's belief in final Republican
victory)[1] means that it is less satisfying aesthetically. *Les Noyers* remains a rather exasperating might-have-been. Here Malraux has
achieved an admirable level of detachment and maturity, but his
powers of characterization, at their highest in *La Condition humaine*, are never properly exercised. Fundamental poetic symbols
—the sun, stars, earth, and trees—are finely presented, but the
balance between the poetry and the ideas remains uncertain, and
subjects outside Malraux's major preoccupations are very cursorily handled. The final impression left is one of unfinished

[1] Cf. Sinkó, op. cit., p. 439.

material: that we have a partial draft of what might have been one of the greatest novels of the century, had Malraux filled out the gaps in his vision with richer characterization and more extended treatment. This, of course, he may yet do; but it looks unlikely. A comparison, once more, with *Doctor Faustus*, shows Mann's much fuller treatment of a somewhat comparable theme. Malraux's dramatic technique—sadly lacking in Mann—does not redeem the general thinness of texture of his novel. *La Condition humaine* was, perhaps, lucky in capturing the atmosphere of the moment, but its extraordinary success with all shades of opinion and at all levels of taste probably had more to do with the blend of violent action, reflection, lyricism, exotic settings, ideas, characters which it contains, and which obviously lends it enormously wide appeal. If the primary function of the poet is to absorb experiences from life—either his own or others'—to transform them into an acceptable form that he can communicate meaningfully to the reader, then it is in *La Condition humaine*, I should maintain, that Malraux has succeeded most richly.

BIBLIOGRAPHY

THIS Bibliography makes no pretence of being exhaustive; a complete bibliography of Malraux's own writings is to be found in Hoffmann, op. cit., together with an extensive list of books and articles dealing with him. I have listed only those of Malraux's writings to which I refer; while other books and articles are also limited to those which I have both consulted and found useful. The editions listed, unless specially indicated, are in every case those actually used. Not normally included are novels and other works to which I refer in general terms. Items which I have found particularly valuable are marked with an asterisk.

1. *Works by Malraux* (listed chronologically)

Lunes en papier, Paris, 1921.

Preface to C. Maurras, *Mademoiselle Monk*, Paris, 1923, pp. 7–9.

La Tentation de l'Occident, Paris, 1926.

D'une jeunesse européenne, in *Écrits*, Paris, 1927 (*Les Cahiers verts*, no. 70, pp. 133–53).

Les Conquérants, Paris, 1928; and *version définitive*, *Livre de Poche* edn., Paris (1959).

Royaume farfelu, Paris, 1928.

Review of H. Keyserling, *Journal de voyage d'un philosophe*, in *N.R.F.*, June 1929, pp. 884–6.

'Les Conquérants, fragment inédit', *Bifur*, 31 December 1929, pp. 5–15.

La Voie royale, Paris, 1930.

'Réponse à Trotski', *N.R.F.*, April 1931, pp. 501–7.

Preface to D. H. Lawrence, *L'Amant de Lady Chatterley*, Paris, 1932, pp. 7–11.

Œuvres gothico-bouddhiques du Pamir, Paris, 1932.

La Condition humaine, Paris, 1933 (editions used: 227th impr., Paris, 1934; édition revue et corrigée, Paris, 1946; and *Livre de Poche* edn., Paris (1960).

Preface to W. Faulkner, *Sanctuaire*, Paris, 1933.

'A l'hôtel des sensations inédites', *Marianne*, 13 December 1933, p. 4.

'L'Art est une conquête', *Commune*, July–August 1934, pp. 68–71.

'L'Attitude de l'artiste', *Commune*, November 1934, pp. 166–75.

Le Temps du mépris, Paris, 1935.

'L'Œuvre d'art', *Commune*, July 1935, pp. 1264–6.

L'Espoir, Paris, 1937 (edition used: 89th impr., Paris, 1948).

'La Psychologie de l'art', *Verve*, December 1937, pp. 41–8

'Laclos', in *Tableau de la littérature française*, Paris, 1939 (edition used: vol. 2, Paris, 1962, pp. 377–89).

Les Noyers de l'Altenburg, Lausanne, 1943 (edition used: Paris, 1948).

Esquisse d'une psychologie du cinéma, Paris, 1946.

'N'était-ce donc que cela?', *Saisons*, no. 3 (Winter 1946–7), pp. 9–24.

La Psychologie de l'art, 3 vols., Geneva, 1947–9.

'The Double Crisis: a Dialogue', with James Burnham, *Partisan Review*, April 1948, pp. 407–38.

Saturne, Paris, 1950.

Les Voix du silence, Paris, 1951.

Le Musée imaginaire de la sculpture mondiale, 3 vols., Paris, 1952–4–6.

Preface to M. Sperber, *Qu'une larme dans l'océan*, Paris, 1952.

Preface to Gen. P. E. Jacquot, *Essai de stratégie occidentale*, Paris, 1953, pp. vii–xvi.

Preface to A. Ollivier, *Saint-Just et la force des choses*, Paris, 1954, pp. 11–29.

La Métamorphose des dieux, vol. 1, Paris, 1957.

2. Books consulted

ALBÉRÈS, R. M. *La Révolte des écrivains d'aujourd'hui*, Paris, 1949.

—— *Bilan littéraire du XXᵉ siècle*, Paris, 1956.

—— *L'Aventure intellectuelle du XXᵉ siècle*, Paris, 1959.

—— *Histoire du roman moderne*, Paris, 1962.

ALDINGTON, R. *Lawrence of Arabia*, London, 1955.

ARLAND, M. *Essais et nouveaux essais critiques*, Paris, 1952.

ARON, R. *L'Opium des intellectuels*, Paris, 1955.

BALMAS, E. *Aspects et problèmes de la littérature contemporaine*, Milan, 1958.

BARRÈRE, J.-B. *Critique de chambre*, Paris, 1964.

BARZUN, J. *Classic, Romantic and Modern*, paperback edn., New York, 1961.

BEAUVOIR, S. DE. *Mémoires d'une jeune fille rangée*, Paris, 1958.

—— *La Force de l'âge*, Paris, 1960.

—— *La Force des choses*, Paris, 1963.

BESPALOFF, R. *Cheminements et carrefours*, Paris, 1938.

BLANCHET, A. *La Littérature et le spirituel*, vol. 1, Paris, 1959.

BLANCHOT, M. *La Part du feu*, 2nd edn., Paris, 1949.

*BLEND, C. D. *André Malraux: Tragic Humanist*, Ohio State U.P., 1963.

BLUMENTHAL, G. *André Malraux—The Conquest of Dread*, Baltimore, 1960.

BOISDEFFRE, P. DE. *Des Vivants et des morts*, Paris, 1954.

*Boisdeffre, P. de. *André Malraux*, 5th revised edn., Paris, 1960.

—— *Métamorphose de la littérature*, 2 vols., 5th revised edn., Paris, 1963.

Brée, G. *Camus*, revised edn., Rutgers U.P., 1961.

Brincourt, A. and J. *Les Œuvres et les lumières*, Paris, 1955.

Brodin, P.-J. *Présences contemporaines*, vol. 1, Paris, 1954.

*Brombert, V. *The Intellectual Hero*, London, 1962.

Chaigne, L. *Vies et œuvres d'écrivains*, vol. 4, new edn., Paris, 1962.

Clouard, H. *Histoire de la littérature française du symbolisme à nos jours*, vol. 2, new edn., Paris, 1962.

Copleston, F. *Friedrich Nietzsche*, 2nd impr., London, 1942.

Cruickshank, J. *Albert Camus and the Literature of Revolt*, paperback edn., New York, 1960.

*—— (ed.), *The Novelist as Philosopher*, London, 1962.

Delhomme, J. *Temps et destin*, 4th edn., Paris, 1955.

Desan, W. *The Tragic Finale*, revised edn., New York, 1960.

Digeon, C. *La Crise allemande de la pensée française (1870–1914)*, Paris, 1959.

Domenach, J.-M. *Barrès par lui-même*, Paris (1958).

Dorival, B. *XX Century Painters*, vol. 2, Paris, 1958.

Duthuit, G. *Le Musée inimaginable*, 3 vols., Paris, 1956.

Éliade, M. *Shamanism*, London, 1964 (English translation of *Le Chamanisme et les techniques archaïques de l'extase*, Paris 1951).

Émery, L. *Sept témoins*, Lyons, n.d.

Erikson, E. H. *Childhood and Society*, New York, 1950.

—— *Young Man Luther*, London, 1959.

Faure, É. *Histoire de l'art*, *Livre de Poche* edn., 5 vols., Paris, 1964.

Fitch, B. T. *Le Sentiment d'étrangeté chez Malraux, Sartre, Camus et Simone de Beauvoir*, Paris, 1964 (the section on Malraux is almost identical with the same author's *Les Deux Univers romanesques d'André Malraux*, Paris, 1964).

Flanner, J. *Men and Monuments*, London, 1957.

Focillon, H. *The Art of the West*, 2 vols., London, 1963 (English translation of *Art d'Occident*, Paris, 1938).

—— *Vie des formes*, new edn., Paris, 1939.

Fowlie, W. *Dionysus in Paris*, London, 1961.

*Frank, J. *The Widening Gyre*, Rutgers U.P., 1963.

*Frohock, W. M. *André Malraux and the Tragic Imagination*, Stanford U.P., 1952.

Gandon, Y. *Usage de faux*, Paris, 1936.

Gannon, E. *The Honor of Being a Man*, Chicago, 1957.

GARAUDY, R. *Une Littérature de fossoyeurs*, Paris, 1947.

GARDINER, P. L. (ed.), *Theories of History*, 2nd impr., Glencoe, Illinois, 1960.

GAROSCI, A. *Gli intellectuali e la guerra di Spagna*, n.p., 1959.

GARTEN, H. F. *Modern German Drama*, London, 1959.

GIDE, A. *Prétextes*, Paris, 1963.

—— *Journal 1889–1939*, Paris, 1951.

—— *Journal 1939–1949*, Paris, 1954.

GLICKSBERG, C. I. *The Tragic Vision in Twentieth-Century Literature*, Carbondale, Illinois, 1963.

GOLDBERGER, A. *Visions of a New Hero*, Paris, 1965.

GOLDMANN, L. *Le Dieu caché*, Paris, 1955.

—— *Pour une sociologie du roman*, Paris, 1964.

GOMBRICH, E. H. *Art and Illusion*, New York, 1960.

—— *Meditations on a Hobby Horse*, London, 1963.

GRAVES, R. *Lawrence and the Arabs*, 4th impr., London, 1928.

GUISSARD, L. *Écrits en notre temps*, Paris, 1964.

HALDA, B. *Berenson et André Malraux*, Paris, 1964.

HAMBURGER, M. *From Prophecy to Exorcism*, London, 1965.

HARTMAN, G. H. *André Malraux*, London, 1960.

HATFIELD, H. (ed.), *Thomas Mann*, Englewood Cliffs, 1964.

HAUSER, A. *The Philosophy of Art History*, New York, 1959.

—— *The Social History of Art*, paperback edn., 4 vols., London, 1962.

HAYS, H. R. *From Ape to Angel*, London, 1959.

HELLER, E. *The Disinherited Mind*, Pelican edn., 1961.

*HOFFMANN, J. *L'Humanisme de Malraux*, Paris, 1963.

HOWE, I. *Politics and the Novel*, London, 1961.

HUGHES, H. S. *Consciousness and Society*, New York, 1958.

—— *Oswald Spengler*, revised edn., New York, 1962.

HUIZINGA, J. *The Waning of the Middle Ages*, English translation, Pelican edn., 1955.

—— *Homo Ludens*, English translation, paperback edn., Boston, 1955.

HUYGHE, R. *The Discovery of Art*, London, 1959 (English translation of *Le Dialogue avec le visible*, Paris, 1955).

ISAACS, H. R. *The Tragedy of the Chinese Revolution*, 2nd edn., Stanford U.P., 1951.

KAELIN, E. F. *An Existentialist Aesthetic*, Wisconsin U.P., 1962.

KAUFMANN, W. *Nietzsche*, Meridian paperback edn., 5th impr., New York, 1960.

KEYSERLING, H. *The Travel Diary of a Philosopher*, English translation, London, 1927.

KNIGHT, E. *Literature considered as Philosophy*, London, 1957.

KRIEGER, M. *The Tragic Vision*, New York, 1960.

KROEBER, A. L. *Style and Civilizations*, paperback edn., California U.P., 1963.

LALOU, R. *Histoire de la littérature française contemporaine*, vol. 2, Paris, 1941.

*LANGLOIS, W. G. *André Malraux: The Indo-China Adventure*, New York, 1966.

LAVERS, A. *L'Usurpateur et le prétendant*, Paris, 1964.

LEHMANN, J. *The Whispering Gallery*, London, 1955.

LEVIN, H. *Contexts of Criticism*, Harvard U.P., 1958.

LEWIS, R. W. B. *The Picaresque Saint*, London, 1960.

*—— (ed.), *Malraux*, Englewood Cliffs, 1964.

—— *Trials of the Word*, Yale U.P., 1965.

LEWIS, W. *The Writer and the Absolute*, London, 1952.

LUBAC, H. DE. *The Drama of Atheist Humanism*, English translation, London, 1949.

MALRAUX, C. *Portrait de Grisélidis*, Paris, 1945.

*—— *Le Bruit de nos pas*, I, *Apprendre à vivre*, Paris, 1963.

*—— II, *Nos vingt ans*, Paris, 1966.

—— *Par de plus longs chemins*, Paris, 1953.

MAURIAC, C. *Malraux ou le mal du héros*, Paris, 1946.

MAURIAC, F. *Journal II*, Paris, 1937.

MAUROIS, A. *De Proust à Camus*, Paris, 1963.

MERLEAU-PONTY, M. *Signes*, Paris, 1960.

MOELLER, C. *Littérature du XXᵉ siècle et christianisme*, vol. 3, Paris, 1961.

MORAND, P. *Papiers d'identité*, Paris, 1931.

MORINO, L. *La Nouvelle Revue Française*, Paris, 1939.

MOURGUE, G. *Dieu dans la littérature d'aujourd'hui*, Paris, 1961.

MUMFORD, L. *The Condition of Man*, London, 1944.

NIETZSCHE, F. *The Birth of Tragedy*, Doubleday Anch. paperback edn., New York, 1956.

—— *Joyful Wisdom*, Ungar paperback edn., New York, 1960.

—— *The Portable Nietzsche*, 11th impr., New York, 1962.

ORTEGA Y GASSET, J. *La Deshumanización del arte*, 5th edn., Madrid, 1958.

PANOFSKY, E. *Meaning in the Visual Arts*, paperback edn., New York, 1955.

PEYRE, H. *The Contemporary French Novel*, New York, 1955.

PICON, G. *André Malraux*, 2nd edn., Paris, 1945.

*—— *Malraux par lui-même*, Paris (1953).

—— *L'Usage de la lecture*, vol. 1, Paris, 1960.

POPPER, K. R. *The Poverty of Historicism*, 3rd corrected edn., London, 1961.

—— *The Open Society and its Enemies*, 2 vols., 4th revised edn., London, 1962.

—— *Conjectures and Refutations*, London, 1963.

PRÉMONT, L. *Le Mythe de Prométhée dans la littérature française contemporaine (1900–1960)*, Laval U.P., 1964.

QUENNELL, P. *The Sign of the Fish*, London, 1960.

*RIGHTER, W. *The Rhetorical Hero*, London, 1964.

ROUSSEAUX, A. *Portraits littéraires choisis*, Geneva, 1947.

—— *Littérature du vingtième siècle*, vol. 3, Paris, 1949.

—— *Littérature du vingtième siècle*, vol. 4, Paris, 1953.

ROY, C. *Descriptions critiques*, vol. 1, 6th edn., Paris, 1949.

SACHS, M. *Day of Wrath* (English translation of *Le Sabbat*), London, 1953.

SACKVILLE-WEST, E. *Inclinations*, London, 1949.

SAINT-EXUPÉRY, A. DE. *Carnets*, Paris, 1953.

SARTRE, J.-P. *Les Mots*, Paris, 1964.

—— *Situations IV*, Paris, 1964.

—— *Situations VI*, Paris, 1964.

SIMON, P.-H. *L'Homme en procès*, Paris, 1950.

—— *Témoins de l'homme*, Paris, 1951.

—— *Le Domaine héroïque des lettres françaises*, Paris, 1963.

SINKÓ, E. *Roman eines Romans*, Cologne, 1962.

SLOCHOWER, H. *No Voice is Wholly Lost*, 2nd impr., New York, 1945.

SMITH, C. *Contemporary French Philosophy*, London, 1964.

SMITH T. M., and MINER, W. L. *Transatlantic Migration* (*The Contemporary American Novel in France*), Duke U.P., 1955.

SPARSHOTT, F. E. *The Structure of Aesthetics*, London and Toronto, 1963.

SPENDER, S. *World within World*, London, 1951.

SPENGLER, O. *The Decline of the West*, English translation, 2 vols., New York, 1947.

STEINMANN, J. *Littérature d'hier et d'aujourd'hui*, Bruges, 1963.

STÉPHANE, R. *Portrait de l'aventurier*, Paris, 1950.

—— *Fin d'une jeunesse*, Paris, 1954.

—— *T. E. Lawrence*, Paris, 1960.

STERN, J. P. *Reinterpretations*, London, 1964.

THOMAS, H. *The Spanish Civil War*, 3rd impr., London, 1961.

TILLIETTE, X. *Existence et littérature*, Paris, 1962.

TROUSSON, R. *Le Thème de Prométhée dans la littérature européenne*, 2 vols., Geneva, 1964.

TYNAN, K. *Tynan on Theatre*, Pelican edn., 1964.

UNAMUNO, M. DE. *Del sentimiento trágico de la vida*, Austral edn., Buenos Aires, 1950.

VAN DEN BOSCH, P. *Les Enfants de l'absurde*, Paris, 1956.

*VANDEGANS, A. *La Jeunesse littéraire d'André Malraux*, Paris, 1964.

VENTURI, L. *Modern Painters*, English translation, New York, 1947.

VILLARS, J. B. *T. E. Lawrence or the Search for the Absolute*, English translation, London, 1958.

VIVAS, E. *Creation and Discovery*, New York, 1955.

—— *The Artistic Transaction*, Ohio State U.P., 1963.

WEIDLÉ, W. *Les Abeilles d'Aristée*, 4th edn., Paris, 1954.

WHEELER, R. E. M. *Rome beyond the Imperial Frontiers*, Pelican edn., 1955.

WILBUR, C. M., and HOW, JULIE L.-Y. *Documents on Communism, Nationalism, and Soviet Advisers in China 1918–1927*, Columbia U.P., 1956.

WILLIAMS, W. D. *Nietzsche and the French*, Oxford, 1952.

WILSON, E. *The Shores of Light*, New York, 1952.

—— *The Bit between my Teeth*, 2nd impr., New York, 1966.

WIND, E. *Art and Anarchy*, London, 1963.

WÖLFFLIN, H. *Principles of Art History*, English translation, New York, n.d.

3. Articles

Esprit, October 1948, and *Yale French Studies*, no. 18 (Winter 1957), entitled 'Passion and the Intellect, or: André Malraux', were entirely devoted to articles on Malraux. These, together with the articles reprinted in Professor R. W. B. Lewis's *Malraux* listed above, I have found especially useful. There are large numbers of articles on Malraux, many of them of limited value to the critic, and I have listed only those which I found of direct use.

Anon., 'Malraux Man', *The Times Literary Supplement*, 26 November 1964, pp. 1–2.

ALEXANDER, I. W. Review of Frohock, op. cit., *French Studies*, October 1954, pp. 377–8.

BALL, B. L., Jr. 'Nature, Symbol of Death in *La Voie royale*', *French Review*, xxxv, pp. 390–5.

BAUMGARTNER, P. 'Solitude and Involvement: Two Aspects of Tragedy in Malraux's novels', *French Review*, May 1965, pp. 766–76.

BLEND, C. D. 'Early Expressions of Malraux's Art Theory', *French Review*, October 1962, pp. 199–213.

BOAK, C. D. 'Jean Hougron and *La Nuit indochinoise*', *France-Asie*, no. 174, July–August 1962, pp. 489–501.

—— 'Malraux—a Note on Editions', *AUMLA*, no. 21, May 1964, pp. 79–83.

—— 'Malraux and T. E. Lawrence', *Modern Language Review*, April 1966, pp. 218–24.

BUROCA, C. 'Réflexions sur l'art chez Camus et chez Malraux', *Simoun*, no. 1, January 1952, pp. 116–20.

CASEY, B. 'André Malraux's *Heart of Darkness*', *Twentieth Century Literature*, v, pp. 21–6.

CHEVALIER, H. M. Translator's introduction to the American edition of *Man's Fate*, New York, 1934, pp. 1–4.

—— 'André Malraux: the Legend and the Man', *Modern Language Quarterly*, June 1953, pp. 199–208.

CLOUARD, H. 'Itinéraire d'André Malraux', *Revue de Paris*, December 1958, pp. 82–95.

CORDLE, T. H. 'Malraux and Nietzsche's *Birth of Tragedy*', *Bucknell Review*, viii, pp. 89–104.

DANIELS, G. 'The Sense of the Past in the Novels of Malraux', in L. J. Austin *et al.*, *Studies in Modern French Literature presented to P. Mansell Jones*, Manchester U.P., 1961, pp. 71–86.

ELLIS, L. B. 'Some Existentialist Concepts in Gide, Malraux, and Saint-Exupéry', *Bucknell Review*, x, pp. 164–73.

ERGMANN, R. 'André Malraux reste un romancier', *La Nef*, March 1958, pp. 67–74.

ERIKSON, E. H. 'Identity and the Life Cycle', *Psychological Issues*, vol. 1, no. 1, 1959, Monograph 1.

ESPIAU DE LA MAËSTRE, A. 'André Malraux und der "postulatorische Atheismus"', *Stimmen der Zeit*, 1960, pp. 180–9.

FROHOCK, W. M. 'Note for a Malraux Bibliography', *Modern Language Notes*, June 1950, pp. 392–5.

—— 'Notes on Malraux's symbols', *Romanic Review*, December 1951, pp. 274–81.

GIRARD, R. 'Le Règne animal dans les romans de Malraux', *French Review*, February 1953, pp. 261–7.

—— 'Les Réflexions sur l'art dans les romans de Malraux', *Modern Language Notes*, 1953, pp. 544–6.

GIRARD, R. 'L'Homme et le Cosmos dans *L'Espoir* et *Les Noyers de l'Altenburg*', *PMLA*, March 1953, pp. 49–55.

—— 'The Role of Eroticism in Malraux's Fiction', *Yale French Studies*, no. 11, pp. 49–54.

GOMBRICH, E. H. Review of *The Metamorphosis of the Gods*, *The Observer*, 9 October 1960, p. 28.

GROETHUYSEN, B. Review of *Les Conquérants* and *Royaume farfelu*, *N.R.F.*, January 1929, pp. 558–63.

JENKINS, C. 'Malraux the Romantic', *London Magazine*, March 1961, pp. 50–7.

—— 'André Malraux', in J. Cruickshank (ed.), *The Novelist as Philosopher*, London, 1962, pp. 55–75.

LANGLOIS, W. 'The Début of André Malraux, Editor', *PMLA*, March 1965, pp. 111–22.

LAWLER, J. R. 'André Malraux and *The Voices of Silence*', *Meanjin*, xix, pp. 282–90.

LEAVITT, R. P. 'Music in the Aesthetics of André Malraux', *French Review*, xxx, pp. 25–30.

LEVIN, H. 'Towards a Sociology of the Novel', *Journal of the History of Ideas*, January 1965, pp. 148–54.

MASON, H. A. 'André Malraux and his Critics', *Scrutiny*, xiv, no. 3, Spring 1947, pp. 162–71.

MATHEWSON, R. W., Jr. 'Dostoevskij and Malraux', *Slavic Printings and Reprintings*, xxi, pp. 211–23.

MATLAW, R. E. 'Recurrent Imagery in Dostoevskij', *Harvard Slavic Studies*, iii, 1957, pp. 201–25.

ONIMUS, J. 'Malraux ou la religion de l'art', *Études*, January–March 1954, pp. 3–16.

OXENHANDLER, N. 'Malraux and the Inference to Despair', *Chicago Review*, xv. iii, pp. 72–4.

RECK, R. D. 'Malraux's Heroes: Activists and Aesthetes', *University of Kansas City Review*, xxviii, pp. 39–46.

—— 'Malraux's Transitional Novel: *Les Noyers de l'Altenburg*', *French Review*, xxxiv, pp. 537–44.

REES, G. O. 'Sound and Silence in Malraux's Novels', *French Review*, xxxii, pp. 223–30.

—— 'Types of Recurring Similes in Malraux's Novels', *Modern Language Notes*, 1953, pp. 373–7.

ROEDIG, C. F. 'The Early Fascinations of Malraux', *American Society of Legion of Honor Magazine*, xxix, pp. 21–31.

ROEDIG, C.   F. 'André Malraux in Asia', *American Society of Legion of Honor Magazine*, xxxii, pp. 145–63.

ST. AUBYN, F. C. 'André Malraux: the Syntax of Greatness', *French Review*, xxxiv, pp. 140–5.

SONNENFELD, A. 'Malraux and the Tyranny of Time', *Romanic Review*, October 1963, pp. 198–212.

TROTSKI, L. 'La Révolution étranglée', *N.R.F.*, April 1931, pp. 488–500.

VAN HUMBEECK-PIRON, P. and M. 'Plaidoyer pour l'art vivant', *Les Questions liturgiques et paroissiales*, January–February 1953, pp. 203–19.

VANDEGANS, A. 'Malraux a-t-il fréquenté les grandes écoles', *Revue des Langues Vivantes*, xxvi, pp. 336–40.

VUILLEMIN, J. 'Les Statues et les hommes', *Les Temps Modernes*, no. 55, 1950, pp. 1921–55.

—— 'Le Souffle dans l'argile', *Les Temps Modernes*, no. 63, 1951, pp. 1224–57.

WATSON, G. D. 'Roquentin in Indo-China', *AUMLA*, no. 22, November 1964, pp. 277–81.

WEIGHTMAN, J. G. Review of G. H. Hartman, *André Malraux*, *The New Statesman*, 9 April 1960, pp. 528–30.

WEST, P. 'Malraux's Genteel Humanism', *Kenyon Review*, xxi, pp. 623–38.

WILKINSON, D. 'Malraux, Revolutionist and Minister', *Journal of Contemporary History*, vol. 1, no. 2, 1966, pp. 43–64.

INDEX